Conversations:
The Autobiography
of Surrealism

EUROPEAN SOURCES

LITERATURE

AMERICAN JOURNALS
Albert Camus

CÉLINE: A BIOGRAPHY
Frédéric Vitoux

CONVERSATIONS: THE AUTOBIOGRAPHY OF SURREALISM
André Breton

DESTINY'S JOURNEY
Alfred Döblin

DIARY OF AN UNKNOWN
Jean Cocteau

FRAGMENTS OF A JOURNAL
Eugene Ionesco

JOURNEY TO POLAND
Alfred Döblin

LOOKING BACK
Lou Andreas-Salomé

ON NEITZSCHE
Georges Bataille

RULES OF THE GAME I: SCRATCHES
Michel Leiris

SKY
Blaise Cendrars

SOUVENIR PORTRAITS
Jean Cocteau

SERIES EDITORS

Russell Epprecht and Sylvère Lotringer

André Breton

Conversations:
The Autobiography
of Surrealism

WITH ANDRÉ PARINAUD AND OTHERS

Translated and with an Introduction by
MARK POLIZZOTTI

PARAGON HOUSE
New York

First American edition, 1993

Published in the United States by

Paragon House
90 Fifth Avenue
New York, N.Y. 10011

Originally published in French under the title Entretiens
by Editions Gallimard in 1952. Revised edition published by Editions Gallimard in 1969.

The translator wishes to acknowledge a grant from the French Ministry
of Culture and assistance from the Cultural Services of the French
Embassy in New York.

Library of Congress Cataloging-in-Publication Data

Breton, André, 1896–1966.
[Entretiens. English]
Conversations : the autobiography of surrealism / André Breton,
with André Parinaud . . . [et al.]
p.   cm.
Includes index.
ISBN 1-55778-423-X
1. Breton, André, 1896–1966—Interviews. 2. Authors, French—20th
century—Interviews. 3. Surrealism. I. Parinaud, André, 1924—
II. Title.
PQ2603.R35E713   1993
841'.912—dc20

92-28131
CIP

[B]

Manufactured in the United States of America

Contents

Chronology

February 19, 1896: André Breton is born in Tinchebray (Normandy), France, and spends his early childhood in Brittany. His father is an ex-policeman and small businessman, his mother a seamstress.

1900–1914: The Bretons live in the Paris suburbs, where Breton attends school, composes Symbolist-inspired poetry, and begins studying medicine.

1915: Breton is drafted as a medical orderly; he discovers Freud's theories and treats psychiatric patients, which profoundly shapes his ideas about the mind and the unconscious. Soon afterward, he meets the enigmatic dandy Jacques Vaché, who inspires a radical reexamination of his views about literature and art.

1919: Following Vaché's mysterious death, Breton composes the automatic text *The Magnetic Fields* (with Philippe Soupault) and becomes interested in the flamboyantly nihilistic Dada movement. When Dada's leader, Tristan Tzara, comes to Paris in 1920, Breton throws himself into the movement's frenzied activities.

1921–1922: Breton marries Simone Kahn and moves into a studio at 42 Rue Fontaine, his address for the rest of his life.

1924: Having broken with Dada, Breton launches the Surrealist movement and publishes the *Manifesto of Surrealism*. The movement, initially defined by its interest in dreams and automatism, counts some of the century's most original minds as its early members: Louis Aragon and Paul Eluard (Breton's closest friends), Robert Desnos, Max Ernst, Antonin Artaud, Jacques

Prévert, Yves Tanguy, Benjamin Péret, Raymond Queneau, Michel Leiris, André Masson, and Man Ray.

1926: Breton meets Nadja, who inspires his best-known work. That same year, seeking to have an impact on social and political mores, he begins a tumultuous association with the Communists, and briefly joins the Party in 1927.

1929: By this time, Breton's political convictions have led to the exclusion of numerous Surrealists from the movement, and to the inflammatory *Second Manifesto of Surrealism*. Several of those excluded respond with the violently anti-Breton pamphlet *A Corpse*. That same year, Breton divorces Simone. Salvador Dali, Luis Buñuel, René Char, and Alberto Giacometti join Surrealism.

1932: Despite Breton's overtures, the Communist party (now heavily Stalinist) remains skeptical about Surrealism. Breton's relations with the Party are further strained that spring, when Aragon leaves Surrealism to become a Communist.

1934: Breton meets and marries Jacqueline Lamba, who inspires his book *Mad Love*, and with whom he has a daughter.

1935: Breton finally breaks with the Communist party, after being denied permission to speak at the Congress of Writers for the Defense of Culture. Although he will remain politically active for the rest of his life, from this moment on he is an outspoken opponent of Stalinism, and will be among the first in France to denounce the infamous Moscow Trials.

1938: Breton, a long-standing admirer of Leon Trotsky, visits the exiled revolutionary in Mexico and drafts with him the manifesto "For an Independent Revolutionary Art." On his return to France, he helps found the Trotskyist association F.I.A.R.I. But the war aborts this project and after the French defeat, Breton, fearing Vichy repression, leaves Europe with his family.

1941–1946: Breton takes refuge in New York, where he organizes various Surrealist activities with fellow exiles Masson, Ernst, Claude Lévi-Strauss, and Marcel Duchamp. During this period, he divorces Jacqueline and marries Elisa Bindhoff, with whom he returns to France in 1946.

1946–1948: Breton tries to renew contact with his former colleagues; but many have conflicting allegiances (particularly to Stalinism, as with Aragon and Eluard), and by the early 1950s few of the prewar Surrealists are left in the group.

1951: The "Carrouges Affair," which alienates many remaining Surrealists, further isolates Breton from his generation.

1952: Broadcast and publication of Breton's *Conversations* with André Parinaud.

1952–1953: Brief collaboration between the Surrealists and the anarchists. Publication of *La Clé des champs*, Breton's last major book.

1950s–1960s: Flanked by an ever-growing circle of younger men and women, Breton continues to lead Surrealism as an organized movement until his death on September 28, 1966.

Introduction:
The "Interviews" of André Breton

André Breton disliked interviews. He gave only some two dozen of them during his lifetime, a small number for someone of his prominence. Even then, they were rarely "interviews" in the usual sense of the word, with its connotations of exchange and spontaneity: Breton's remarks showed every sign of having been carefully prepared beforehand. Beginning with his first published interview in 1923, his comments for the press have always had the slightly artificial, larger-than-life quality of a stage play.

In fact, fundamentally suspicious of both interview and interviewer, Breton required that written questions be submitted to him in advance as a way of avoiding unpleasant surprises later. He often took the liberty of editing both questions and answers, and always insisted on approving the text before publication. This distrust is not so surprising. For one thing, Breton himself was quite accomplished at turning others' statements against them: in his own published conversations with Sigmund Freud and André Gide from the 1920s, he had vented resentment of his elders' snubs by cannily editing their comments, to make one appear a senile pedant and the other a vainglorious has-been. (He later repented his cavalier treatment of Freud, and dismissed it—somewhat conveniently—as a "regrettable sacrifice to the Dada spirit.") More to the point, by midcentury Breton had become a prominent intellectual figure in his own right, the undisputed "Pope" of Surrealism (or so went the nickname he despised), and was less inclined than ever to give interviewers a chance to reinterpret his words. As the primary spokesman of a movement caught up in controversy since its inception, Breton knew how easily unguarded remarks could come back to haunt him.

For the radio interviews that constitute the present volume, not only was Breton's text composed in advance, but André Parinaud's questions were themselves subjected to extensive correction, reformulation, deletion, and addition. One former Surrealist even claims that Breton first wrote his answers in their entirety, then had Parinaud insert his questions as prompts or transitions; and Breton himself suggested eliminating the questions altogether in the published version of the interviews. What is certain is that, Breton's periodic exclamations of surprise or dismay notwithstanding, both sides of the conversation were fixed long before the broadcast date, then read like a script. Regardless of the interview format, Breton's authorship of these *Conversations* is just as complete as it is for *Nadja* or the *Manifestoes of Surrealism*, and his control over the text is just as absolute.

And yet, of all Breton's interviewers, André Parinaud would seem the least likely to rouse his distrust. His admiration for his subject is patently visible throughout these conversations, and the tone of his questions conveys a respect that sometimes borders on obsequiousness. Parinaud had in fact wanted to interview Breton since the latter's return to France in 1946, although the project did not materialize until 1950, when Parinaud was a journalist for French National Radio. The discussions themselves were taped the following year, then aired from March to June 1952.

Breton's own reasons for agreeing to these interviews are more complex. On the most basic level, they were a way of securing desperately needed income, not only from the radio sessions themselves but also from the resulting book, which Editions Gallimard published in July 1952 in an edition of 5,500 copies. (In this regard, the *Conversations* was less than triumphant: Breton received a modest advance for the volume, and barely 3,000 copies were sold in the first ten years. Only after Gallimard reissued the book in paperback, three years after Breton's death, did it become a relative economic success.)

More importantly, they were a means of pushing Surrealism back into the public eye, and of countering the commonly held view that it had lost its audience with the Second World War.

Breton was only too aware that a rising tide of neglect threatened to engulf his movement to the benefit of the newer, seemingly more relevant current called Existentialism. On top of which, Surrealism's open rejection of Stalinism, which had already cost it influence in the 1930s, now isolated it almost entirely from the postwar intellectual Left, at a time when the French Communist party was fully enjoying its association with the Resistance. To a generation that looked admiringly upon the "Party of the executed ones" (as the Communists called themselves) and flocked around Sartre at the Deux Magots, Breton seemed to be less an intellectual power broker than a grand old man of letters—listened to, perhaps, but not really heeded.

Finally, Breton was struggling with his own diminished output, a situation that both furthered his erasure from public awareness and caused him fits of deep depression. He had written no new books since *Arcane 17* in 1944, limiting himself in the interim to a volume of selected poems, new editions of earlier works, and a smattering of essays, articles, and prefaces to art exhibit catalogues. Gone were the days when he could yield such major writings as the *Second Manifesto* and *The Immaculate Conception*, plus a book of poems, all in the space of twelve months. In fact, apart from a collection of previously published essays and a collaborative tome on "magic art," *Conversations* is Breton's last important work. It is as if, through this excavation of the past, he were making a final effort both to combat his creative paralysis and to regain his place in the here and now.

Still, while the *Conversations* did draw attention back to Surrealism, its ultimate importance lies far beyond the strategic and personal factors surrounding their composition. For one thing, this book is the closest Breton ever came to writing his intellectual autobiography, albeit a rather selective one. Breton had an aversion to intimate confidences, and the reader will find few personal details here: not a word about his childhood; and despite his insistence on the importance of love, barely an allusion to his three wives or dozen love affairs. But he was an unequaled commentator on his own experience when it reflected his lifelong identification

with Surrealism's ideals—"No one can deny that my life has formed one body [with the movement]," he tells Parinaud—and on this level one could hardly ask for a more articulate or knowledgeable guide.

Indeed, though many books have been written about Surrealism, this is the only one to chronicle its history as lived from within, to combine the wisdom of first-hand experience with the passion of undying commitment. Detailed here are the movement's most spectacular highs and lows: from the discovery of automatic writing in 1919, through the group's tumultuous association with Dada and the notorious public scandals of the 1920s, to Breton's ideological debates with the Communist party and wartime exile in New York. Included as well are myriad personal anecdotes about the figures whose lives coincided for a time with Surrealism—Apollinaire, Duchamp, Tzara, Picabia, Dali, Eluard, Aragon, Desnos, Artaud, Ernst, and many others—related with a lucidity and verve that place them among Breton's best prose writings. And, most important of all, throughout the book are privileged insights into the Surrealist movement itself, by the man who embodied it for nearly half a century.

What this account is *not* is impartial, nor should we expect it to be. Surrealism was marked by frequent controversy, and its weapon of choice was the polemic. As such, Breton is often clearly tendentious in his presentation of events. Occasionally he even bends the facts to suit his own interpretations, as in his rather heroicized rendering of the 1929 "Bar du Château" incident, in which the young members of the *Grand Jeu* group were publicly disgraced for reasons that had to do with personality as much as with ideology; or his erroneous claim that only he knew the mysterious Jacques Vaché (whereas Vaché had certainly met Breton's longtime friend Théodore Fraenkel—someone never mentioned in these pages); or the dramatic, if skewed, version of his firing by arts patron Jacques Doucet. At other times Breton omits whole episodes from his narrative, perhaps the most notable being the so-called "Carrouges Affair" of early 1951, Surrealism's last great internal upheaval, during which a number of

Surrealists tried with great fracas to stage a *coup d'état* against Breton himself. These omissions and historical revisions are surely not accidental, but instead reveal—as does the tone of embattlement pervading Breton's tales of earlier polemics—that every one of these polemics was stillongoing for him. However long ago these disputes might have taken place, their original vigor was undiminished for Breton, the issues they raised as pressing as ever, as if the battles of a lifetime were eternally being waged in a timeless field.

In fact, although ostensibly about the past, these interviews really concern the present and the future. Breton's remarks on the 1920s, just as much as his dyspeptic assessments of the post–World War II era (particularly in the newspaper interviews at the end of this volume), are constantly subtended by an ardent involvement in current developments, and by a desire to keep Surrealism's precepts alive. Breton was wary of doing what he had accused Maurice Nadeau of doing in his 1945 *History of Surrealism*: turning the movement into an artifact, good only for museums and study guides. To the end of his life he fought, wrote, and argued for Surrealism's continued relevance, stressing those aspects that both concerned and transcended the political and social realities of the moment. Some of his assertions, particularly about the future of Stalinism, now seem remarkably prescient; while others, such as his belief in a Fourieristic utopia, will no doubt appear naive. But above and beyond the specifics, Breton's plea for a redefinition of human values, particularly in an age of corporate cynicism and spiritual impoverishment, rings with even greater urgency today than it did forty years ago. The *Conservations* might be Breton's swan song as a writer, but his preservation of Surrealism's works and days, and his delineation of its philosophical constants, go a long way toward assuring the movement's lasting place in the history of ideas.

It is in this spirit that we should read the *Conversations*: not as history, but as a stocktaking, a defense and illustration of Surrealism as it existed in 1952, and—Breton felt he had every reason to believe—as it would continue to exist until "a new movement

with an even greater power of liberation" came along to take its place. At the end of their sessions he tells Parinaud, "With all due respect to those who, as you know, have dug Surrealism's grave two or three times yearly for the past quarter century, I maintain that the principle of its energy remains intact." Despite their retrospective aspect, these interviews reveal a man who, in the face of every obstacle, could still afford the luxury of looking forward.

M.P., August 1992

Translator's Note

Titles of works that exist in English are given in translation. All others are given in the original, with a translation in square brackets.

In a few instances I have corrected Breton's spelling of proper names, and in a few more I've supplied first names where only the last was given. Unless otherwise indicated, footnotes are the translator's.

Although originally published in English, the interview with Charles Henri Ford was actually conducted in French, and so readers should consider my translation simply an alternative to the one that appeared in *View* in 1941. I have nonetheless used the *View* text to restore several passages cut for the French book edition, which are here given in footnotes.

I

Radio Interviews
with André Parinaud
(1913–1952)

Merry, and perhaps so imprudently laureled
With youth that a hastening fawn would enlace
This Nymph on the rocks who the soul (If not depict
Did I at least catch her in the blue of some forest edge).

On the gilded barque of a ventured dream
—Who sparked your hope? Your faith in life?—
Beyond eyes the steady rise would gleam
Under cool azure, in the whispered light . . .

—Rather than the Eden to which her hand invites,
She, ecstatic, undressed in white,
Whom reality has not yet enchained:

Caress of dawn, a statue's awe foretokened,
Awakening, avowal that one daren't, and modesty ill-feigned,
Chaste candor of a single prayer unspoken.

—Poem from 1913, in Mont de Piété [*Pawnshop*]

1.

BEFORE 1914. THE LAST GLIMMERS OF SYMBOLISM. THE PRESTIGE OF PAUL VALÉRY.

ANDRÉ PARINAUD: André Breton, exactly when did you begin to feel the stirrings of the new sensibility that would lead to Surrealism? Following which events?

ANDRÉ BRETON: You know, it's not easy to retrace the development of one's own sensibility. One can readily see what one has *become*, which events have shaped the course of one's life. But what always stays out of reach, what remains more or less concealed, is precisely what might have catalyzed these events, the "something" that caused one's mental life to take a particular turn. As some occultists have pointed out, light or fire is indispensable to certain chemical operations, and yet the formula describing these operations never speaks of fire or light. It's obviously a lacuna. I believe the same holds true for sensibility.

AP: No doubt. But what made you receptive to new currents? What originally led you, first to write, and then to define yourself as a Surrealist?

AB: Perhaps only psychoanalysis could explain that, if it delved very deeply into my childhood. For me to answer you, I'd have to begin at a much later date—say, toward the end of my adolescence; in other words at a moment when I had already developed a certain number of my own likes and dislikes. We can situate that moment in 1913.

3

AP: 1913 . . . when you were seventeen years old. I believe you were then taking premed courses, with an eye toward the medical profession?

AB: Yes, but you must understand that this was an alibi, pure and simple. The truth is, I was drawn to other things. My physical presence on the lecture-hall benches or at the laboratory tables should not imply the same presence of mind. And yet, the demon that possessed me was hardly the "literary" demon: I wasn't burning with the desire to write, to make "a name for myself" in literature, as they say. At that age, I was subject to an indistinct call; within those school walls, I felt a vague hunger for whatever was happening outside them, where I was forced not to be. I was convinced that it was *there*, on the aimless streets, that what really concerned me—what was *specifically* relevant to me, what had the most to do with my destiny—was being played out. It's not easy to explain.

AP: Still, let's stay with this. To the extent that this mood seems related to a way of feeling and acting that was not only yours, but that later took root in Surrealism, such an attitude has something of an historic value.

AB: In 1913, all I knew of Rimbaud's work were a few poems in anthologies. I hadn't yet come across his famous declaration of refusal: "The writer's hand is no better than the ploughman's. What a century of hands! I'll never have my hand." But I felt repelled—no less than Rimbaud had—by the notion of a "career," including that of professional writer. "I loathe all trades," Rimbaud also said . . .

AP: What did find favor in your eyes at the time?

AB: The greatest *rarities* that poetry and art had managed to produce (at that time: Stéphane Mallarmé, Joris-Karl Huysmans, and Gustave Moreau). You cannot know how I longed to

approach the men who were carrying on that tradition. The first one I met was Jean Royère. "My poetry," he said, "is obscure as a lily." And in fact, that superbly hermetic poetry still has resonance for me. At the time, Jean Royère edited a beautiful magazine called *La Phalange*, which published my first poems, notably a sonnet dedicated to Paul Valéry and a tribute to Francis Vielé-Griffin.

AP: What you say is all the more interesting in that, as we well know, Surrealism has not been kind to the Symbolists. So you yourself burned what you once loved!

AB: Not entirely. I believe that in those days, the literary conscience had not sunk nearly so low as it has today. At least there were *reserved territories*, where expression itself was worshipped unequivocally. A magazine such as Paul Fort's *Vers et Prose* could, without making false claims, carry as its epigraph: "Defense and illustration of high literature and lyricism in prose and poetry." The mainstream public didn't enter, of course, but the important thing is that the promise was kept.

Today, critics are unjust toward Symbolism. You say that Surrealism didn't exactly raise Symbolism's standing. Historically, it was inevitable that we should oppose Symbolism, but the critics didn't have to follow in our footsteps. It was their task to find the "driving belt" linking the two movements and put it back in place.

AP: Most of these poets and writers, who were then reaching their prime, had met some twenty-five years earlier at Mallarmé's "Tuesdays," I think it was, in his little salon on Rue de Rome. What was so exemplary about them?

AB: In retrospect, I'd say it was their *manner*. Again, nothing was more important to them than quality, nobility of expression. The kind of beauty they honored was not the same as ours, of course, and even at the time it gave the impression of a veiled woman fading into the distance. Nonetheless, it was thanks to them that a corpus of essential values was preserved and kept untarnished.

Even today, this alone should warrant our taking our hats off to them (but no one wears hats anymore) . . .

AP: Admittedly, the times were much less bitter than the period following. But already a new generation was ushering the Symbolists out: the Cubists and the Futurists had made their presence felt during the four preceding years, and no less a work than Guillaume Apollinaire's *Alcools* was published in the same year, 1913. Were you already "aware"?

AB: Only vaguely. Mostly I retained my veneration (the word is not excessive) for those great witnesses of a bygone era, even as the shadows were deepening around them—shadows they had loved and that suited them so well. These men had resisted any compromise, and looked upon the pitiful place the critics reserved for them without bitterness. They truly were above all that. As for me, I was endlessly enchanted by some of their poetry and prose; and if they happened not to write for several years, their silence was just as precious to me as their voices. It's important to say this today, at a time when young people are constantly demanding that their elders go further, that they "speak out" at the drop of a hat, on the pretext that some of them have already spoken out so often before—even though it's obviously youth's turn to speak out.

AP: Perhaps it's because we no longer know the quality of that silence you found so precious . . .

AB: Perhaps. My feeling was that those writers, whose words had moved me and permeated me forever, had given me an invaluable gift. What dignified them once and for all in my eyes was that they *alone* had given me this gift—without knowing me, and in a world that already appeared strangely impoverished. If I wanted anything more from them, it was at most a *sign of life*, addressed to me personally in the form of an answer to a letter or the acceptance of a requested meeting. On certain days, nothing mattered more to me than obtaining one or the other of these from a Vielé-

Griffin, a René Ghil, a Saint-Pol Roux, or a Paul Valéry: it was as if they were granting me a particle of their secret. Not that this diminished their secret—on the contrary. It's been a long time since we wrote letters with the same tone as theirs; even if we were tempted to try, we'd hold back. A sense of propriety has gotten in the way. Today, to slip a wisp of eternity into a letter, to be inclined even slightly toward a lapidary statement, would seem as out of place as it would on the telephone.

AP: What made you decide to contact these poets in particular, as opposed to others with similar tendencies?

AB: Actually, there was a deliberate choice on my part. Vielé-Griffin, although he has been unjustly forgotten today, was considered a master within Symbolist and post-Symbolist circles. For me, he was the one who had dedicated a collection of poems "to the refined speech of France." His verse was the sunniest of the period, the most fluid. A vast fresco like *La Chevauchée d'Yeldis* [Yeldis's Ride] takes up and renews the theme of Victor Hugo's "La Chanson des aventuriers de la mer" by turning it inward. (I was greatly surprised, the first time I visited Vielé-Griffin in his sumptuous apartment on Quai de Passy, to discover a bust of Hugo on his desk.) A collection like *La Partenza* [The Departure], twenty-three poems that bid farewell to the beautiful side of life, is a masterpiece of both effusion and restraint. What else? Of the two or three great "starters" of 1885, Vielé-Griffin was the one who had truly kept his distance from honors and popularity. I saw him as an antidote to Henri de Régnier, for instance.

AP: And René Ghil?

AB: I liked him in a way I'd qualify as more subversive—more distant as well. His works, which when read silently yield only a small portion of their meaning (but given some of the author's pseudoscientific preoccupations, so much the better, perhaps), plunged me into a kind of verbal night, punctuated by rare sparks, which at once annoyed and attracted me. If the words "recondite"

and "abstruse" could legitimately be applied to anyone's language, then it's certainly to his. And yet, when Ghil's poems unfurled over an auditorium (during one of those "poetry matinees" they used to hold back then), their musical intensity eclipsed all the others. Ghil was—possibly along with Saint-Pol Roux, whom I met only later—the most disparaged poet of Symbolism. While the critics continued to heap only insults and sarcasm on him, I found it touching that, against all odds, he maintained his "will," as he said, toward a "difficult and sacred art."

The year 1913 more or less marked the outer edge of a fringe: the shadow that the pyramid of the nineteenth century threw on the pyramid of the twentieth, construction of which had only just begun. It's true that we were going to have our fill starting the following year! But in the meantime, the field of exploration seemed open (forty-two years of peace, relative prosperity, the persistent illusion of progress). Still, later accounts would suggest that everything was topsy-turvy, on the intellectual plane . . .

AP: I'd like to know if you found at least one man who was able to bridge the gap from one century to the next?

AB: Yes, of course; his name was Paul Valéry, and he was unique. For a long time I considered him the great enigma. I practically knew by heart his *Evening with Mr. Teste*, which had appeared in 1896, the year of my birth, in *Le Centaure*, the magazine he had cofounded.

I could not stop praising that work to the skies, to the point where, at times, the character of Mr. Teste seemed to emerge from his frame—Valéry's story—to come mutter his harsh complaints in my ear. Still today, there are plenty of circumstances in which I hear this fellow grumbling the way no one else can; he's still the one who is always *right*. For me, Valéry had reached the supreme point of expression with Mr. Teste: a character created by him (at least I suppose so) had truly set himself in motion, had come forward to meet me.

AP: Were you equally taken with Valéry's early poems?

AB: Perhaps, but in a different way. Still, it's likely they used the same ellipses to mentally ensnare me as *Teste* did. These poems were hard to find, scattered as they were in long-lost periodicals. But even when I got hold of one, I never managed to exhaust its mystery or disturbing power. They glided down the slippery slope of reverie—an often erotic reverie, moreover. I'm thinking of a poem such as "Anne" the first time I read it, and even afterward:

> *Anne who blends with the pale sheet, leaving forlorn*
> *The hair drowsing over her just opened eyes,*
> *Gazes remotely at her arms weakly folded*
> *On the colorless surface of the uncovered belly . . .*

I'm convinced that frequenting Valéry gave me a certain taste for the risqué, mentally speaking.

AP: Is it true that, for you, his prolonged silence only added to the appeal?

AB: It's by far what made him most fascinating. After having given so much of himself, he seemed to have left the literary life behind for good. He had published nothing in fifteen years. He was said to be completely absorbed in speculations that fell outside of his normal field, in which mathematics no doubt played a large part. For me it was very tempting—and pleasantly distracting—to imagine him following Mr. Teste's imperatives. I felt that in Valéry, Mr. Teste had supplanted the poet and even the "lover of poems," as he had earlier enjoyed defining himself. In my eyes, he benefited from the prestige inherent in a myth that we've seen built around Rimbaud: that of a man turning his back on his life's work one fine day, as if, once he had reached certain heights, the work somehow "rejected" its creator. Such behavior on his part lent these heights an unsurpassable, somewhat vertiginous character, and, I repeat, made them all the more fascinating. Rimbaud's adventure in Harrar (the questions it raises) accounted, and still accounts, for a large share of our passionate interest in

him. For me, Valéry stood in the same light, as only Marcel Duchamp has since then.

AP: Would you describe your meetings with Paul Valéry?

AB: I can still see myself entering his home for the first time, at 40 Rue de Villejust, which I so little suspected would one day exchange its name for his own.* Beautiful Impressionist canvases crowded onto the walls as best they could, covering over the mirrors. This man—he and no other—greeted me quite graciously, even though I had never seen his face before reaching the top of the stairs. His eyes, which were the pretty transparent blue of the sea at low tide, stared at me from beneath sharp-edged lids. I remember that he greatly disconcerted me right off the bat by praising my luck at living in Pantin at the time, which for him meant the perfume factories on Rue de Paris. He envied me for having grown up, as he said, "among the skirts of tarts." He might have acquired that turn of mind from Huysmans, but in any case fetishism was pretty typical of him. The charms and exceptional resources of his conversation have been sufficiently celebrated. But perhaps the most titillating aspect of this conversation was when his "profoundly destructive, even nihilistic mind," which so rightly impressed T. S. Eliot, showed through.

AP: This is no doubt what provided his link with Surrealism—a link that began to crack in around 1921, if I'm not mistaken, and shattered several years later.

AB: Exactly. The fact nonetheless remains that I learned a lot from Valéry. For several years, with inexhaustible patience, he answered all my questions. He made me—he took great pains to make me—be hard on myself. It's to him that I owe my lasting concern with various elevated disciplines. Moreover, as long as I had met certain fundamental demands, he would allow me great latitude. He told me, "I'm not at all anxious to make others share

* Rue de Villejust was rebaptized Rue Paul Valéry in 1946, the year after the poet's death.

my ideas. Proselytism is antithetical to me. People see what they will . . ."

And yet, the myth I spoke about must have won out. Nothing could withstand the disappointment, the disillusionment of seeing him suddenly contradict his attitude, publish new poems, revise his old ones (clumsily, I might add), and try—but quite in vain—to revive Mr. Teste. I won't dwell on this spectacular phase of his evolution. I chose the day of his induction into the Académie Française to part with his letters, which a rare book dealer coveted. It's true that I had the weakness to keep copies, but I had treasured the originals for years.

AP: Much time had passed. I suppose that quite a few things had occurred meanwhile . . .

AB: Yes. The Symbolist sanctuary had finished crumbling. Other passersby, who had attained various degrees of eminence and become famous almost overnight, had had time to appear, and even, in some cases (not necessarily the least important), to disappear.

Overall, they bore a message of an entirely different order, which demanded immediate examination and tended to move one *forward*, rather than backward. Cubism and Futurism had been significant explosions. The war was quite another sort of explosion. Straddling (as was his wont) the period of time between them was a poetic figure whom I regarded as being of primary importance: Guillaume Apollinaire.

AP: And with your permission, we'll devote our second program to the years 1914 to 1919, and to the circumstances that showed you who you really were.

Vaché shook hands to say neither hello nor goodbye. He lived in Place du Beffroi, in a pretty room with a young woman whom I knew only as Louise, and whom, when I visited, he obliged to stand still and silent for hours in a corner. At five o'clock she served tea, and his only thanks was to kiss her hand. As he told it, they had no sexual relations; rather, he was content simply to sleep beside her in the same bed.

—*"La Confession dédaigneuse," in* Les Pas perdus [*The Lost Steps*]

2.

WORLD WAR I. FROM GUILLAUME APOLLINAIRE TO JACQUES VACHÉ. THE MAGIC OF RIMBAUD. FACING THE "ABERRATIONS OF THE HUMAN MIND."

ANDRÉ PARINAUD: In this second broadcast, we will discuss the period from 1914 to 1919. The first important factor of this period is your state of mind at the outbreak of the war. Could you share some of your memories with us?

ANDRÉ BRETON: Why not? "Sac au Dos" . . . Do you know Huysmans's story? One of the masterpieces of Naturalism, from *Les Soirées de Médan* [Evenings of Médan]. Well, you need only transpose that a little, raise it slightly above ground level, in order to grasp the *mood* of certain young men, myself included, whom the war had just torn from their aspirations and flung into a cesspool of blood, mud, and idiocy.

AP: You were in a position of rebellion. Can you be more specific about your state of mind?

AB: As soon as my initial stupor had passed—after several months of artillery "training"—I began to look more questioningly around me. Right nearby, in the "camp" itself, the most sensitive among us had secretly found a refuge. One spent his rare moments of leisure sketching new dress designs; at the recital of punishments that his total ineptitude at military exercises earned him, he merely lifted a minuscule flask of oil of amber to his nostril. Another, at the first mention of "rest" or "halt," dove into

13

the *Epistles to the Corinthians*. The disasters of the early days, the dark prospects of trench warfare, the uncertain outcome of the conflict—even if these were all more or less concealed— engendered a mood that left little place for resignation.

AP: From what source did you, as a poet, nourish your spirit?

AB: My first coherent reaction was to turn toward those whom I thought might shed some light on that snakepit, and first and foremost those who had let their voices be heard up until then, and whom one could reasonably expect to be the most likely to "master the situation." What an immediate disappointment! Who today could stomach the articles that the likes of Maurice Barrès and Henri Bergson inflicted on us at the time? Nothing in those articles rose above the level of expression found in mercenary journalism, or was even apt to make me suffer my condition with greater patience. Nationalism had never been my strong point. If, in this regard, my thought was influenced by someone—and it still is—it was by the Jean-Jacques Rousseau of the *Discourse on Inequality* and the *Social Contract*. Already the shouts of the mob were powerless to alter that. I even think that it was on the branch planted by Rousseau—to my mind, the first one to grow at man's height—that poetry began to flower.

Under such conditions, how could I not have been tempted to seek help from the poets? What did *they* think of this horrible adventure? What had become of the values they placed above all others? Their only concern during the preceding years, for example, had been with breaking out of fixed frameworks, promoting the greatest possible freedom of expression: what was going to happen to this, at a time when everyone wore a gag over his mouth, not to say a blindfold over his eyes? . . . I won't even mention the poets—or those who passed for such (Régnier, Charles Péguy, Paul Claudel, and the like)—whose primary concern was to espouse the national spirit and burst into the circumstantial *Gloria*. Others kept silent: this wasn't much, but all things considered it was vastly preferable. Very rare human accents came through later, but weakly, either because they were stifled or

because they didn't have the requisite timbre (I'm thinking in particular of Pierre-Jean Jouve's first collections of poems); personally, I found them to be of no help. At the time, there was only one man whose poetic genius eclipsed all others for me, who constantly remained the focal point. That man was Guillaume Apollinaire.

AP: Guillaume Apollinaire: the great name has been dropped. I'd like you to describe the importance that this poet and his works had for you.

AB: Our relations, which were short-lived but quite assiduous on my part, had begun by correspondence. The first time he physically appeared before me was on his hospital bed, on May 10, 1916, the day after his trepanning operation, as his inscription on my copy of *Alcools* reminds me. From then on I was to see him almost every day until his death.

He was a very great man, the likes of whom I've never seen since. Fairly haggard, it's true. Lyricism in person. He trailed the Parade of Orpheus behind him. He was the author of "The Song of the Poorly Loved" and "Zone," of "The Emigrant of Landor Road" and "The Musician of Saint-Merry," the champion of the *poem-event*. In other words, he was the apostle of a concept that required every new poem to be a total recasting of its author's means; to live its own adventure, away from any preexisting paths, disdaining any innovations made prior to it. What a caution against the clichés that so few poets have spared us since! And you know that he had the strength to carry out this impossible task.

AP: Oh, no one could deny it! I'd be interested in having you comment on Apollinaire's poetic procedure, his way of working.

AB: His motto was, "I fill with wonder." I still believe today that it was not too grand a claim on his part, given the vast knowledge that practically he alone possessed in rarefied domains (myths, anything having to do with the great curiosities, and whatever was buried away in the restricted sections of libraries). This

knowledge made him no less open to the future. Not content merely to support the most daring artistic initiatives of his time, he felt the need to become part of them, to put in their service everything he possessed in the way of specialized knowledge, ardor . . . and influence. Just as he was conquered by at least the *character* of Alfred Jarry, of whom he painted a moving portrait in his *Contemporains pittoresques* [Colorful Contemporaries], and just as he immediately recognized the genius of Henri Rousseau, so too did he situate once and for all the processes of a Matisse, a Derain, a Picasso, a De Chirico. He did so by means of a mental range the likes of which hadn't been seen since Baudelaire. Though so imbued with multiple traditions, he had been proud to draft the manifesto of the "Futurist antitradition." Whereas Valéry in this regard proved to be old-fashioned, even stubbornly resistant (which is interesting in itself, moreover), Apollinaire pushed forward, even if it sometimes meant coming down on the wrong side of the fence. I loved him, and persist in honoring him as such. He was a considerable "seer." While many continue to speak of him with sympathy, or even enthusiasm, few truly understand him. The lamps that lead from *L'Enchanteur pourrissant* [The Rotting Enchanter] to *The Poet Assassinated* are still dim, and they illuminate precious little of a road on which afterthoughts cross paths with premonitions.

AP: What was Apollinaire's conduct vis-à-vis the war?

AB: We knew right away that he had volunteered for the army; the friends who had managed to stay in touch with him sent each other his new poems. These poems were still lit by the same flame, but nothing in them showed an appreciable awareness of events. Apollinaire was trying to resolve everything with an enthusiasm that was surely sincere, but that sounded forced; despite the ever-renewed expression of feeling, to my mind it couldn't help lapsing into conformity. The worst realities of the times were sidestepped, the most legitimate worries ignored, in favor of a playfulness that went unchecked in the *Calligrammes* proper; while his mind kept trying, as irrationally as you please, to take

comfort in the "scenery" of war. Apollinaire reacted to the ap-
palling *fact* of war with a desire to plunge back into childhood, a
desperate "reanimism" that fell far short of being the talisman he'd
hoped. Whatever great successes he achieved in this vein—I'm
thinking of such poems as "April Night 1915"—I believe that in
his person, poetry had been unable to rise to the task. In my eyes,
it was stricken by inadequacy. This is no doubt what made me so
attentive to a message of an entirely different order.

AP: You're speaking of Jacques Vaché, of course.

AB: Yes. If ever someone's influence touched me to the core, it
was his.

AP: Many have commented on Vaché's attitude, but you were
the first to underline the importance of his example. What made it
so exceptionally interesting for you?

AB: First of all, through him, *everything was defied*. Faced with the
horror of those times, which those around me protested only
haltingly and in whispers, he seemed to be the only one who
remained absolutely untouched, the only one capable of develop-
ing the crystal armor that would keep us immune to contagion . . .
We met—yes, quite a few lines have already been written about
this—in a hospital in Nantes, where I was an intern and he was
being treated. This was in the early months of 1916. I was struck
both by the very studied nature of his appearance and by the
ultracasual tone of his statements. He could very well have passed
for Mr. Teste's *grandson*, if he hadn't held as offhand a view of the
family as he did of everything else. The "enormity" of what was
happening at the time and, so to speak, of what was being thought
communally, left him remarkably unfazed.

I also think today that he was a kind of Des Esseintes of action.*
His "against the grain" was exerted under such conditions of
surveillance and, despite this, with such meticulousness, that a

* A reference to the antihero of J.-K. Huysmans's *Against the Grain*.

kind of vengeful, muffled, purely internal laughter rippled in his wake . . .

AP: Isn't this where his new and, I believe you have gone so far as to call it, "initiatory" concept of humor resided?

AB: That is to say, *umor*, which out of weariness—and pressed by me—he defined as possibly being "the sense of the theatrical (and joyless) pointlessness of everything," hardly confined itself to the realm of contemplation, however jaded. This "umor" was not above committing tiny acts against those whom André Gide's character Lafcadio called "dromedaries." I've given several examples in the recollections I gathered for the republication of Jacques Vaché's *Letters from the Front* [Letters de guerre]. They did not exclude the kind of joke said to be "in very poor taste," if only as a way of flouting that very taste. In Vaché's person, in utmost secrecy, a principle of total insubordination was undermining the world, reducing everything that then seemed all-important to a petty scale, desecrating everything in its path. Art itself was not spared. "We like neither art nor artists," proclaimed Jacques Vaché who, at best, judged it permissible to "create one's own sensations with the help of a flamboyant collision of rare words," or, better still, to "neatly draw the angles, the squares, all the geometry of feelings." To my mind, his attitude, in this and every other respect, represents the most evolved form of dandyism . . .

AP: Excuse me for interrupting, but there's a profound antagonism between Vaché's attitude and Apollinaire's. How were you able to reconcile them?

AB: Indeed, these two life-styles were profoundly antagonistic, and for me they would never confront each other more tellingly than on June 24, 1917, at the "premiere" of Apollinaire's play *Les Mamelles de Tirésias* [The Teats of Tiresias]. I've had occasion to tell how Vaché, on leave from the front, had arranged to meet me there. The play had begun almost two hours late. Disappointing enough in itself, it was furthermore poorly acted, and the audi-

ence, already annoyed by the delay, had greeted the first act with shouts of protest. The reason for a new outburst in one part of the orchestra seats soon became clear: it was Jacques Vaché who had just entered, wearing the uniform of a British officer. To put himself immediately in tune with the situation, he had unholstered his revolver and appeared to be of a mind to use it. I calmed him down the best I could and managed to make him endure the rest of the show, not without great impatience. Never before, as I did on that evening, had I measured the depth of the gap that would separate the new generation from the one preceding it. Vaché—who as it turned out was exasperated both by the poor-man's lyricism of the play and by the hackneyed Cubism of the sets and costumes—Vaché, standing defiantly before an audience that was at once used to and tainted by this kind of performance, cut the figure of an enlightener. A few more years would pass—maybe three or four—before the break between these two conflicting modes of thought would be complete.

AP: Didn't the war experience also heighten Rimbaud's influence on you?

AB: Yes. Paradoxically, my time in Nantes—when the meeting with Jacques Vaché led to the revision of most of my former opinions—was also the time when I was truly initiated into Rimbaud, when I began to study his work in depth and with unbridled passion. You have to remember that in 1916, major documents, such as the letters to Delahaye from 1875, had only recently come to light. Until then we had been lacking an essential signpost. These documents, in fact, mark the crucial turning point in Rimbaud's evolution, his definitive farewell to poetry and his passage to a totally different kind of activity. All through the streets of Nantes, Rimbaud possessed me completely: what he had seen, albeit in an entirely different place, interfered with what I was seeing, and even went so far as to replace it. Never again since then have I experienced that kind of "trance-like state." The long road that took me every afternoon, alone and on foot, from the hospital on Rue du Bocage to the beautiful Parc de Procé,

opened all kinds of vistas onto the sites of the *Illuminations* themselves: here, the general's house in "Childhood"; there, "this wood bridge, arched"; farther on, certain unusual movements that Rimbaud had described: all this was swept into one particular bend of the little stream bordering the park, which merged with "the Cassis River." I can't give a more rational idea of these things. My entire quest for knowledge was concentrated on, was aimed at Rimbaud. I even wearied Valéry and Apollinaire with my constant requests for information about him, and what they were able to tell me, as you can imagine, fell terribly short of what I had hoped for. It goes without saying that Vaché showed only the greatest intolerance toward Rimbaud, but on this subject his power over me was ineffective. It's as if I had been under a spell . . .

What finally distracted me from him was the change of assignment that, from one day to the next, made me the assistant of Doctor Raoul Leroy at the psychiatric center of the 2nd Army in Saint-Dizier. This center took in men who had been evacuated from the front for reasons of mental distress (including a number of acute delirium cases), as well as various delinquents who were facing court-martial, and for whom they wanted a medicolegal report. My stay in this place and the sustained attention I paid to what happened there counted for a lot in my life, and no doubt had a decisive influence on the development of my thought. It was there—although this was hardly common practice at the time— that I was able to try out the investigative procedures of psychoanalysis on patients, notably recording their dreams and free associations, which I then interpreted. We might already note in passing that these dreams, these kinds of associations would initially constitute almost the entirety of Surrealism's raw materials. We only amplified the *ends* toward which those dreams and associations were being collected; yes, still interpretation, but above all *liberation* from constraints—logical, moral, and otherwise— with an eye toward recuperating of the mind's original powers. The medicolegal reports, neatly written out as if for school, on whose conclusions a man's entire future depended, left me feeling rather critical of the notion of responsibility.

Finally—this is no doubt more subjective—I met someone there, the memory of whom has never left me. He was a young, well-educated man who, in the front lines, had aroused the concern of his superior officers by a recklessness carried to extremes: standing on the parapet in the midst of the bombardments, he conducted the grenades flying by with his finger. His explanation for the doctors was as simple as could be: strange as it may seem, and although this ploy was not new, he had never been wounded. But underneath, some clearly heterodox certainties were being articulated: the supposed war was only a simulacrum, the make-believe shells could do no harm, the apparent injuries were only makeup and, moreover, under cover of asepsis no one undid the bandages to make sure. He also maintained that the corpses removed from the operating tables were distributed at night around the fake battlefields, etc. Naturally, the doctors did everything in their power to make this man admit that the outsized costs of such a spectacle could not simply be for his personal benefit, but it seemed to me he didn't really believe it. His arguments—among the richest I've ever heard—and the impossibility of making him give them up made a great impression on me. I've often thought, after the fact, of the extreme point he represented on a line linking the speculations of an idealist such as Fichte to certain of Pascal's radical doubts. There's no doubt that for me a certain temptation originated there, which would see the light of day several years later in my "Introduction to the Discourse on the Paucity of Reality."

AP: Your stay in Saint-Dizier evidently left a deep impression. Can you clarify the impact this period had on your future?

AB: From my stay at the center in Saint-Dizier, I've retained a keen curiosity and a great respect for what are commonly called the aberrations of the human mind. Perhaps I also learned to guard against these aberrations, given the intolerable living conditions that go with them.

AP: We now come to the year 1918, when the war was about to end. Did poetry show any signs of release or renewal?

AB: Paris was coming back to life. On Wednesdays, at around six in the afternoon on the sidewalk of the Café de Flore, Apollinaire, still girded in his sky-blue artilleryman's uniform—worried eye against the leather disk protecting his temple—went from table to table, making the rounds of his friends, who were gathered into very disparate, if not openly hostile, groups. It had already been a year since the thin but historically important periodical *Nord-Sud* had begun to appear. Although still centered on the Cubist aesthetic (Apollinaire, Max Jacob, and Georges Braque contributed to it), *Nord-Sud* also welcomed younger poets (at the time, Philippe Soupault, Tristan Tzara, Louis Aragon, and myself). Most importantly, under the signature of its editor, Pierre Reverdy, it put forth several lasting principles and major themes on the subject of poetic creation.

But the unkindest cuts were still to happen: within several months both Apollinaire and Vaché would be gone. These disappearances, and everything they entailed for some of us on an emotional level, imposed a total reorganization.

AP: It is, then, to these new imperatives that we'll devote our third program.

. . . That dazzling figure of black light, the Comte de Lautréamont. In the eyes of certain contemporary poets, Maldoror *and the* Poésies *sparkle with incomparable brilliance. They are the expression of a total revelation that seems to exceed human possibility. All of modern life, in its most specific aspects, is sublimated in one stroke. His backdrops revolve on the swinging doors of ancient suns that illuminate the sapphire floor; the silver-beaked gaslamp, winged and smiling, that glides over the Seine; the green membranes of space and the shops of Rue Vivienne, prey to the crystalline rays from the center of the earth. An absolutely virgin eye lies in wait for the scientific perfection of the world, disregarding the consciously utilitarian nature of this perfection, situating it with all the rest in the light of apocalypse.* Definitive apocalypse: *in this work, the great instinctive pulsebeats are lost and exalted on contact with an asbestos cage containing a white-hot heart. For centuries to come, the most audacious things that can be thought or undertaken will find their magic law formulated here in advance.*

—Anthologie de l' humour noir [*Anthology of Black Humor*]

3.

BRETON MEETS SOUPAULT AND ARAGON (THE "THREE
MUSKETEERS"). PIERRE REVERDY ON RUE CORTOT.
THE PACT WITH THE COUNT. THE DEATH OF VACHÉ.
LITTÉRATURE.

ANDRE PARINAUD: The period we'll discuss in this third broadcast takes place in the months that immediately preceded the end
of the First World War. The creation of the magazine *Littérature*
will be our main focus, along with your friendships with others
who shared your activities at the time.

ANDRE BRETON: In my first meetings with Soupault and Aragon reside the origins of the activity that, starting in March 1919,
was to begin its explorations in *Littérature*, soon explode into
"Dada," and then be forced to revitalize itself from top to bottom
as Surrealism.

AP: How did your friendship with Philippe Soupault come
about?

AB: I met Philippe Soupault through Apollinaire; the elective
admiration we both felt for the latter was the basis of our coming
together. Shortly afterward I met Louis Aragon at Adrienne Monnier's bookstore, "La Maison des Amis des Livres," on Rue de
l'Odéon. Leaving the store, we walked together back to the Val-
de-Grâce hospital, where we were both confined by our military
obligations, which alternated with courses in wartime medicine.

Keep in mind that at the end of the war, those of the coming
generation who had a vital interest in poetry and its problems
could be counted on the fingers of one hand. There was none of
that plethora of periodicals and pamphlets that marked the end of
the following war, engendering total confusion in the poetic domain, as in so many others. The discussions between Soupault,
Aragon, and myself were all the more intense in that the field of
exploration was wide open. Moreover, resolved as we were to walk
a common road, we had nonetheless each started out from very
different sets of ideas. Each of us showed the other two what we
considered our most significant, most precious possessions.

AP: Could you highlight Soupault's original contribution to your
little group?

AB: Soupault's contribution consisted in a keen sense of what
was modern (what we then called "modern" among ourselves, all
the while knowing how unstable this notion was). As we defined
it, Apollinaire, for example, was "modern" to the fullest extent in
the poem "Monday on Rue Christine" and in several chapters of
The Poet Assassinated; he stopped being modern—to say the least—
in some of his later poems, such as "Honor's Hymn." Gide, albeit
to a lesser degree, was "modern" in the creation of Lafcadio in
Lafcadio's Adventures, and even in certain attitudes of *Marshlands* or
Prometheus Misbound. All things considered, the issue was one of
total liberation, not only from ways of thinking but also from
preestablished means of expression. Our goal was the necessary
promotion of specifically new ways of feeling and *saying*, the
search for which implied, by definition, a maximum of *adventure*.
Soupault brought very enviable natural inclinations to this search:
in particular, he seemed to have done away with the "poetic old-
fashionedness" that Rimbaud, by his own admission, had never
managed to eliminate. He was probably the only one at the time (I
believe Apollinaire forced himself to do it—at rare intervals, for
that matter) who left his poems as they came, safeguarded them
from any regrets. Anywhere, in a cafe, for instance, in the time it
took to ask the waiter for "something to write with," he could

satisfy the request for a poem. The poem ended—I almost said, landed on its feet like a cat—at the first outside intrusion. The results of such a method, or absence of method, were of rather variable interest, but at least they were always valid from the point of view of freedom, and of freshness. I'm thinking of one poem of his, later published in *Rose des vents* [Compass Rose]:

Sunday

The airplane weaves telegraph lines
and the source sings the same song
at the Coachmen's Meeting House the drinks are orange
but the train mechanics have white eyes
The lady has lost her smile in the woods

AP: And could you describe Soupault at the time?

AB: He was like his poetry, extremely refined, a shade distant, likable, and *airy*. In daily life you couldn't pin him down for long. He liked all the travelers, without great discernment—Rimbaud, perhaps largely for this reason; the Valéry Larbaud of *Barnabooth*; the Blaise Cendrars of the *Prose du transsibérien*, whom he knew personally and who had put him onto Arthur Cravan. He wasn't all that well-read, although he was rather strongly imbued with English literature. In that domain he seemed keener on novels than on poems, although, thinking in retrospect of his *Chansons* [Songs], which rendered such a new sound, I wonder if they didn't owe a lot to the "nonsense verse" of Edward Lear.*

AP: Aragon must have made quite a contrast with Soupault . . .

AB: Aragon was of very different character and education. When we first met, he put Villon far above the moderns and, among his contemporaries, vastly preferred the Jules Romains of *Odes et prières* [Odes and Prayers] to the Apollinaire of *Alcools*. You can imagine the heresy this constituted in Soupault's and my eyes,

*They were, in fact, almost direct translations of Lear.

but it was an opinion that was current around Adrienne Monnier—one that she encouraged as much as possible—and Aragon was among the principle habitués of her bookstore. He had all the talents needed to shine there.

AP: I think it would be good for us to hear about Adrienne Monnier and her bookstore, the "Amis des Livres."

AB: Adrienne Monnier had made her store the most attractive intellectual meeting place of the time. The nice touches she could introduce into the conversation, the opportunities she gave young people, and even the provocative bias of her tastes: there was no lack of trump cards in her hand. The most enticing figures of the day showed up sooner or later at the "Amis des Livres": Léon-Paul Fargue, Pierre Reverdy, Valéry Larbaud, Erik Satie. I made sure that Valéry and Apollinaire found their way there—and they never lost it. Speaking of which, Paul Léautaud once said without too much exaggeration that Valéry's entire reputation and his unprecedented official successes started at the "Amis des Livres."

AP: Was Aragon already the seductive and original mind that *Paris Peasant* later revealed?

AB: In person. In short order he jettisoned whatever tastes might have conflicted with Soupault's or mine. I can still recall the extraordinary walking companion he was. The areas of Paris I visited with him, even the most nondescript, were enhanced several notches by a magic, romantic fantasizing that was never caught short for long, and that burst forth at a bend in the street or before a shop window. Even before *Paris Peasant*, a book such as *Anicet* already gives an idea of these riches. No one was ever a more able detector of the unusual in all its forms; no one was ever more inclined toward such intoxicating reveries on a kind of hidden life of the city (who else could have tipped Jules Romains off—the latter speaks of it in *Vorge Côntre Quinette*—about the renowned fable of the 365 secretly connected apartments that

supposedly exist in Paris?). In this sense, Aragon was staggering—even for himself.

By then, he had already read everything. His infallible memory could recall the plots of countless novels, no matter how far back he had read them. His mental agility was unequalled, which might account for the rather pronounced laxity of his opinions and, alongside this, a certain suggestibility. He was extremely warm and generous in friendship. The only danger he courted was his excessive desire to please. *Scintillating* . . .

AP: Was he already something of a rebel?

AB: At the time, he was not very rebellious. He rather flirtatiously displayed a taste for subversion, but in reality the impositions of war and of his professional orientation (medicine) were borne lightheartedly. Decorated at the front with the Croix de Guerre. He always managed to "cram" for the intern exams a little better than the others.

AP: So the moral crisis he later passed through wasn't yet in the offing.

AB: He wasn't suffering any deep crises right then . . . Yes, one did come about later on—by contagion, as far as I can tell.

AP: And what about yourself?

AB: Ah! I had been adrift for quite some time: there was no possible compromise with a world that had learned nothing from such a horrible adventure. Under such conditions, why should I devote even one iota of my time and availability to things not motivated by my own desire? Indeed, where was I? Perhaps I was expecting some kind of—strictly personal—miracle that would start me down a different path. When I look at my life since then, I suppose such a miracle must have occurred, but imperceptibly. It's nonetheless true that I saw everything others pushed me toward as a deception, a trap. Wartime censorship had been vig-

ilant: in circles such as ours, events of such *political* significance as the Zimmerwald and Kienthal conferences* had had little impact, and the Bolshevik revolution itself was far from being recognized for what it was. Had someone told us then that our different ways of understanding the implications of these events would give rise to ferments of discord between us, naturally we would have been totally incredulous. What is generally called "social conscience" didn't exist among us.

AP: I suppose that at the time you were still in contact with Valéry and Apollinaire?

AB: I continued to see Valéry, no doubt with less enthusiasm since I'd learned he was grappling with the more or less Racinian alexandrines of *The Young Fate*. Was it really worth having hidden for so long, only to reappear in that garb? I've already said that, for me, a very demanding myth was at stake: with *The Young Fate*, it was as if Mr. Teste had been *duped*, betrayed. Apart from several flashes of brilliance, this long poem—which its author called an "exercise"—hardly seemed worthwhile.

Apollinaire had returned to his garret at 202 Boulevard Saint-Germain. You edged your way in between bookshelves, rows of African and Oceanian fetishes, paintings of the most revolutionary kind for the times, like so many sails heading for the mind's most adventurous horizons: Picasso, De Chirico, Larionov . . . There was no path more sinuous than the one leading to the desk where he sat, half-present and half-absent. Without letting the conversation drop entirely, now and then he would jot several words on a scrap of paper—and his pen plunged into this terrible gilded-bronze inkwell that was shaped like the Sacré-Coeur (he

---

* Held in Switzerland in 1915 and 1916, respectively, these conferences were sponsored by pacifist Socialists of various countries. At both, Lenin tried to persuade the organizers to turn the world war into a Socialist civil war, but instead the 1916 conference finally adopted the more moderate demand for "an immediate peace without annexations or indemnities and the right of the peoples to self-determination." In any event, the conferences amounted to little, for the pacifist Socialists were themselves only a small minority of the international movement, as compared to their prowar counterparts.

was wild about such objects). It also happened that he would leave me alone in his home for hours, after having handed me some rare work, something by Sade or a volume of *Monsieur Nicolas*. Soupault and I, and later Aragon, preferred to pay him separate visits.

Much more suited to our gatherings was the almost naked room into which Pierre Reverdy welcomed us, usually on Sundays. He lived at the crest of Montmartre, on Rue Cortot, a few steps away from Rue des Saules. Nothing can give a better idea of the astounding "climate" that reigned there than this admirable sentence by Reverdy himself, which opens *La Lucarne ovale* [The Oval Skylight]:

> In those days coal had become as precious and scarce as gold nuggets, and I wrote in an attic where the snow, falling through the cracks in the ceiling, turned blue.

I have never stopped being enchanted by such a way of speaking. It immediately takes me into the heart of the verbal magic that, for us, was the domain where Reverdy operated. Only Aloysius Bertrand and Rimbaud had advanced so far down that path. As for me, I loved and still love poetry immersed in the things that suffuse everyday life, the halo of apprehensions and clues that floats around our impressions and our acts. Reverdy dipped into it as if by chance. The rhythm he had created for himself seemed to be his only tool, but that tool never failed him. He was marvelous. Reverdy was much more of a theoretician than Apollinaire: he would even have been an ideal master for us if he'd been less passionate in discussion, if he'd cared more genuinely about the objections we raised. But it's true that his passion was a large part of his charm. No one was ever more thoughtful, or made you more thoughtful, about the deep wellsprings of poetry than he. Once you knew him, nothing seemed as important as his theses on the image in poetry. Nor has anyone else shown such exemplary detachment toward fate's long ingratitude.

AP: So there wasn't a single difference of opinion with Reverdy?

AB: Oh, with him subjects of controversy were never in short supply. Despite everything, we found him a bit too wrapped up in his own world, too exclusively attentive to the kind of poetic expression associated with Cubism. We thought—or we foresaw—that other sensory currents were on the march, and that nothing would hold them back. A good number of our objections, furthermore, were dictated by the recent discovery of the Comte de Lautréamont—"Count Lautréamont"—who had sent all three of us into raptures. Nothing, not even Rimbaud, had stirred me so deeply . . . Still today, I am absolutely incapable of thinking dispassionately of that dazzling message that seems to exceed human possibility from every angle. To get an idea of how far our exaltation could go in this regard, you need only read these lines by Soupault: "It's not for me, nor for anyone (do you hear, Gentlemen? who wants my witnesses?) to judge the Count. One does not judge M. de Lautréamont. One recognizes Him as He passes and one bows down to the ground. I pledge my life to him or her who can make me forget Him forever." Had this declaration taken the form of a *pact*, I would have signed it without hesitation.

Reverdy had not gone that route, so he had no idea how violent the imperatives to which *Maldoror* subjected us were. How could Léon Bloy, Rémy de Gourmont, and, more recently, Valéry Larbaud (who had nonetheless felt the mesmerizing power of that unique message) have arbitrarily brushed him aside as a pathological case, or not have been more shaken by him? Only Jarry, no doubt . . . but Jarry had only alluded to him in his writings. For us, from the outset, there was no genius that could hold a candle to Lautréamont. We felt that a great sign of the times resided in the fact that his hour still hadn't come, whereas for us it was indisputably here.

AP: To summarize, then, what were your mutual concerns in those last months of the war?

AB: You'll have to forgive me, but here we enter the technical realm. Our preoccupations tended toward the elucidation of the *lyrical* phenomenon in poetry. At the time, I understood lyricism

to be the spasmodic surpassing of controlled expression. I was convinced that this surpassing could result only from a considerable emotional rush, and that in return, only this surpassing could generate deep emotion. But—and here's the mystery—the emotion induced would differ in every respect from the inductive emotion. There would be a transmutation. The highest examples I knew were contained in the exuberance of Lautréamont's "Beautiful as" series, the most famous of these being: "Beautiful as the chance meeting, on a dissection table, of a sewing machine and an umbrella"; or else in the memory lapses that surround the evocation of "Falmer's hair" at the end of Canto 4 of *Maldoror*. In Rimbaud, it seemed to me that these *summits* were reached in "Devotions" and "Dream."

AP: Were you able to objectify your thoughts on this subject?

AB: Objectify, no, but verify, yes. It was around that time that Apollinaire, in *Le Mercure de France*, published a rather long, manifesto-style text entitled "The New Spirit and the Poets"—a text that, if the truth be told, won only our partial support. While we were pleased to have him confirm that in poetry and art "surprise is our greatest new resource," and to see him demand "freedom of unimaginable oppulence," we were worried about the importance he placed on reviving the "critical spirit" of the classics, which to us seemed terribly limiting, as well as on their "sense of duty," which we considered debatable, in any case outmoded, and, regardless, out of the question. The will to situate the debate on a national, even nationalistic, level ("France," said Apollinaire, "keeper of the entire secret of civilization") seemed still more unacceptable to us. Nor did we like seeing art humiliated by science. We especially deplored that the "new spirit" thus conceived was seeking to base itself on external artifice (typographical or otherwise): lyrical means themselves were neither deepened nor renewed. But maybe it was Apollinaire's wound that limited his audacity and reduced his field of prospection . . .

In a few more months, that prestigious voice would be

silenced—by a paradox of fate it was on the eve of the Armistice—that voice that had combined those of Simon Magus and Merlin, and also the one that (and this was strictly *unheard-of*) he had lent to Croniamental, the "poet assassinated."

AP: Were you telling me before that it's still possible to hear his voice?

AB: Here's a record on which Apollinaire recorded four poems, under the direction of Charles Bruneau of the Sorbonne. The technology was mediocre. The great, and sole, value of the document is that it lets us hear Apollinaire. Here is the great poet's voice as it emerges from the shadows:

> Open this door where I knock weeping
> Life is uncertain as the tides of Euripos . . .

AP: Maybe it isn't worth listening to the rest?

AB: No, and it's too bad. He had such high hopes for the phonograph . . . Well, enough. Barely two more months had gone by when a new crack appeared in the sentient edifice that Soupault, Aragon, and I had built together. What was even more serious about this one is that it occurred not at the top, but in the very foundation of that edifice. Around January 10, 1919, we learned of the death of Jacques Vaché, which had occurred, seemingly by accident, after he'd taken too much opium in a hotel in Nantes. Vaché—whom I was the only one to know personally, even though Aragon had exchanged a letter with him—exerted an unparalleled seduction over us. His behavior and his statements were an object of continual reference. His letters were an oracle, and the nature of that oracle was to be inexhaustible. Today I think that he harbored a great secret, which consisted in *unmasking* and *masking* at the same time. The fact remains that for us he incarnated the highest power of "disengagement" (maximum disengagement from everything that was hypocritically being

propounded; disengagement from art: "Art is folly"; disengagement especially from the reigning "moral law," which had just shown us precisely what it was worth). Whatever action we sought to undertake, since this was becoming more and more urgent, always seemed to lead us back to him. Indeed, we were only awaiting his return to begin these actions, for, like us and those our age, he was still in uniform. Suffice it to say that his loss was irreparable . . . Anyway! We were—I was—at an age when life is stronger . . . In retrospect, I'm amazed that my recovery was so rapid, since in March 1919, under our triple editorship (Aragon, Breton, Soupault), the first issue of our magazine *Littérature* appeared. Valéry had suggested the title, which for him was already laden with ambivalence because of the last line of Verlaine's poem "Art poétique": "And all the rest is literature." From Valéry's point of view (that of the intellect) he couldn't help being more interested in "literature"—"all the rest"—than in what Verlaine took to be its opposite. But Valéry was also laughing up his sleeve, and there was surely a certain perverseness in his advice. As far as we were concerned, if we adopted this word as our title, it was as an antiphrasis and in a mocking spirit in which Verlaine played no part.

AP: And how did *Littérature* look, at the beginning?

AB: Oh, very well-bred! What more could one ask? The great survivors of Symbolism—Gide, Valéry, Léon-Paul Fargue—led the way, followed by the poets who had gravitated around Apollinaire: André Salmon, Max Jacob, Reverdy, Blaise Cendrars. A little later they were joined by Paul Morand and Jean Giraudoux, then Pierre Drieu la Rochelle. The link between them and us was provided by Jean Paulhan, through whom I met Paul Eluard soon afterward. It seemed that everyone was getting his due, and also that we had a fair wind in our sails: in the first four issues (from March to June 1919), the magazine published the *Poésies* of Isidore Ducasse, a.k.a. the Comte de Lautréamont, which I had taken down by hand from the only known copy in the Bibliothèque

Nationale; and an extremely important unpublished work by Rimbaud, "The Hands of Jeanne-Marie." But various cracks soon began to appear, harbingers of "Dada."

AP: With your permission, that will be the subject of our next interview.

The world that writes 365 in Arabic characters has learned to multiply it by a two-figure number.

*   *   *

I have a sinister mark on the inner side of my arm, a blue M that threatens me.

*   *   *

Getting bored cannot be done; that would be to the detriment of caresses and before long we will be there no more.

*   *   *

God the Father's will to grandeur does not in France exceed 4,810 meters' height above sea level.

*   *   *

Between the manifold splendors of anger, I watch a door slam like the corsage of a flower or the erasers of schoolchildren.

*   *   *

Temptation to order a new drink: a plantain demolition, for instance.

—The Magnetic Fields

4.

AFTER THE WAR. AUTOMATIC WRITING: *THE MAGNETIC FIELDS*. TZARA IN PARIS. THE DADA DEMONSTRATIONS.

ANDRE PARINAUD: This fourth broadcast touches on the period of your life between the spring of 1919 and the end of 1920, in other words the period that stretches from the first issues of *Littérature* and your return to civilian life through your break from Dada. What was your state of mind and what were your ambitions in 1919?

ANDRE BRETON: Bear in mind that, during the spring and summer of 1919 when the first six issues of *Littérature* came out, we had very little freedom of movement: I wasn't discharged until September, and Aragon several months after that. The powers that were took great care to ease the transition between the kind of existence to which the war had introduced us, and the kind that the return to civilian life held in store. This precaution was hardly superfluous. The inevitable contact between soldiers returning from the front soon ended up retrospectively heightening the reasons for anger: their feelings about the pointless sacrifice of so many lives; their desire to "square accounts" with the rear guard, whose famous hard-line policies had for so long gone hand in hand with ruthless racketeering; the innumerable broken homes; and the extreme mediocrity of any future prospects. The headiness of military victory had died down . . .
We had gotten away from the war, that much was certain. But

what we couldn't get away from was the "brain washing" that for four years had been turning men—who asked only to live and (with rare exceptions) get along with their neighbors—into frenzied and fanatical creatures who not only did their masters' bidding, but could also be ruthlessly decimated. Naturally, some of these poor fellows were now looking rather angrily at the ones who had given them such good reasons to go fight. One couldn't keep these former soldiers from comparing notes or sharing their individual experiences, which the censorship office had made sure were never broadcast. No more than one could keep them from discovering the extent of the war's ravages, the limitless passivity it had generated and, when this passivity had tried to rouse itself, the terrible harshness of the repression that followed. As you might imagine, they were not in the best of moods.

AP: Still, the general atmosphere was not one of revolt, but rather of apathy—or so it seems at this remove.

AB: It's true that most of these soldiers soon chose their camps. Little by little, they formed associations whose leaders quickly managed to channel their dissatisfaction. Moreover, even when their interests began to diverge sharply, as "war veterans" they maintained a certain measure of purely sentimental solidarity (which in retrospect is rather amusing). The powers I spoke of— who had braved extreme unpopularity during the war years—had no trouble staying in office, simply by promoting darkly destitute ceremonies to absorb the unrest that threatened to spread like a stain. These ceremonies foreshadowed the constant inauguration of monuments to the dead that live on today as testaments to an age of vandalism, such as the shrine of the "unknown soldier" in Paris's Place de l'Etoile . . . As far as I was concerned, now that I was freed from the military yoke, I was determined to avoid any new obligations. Come what may.

AP: How did you envision the future at that moment?

AB: My future was impossible to envision. It's difficult for me,

today, to recapture that state of mind. For hours on end I paced around the table in my hotel room. I walked aimlessly throughout Paris, and spent evenings alone on a bench in Place du Châtelet. I don't believe I was pursuing an idea or solution: no, I was prey to a kind of daily fatalism, translated by a not-unpleasant "drifting with the tide." This stemmed from an almost total indifference that spared only my few friends, in other words those who in some way or another were feeling the same distress as I. This distress was surely of a new kind, although it could hardly be objectified.

AP: It was nonetheless in that period that you seemed to make certain resolutions, at least as far as the orientation of *Littérature* was concerned.

AB: Yes. One thing I quickly realized was that the orientation of *Littérature*'s early issues was no longer viable. What good was it to keep attempting an impossible synthesis between elements whose juxtaposition satisfied a certain desire for quality, but that had absolutely nothing in common with one another? We needed to counter the magazine's anthological side.

In the path that was more specifically becoming our own, Aragon, Soupault, and I no longer had to rely strictly on ourselves. In the interim we had met Paul Eluard and, shortly before, I had begun corresponding with Tristan Tzara.

AP: What led Eluard your way?

AB: Before becoming our friend, Eluard was the friend of Jean Paulhan, and for a long time he shared the latter's concerns; he cultivated his learned objections in matters linguistic and poetic. At the time, we were very much in tune with what Paulhan said and, even more so, what he implied, the afterthoughts he was so good at suggesting. Paulhan's extreme moderation, the muffled nature of his observations, the singular sharpness of his perspective on things interested me as much as they interested Eluard.

And many other affinities besides led Eluard to make common cause with us.

AP: What did you know about Tzara before meeting him?

AB: Tzara was still in Zurich, where he was causing quite an uproar. In the preceding years, the so-called "Dada" activity had remained fairly unclear to me. I discovered the first two issues of *Dada* at Apollinaire's; he viewed them with some distrust, suspecting certain of its editors of not being entirely squared away with their countries' military authorities, and even fearing that to receive such a periodical in the mail might compromise him . . .

These issues still showed a certain dependency on experiments from before the war (Cubism, Futurism), even though a distinctly negative spirit was already evident, along with a tendency toward extremism. But it was only *Dada 3*, which reached Paris at the beginning of 1919, that lit the powder keg. Tzara's "Dada Manifesto 1918," which opened it, was violently explosive. It proclaimed art's break from logic, the necessity of making a "great negative effort"; it praised spontaneity to the skies. What impressed me most, even more than what was said, was the quality that emanated from it: exasperated and nervous; provocative and distant; poetic, too. A little later, Tzara said, "I am not a professional writer and I have no literary ambitions. I should have become a successful adventurer, making subtle gestures, if I had had the physical force and nervous stamina to achieve this one exploit: not to be bored." It was statements such as these that got me so interested in him at the time.

AP: That statement of Tzara's could have been signed by Vaché . . .

AB: It's obvious that such an attitude likened him especially to Jacques Vaché, which is what led me to transfer onto him much of the confidence and hope that I had placed in Vaché. As a result, *Littérature's* orientation was drastically altered.

While all this was happening, moreover, a widespread move-

ment was converging from various parts of the world. This conflu-
ence encouraged a confrontation of attitudes that until then had
had little to do with each other, but that held numerous points in
common—which we still haven't fully explored. Founded during
the war in America, then continuing its publication in Paris,
Francis Picabia's magazine, *291*, which later became *391*, called
our attention to the activities of Arthur Cravan, "poet and boxer,"
who claimed to be Oscar Wilde's nephew. Right before the war,
Cravan had published a little magazine called *Maintenant*, the tone
of which was unprecedentedly direct. After that, in America, he
constantly drew attention to himself by challenging everything
that could be considered good sense and good taste, and by doing
it with inexhaustible vigor and youth. I don't have time here to
recount his exploits in detail, but I did give a glimpse of them in
my *Anthologie de l'humour noir* [Anthology of Black Humor].

AP: Wasn't it also at that time that Marcel Duchamp's activities
became extremely important to you?

AB: Yes. It was also through Picabia that we received news—
very unsettling news—of Marcel Duchamp. His evolution was
one of the strangest ever: after having paid a wholly original
tribute to Cubism and Futurism from 1911 to 1913, in such now-
famous canvases as *Nude Descending a Staircase* and *The King and
Queen Surrounded by Swift Nudes*, he played the iconoclast by signing "ready-made objects," such as a bottle rack, a snow shovel, or
a urinal, which, he was convinced, were promoted to the stature
of works of art by the sole virtue of his "choice." With still more
flagrant nonchalance, he signed a color reproduction of the *Mona
Lisa* after having embellished her with a mustache. They said that
for several years he had been working on a giant painting on glass,
The Bride Stripped Bare by Her Bachelors, Even, about which no one
had any details yet, but which opened in every direction onto the
unusual, the unknown.

AP: Picabia was also very active at the time. What was your
opinion of his poetry, painting, and attitude?

AB: Picabia, who had just returned to Paris (passing through Switzerland in order to meet Tzara), indeed seemed quite "worked up." In his magazine, *391*, he threw numerous darts, which he seldom neglected to dip in poison first, against all and sundry. Among the living—apart from Tzara, who had obviously won him over—he spared only Duchamp, whose influence over him was very strong then, and Georges Ribemont-Dessaignes, who shared most of his views. Certain elements of his behavior struck us as a little histrionic, a bit paroxysmal, but I appreciated both the insolent liberty of his poetry (*52 miroirs* [52 Mirrors], *L'Athlète des pompes funèbres* [The Funeral Parlor Athlete]) and his taste for "adventure-for-adventure's-sake," which his visual experiments demonstrated to an unsurpassable degree (*Udnie, Very Rare Picture on the Earth, Amorous Procession*, and many others).

AP: These details about yourself and your friends clearly show both your desire for and your misgivings about revolution. They provide a better understanding of your reasons for joining Dada, and for later breaking away from it. We're still in 1919. How much did you know about Dada?

AB: At that time, we still had very little information about what the "Dada movement" might have been in Berlin, under the impetus of Richard Huelsenbeck; but we would soon see it dazzlingly and crucially reaffirmed in Cologne around Max Ernst. The link between Max Ernst's mind and Tzara's was supplied by Hans Arp, who spent the war with Tzara in Zurich—Arp, whose drawings and "woodcuts" were probably, in those days, the newest and freest things around, and whose poems of the time, written in German, were also what rendered the most original and most moving sound. The important thing for us was that the same currents were forming in two countries that only yesterday had been enemies. As far as we were concerned, there couldn't be a better justification.

I repeat, it was the convergence of these lines that convinced me to join the "Dada movement" (Soupault, as with all things, ac-

corded it less importance; Aragon was hesitant for a long time). Dada, as it was formulated in the "1918 Manifesto," seemed to respond to a form of the necessity of the times, seemed historically to *link*—in order then to *overcome*—certain major objections that had surged from all over.

AP: Was the "Dada spirit" already influencing the direction of *Littérature?*

AB: As undermined as it might have been by the "Dada" spirit, *Littérature* as a magazine nonetheless stayed relatively true to its initial format. Typographical artifices, which were the principal affectation of *Dada* and *391*, played no part here. The inclusion of elements that were, if not hostile to this new state of mind, at least immune to any possible contagion—Valéry, Gide, Max Jacob, Cendrars, Morand—continued until February 1920, when the twelfth issue came out. If there was any attempt at subversion, it was on grounds other than "Dada": after the publication of Lautréamont's *Poésies*, *Littérature* began publishing Jacques Vaché's *Letters from the Front*; in a spirit of mockery, it asked popular novelist Jules Mary for his reminiscences of Rimbaud; it led the literary community into a trap it still hasn't forgotten, by sending writers a survey that asked "Why do you write?" and by publishing their answers—the vast majority of which were pathetic—by order of mediocrity.

But even more significant—and we should take note of this once and for all—is that in the October to December 1919 issues, *Littérature* published, under my signature and Soupault's, the first three chapters of *The Magnetic Fields*. Without a doubt, we are dealing here with the first *Surrealist* (and in no sense Dadaist) work, since it was the fruit of the first systematic applications of automatic writing. This book had already been finished several months earlier. The daily practice of automatic writing—at times we spent eight or ten consecutive hours at it—led us to make observations of great portent; but only later were these observations coordinated and shown to be significant. Be that as it may, at that moment we lived in a state of euphoria, almost in the intoxica-

tion of discovery. We felt like miners who had just struck the mother lode.

AP: So in 1919 you had already acquired the drilling and extraction techniques that Surrealism later used on a larger scale.

AB: Yes, the initial, all-important observations had been made. All that remained was to shed light on the operation's various implications, psychological and otherwise. Therefore it's inaccurate and chronologically incorrect to present Surrealism as a movement that evolved from Dada, or to see it as the constructive rectification of Dada. The truth is that, in *Littérature* as well as in the Dada magazines properly speaking, Surrealist texts constantly alternated with Dadaist texts. Although the necessities I alluded to earlier momentarily converged to make us put the accent on Dada, Dada and Surrealism—even if the latter was still latent—can only be considered correlatively, like two waves that cover each other by turns.

AP: What was this "Dada activity" like at the beginning of 1920?

AB: I think we can distinguish three phases of Dada activity as it developed in Paris. There was a phase of great agitation, which began shortly after Tzara's arrival and was under his direct control; this period ran from January to August 1920, and was not really resumed at the end of the year. There was a more halting period, which still aimed at pursuing the same goals but by radically renewed means, in particular those devised by Aragon and myself; this period stretched from January to August 1921. Finally there was a phase of unease, during which the attempt to return to the original format of our performances quickly discouraged the last remaining participants, and during which dissension mounted until August 1922, the date of Dada's ultimate extinction.

AP: Let's examine this activity phase by phase. What came first?

AB: The first phase (in the early months of 1920) was, in retro-spect and viewed from outside, quite dazzling. A number of periodicals burst onto the scene: *Bulletin Dada* and *Dadaphone*, edited by Tzara; *Cannibale*, edited by Picabia; *Proverbe*, edited by Eluard; issue number 13 of *Littérature*, devoted to the publication of "23 Dada Manifestoes"; and several other magazines of lesser importance attested to the movement's vitality. We weren't con-tent simply to write, moreover, but also staged a number of public demonstrations: in short order came the "First Friday of *Littéra-ture*" at the Palais des Fêtes (January), the demonstration at the Salon des Indépendants (February), the one at the Théâtre de l'Oeuvre (March), and the "Festival" at the Salle Gaveau (May). At first glance, we had apparently obtained the desired effect: con-formism was made to look bad, common sense was beside itself, and the press was seething with rage. It might seem that every-thing was for the best, and yet from within—at least as far as Aragon, Eluard, and I were concerned—the situation was per-ceived differently. Of course we exploited, ad nauseam, methods of stupefaction, of "cretinization" in the Maldororian sense of the word; but these were mainly harmless provocations that had been perfected in Zurich or elsewhere. Each time a Dada demonstra-tion was planned—by Tzara, of course, who never tired of them—Picabia gathered us in his salon and *enjoined* us, one after the other, to come up with *ideas* for it. In the end, the harvest was not very abundant. The crowning touch was inevitably the first, or the second, or the *n*th "adventure of Mr. Antipyrine" by Tris-tan Tzara, acted out by his friends, who were perennially stuffed into tall cardboard cylinders (this was his favorite "idea" of last resort; Zurich had no doubt been flabbergasted by it). Of course, most of us were young, and the lack of perspective in such activ-ities didn't bother us. Soupault and I, for example, derived no small satisfaction from that fact that a skit we'd written called *Vous m'oublierez* [You'll Forget Me], performed by the two of us at the Salle Gaveau, warranted a bombardment of eggs, tomatoes, and steaks that the audience had rushed out to buy during intermis-sion. What the public thought of us we returned in kind a hun-dredfold. Still, two or three of us couldn't help wondering if this

"battle over *Hernani*," newly joined every month with the same self-satisfaction, and whose tactics had so quickly become stereo-typed, was sufficient in and of itself. I had nothing against the "scarlet vest,"* on the condition that beneath it beat the heart of Aloysius Bertrand or Gérard de Nerval, and beneath their hearts, the hearts of Nervalis or Hölderlin, and still others beneath theirs . . .

AP: So not everything you collectively published hit the Dada "note" in the proper sense?

AB: The specifically "Dada" *note*—Surrealist infiltrations excluded—was sounded only by Tzara, Picabia, and Ribemont-Dessaignes. Duchamp's activities were continually invoked, but from afar. Arp stayed within poetic and visual limits. Ernst was not the sort to choose between Dada and Surrealism: he brought grist to both mills at the same time.

AP: Was this the source of the unease that was already preparing the ground for your reaction?

AB: I believe so. The great disappointment at the time—for several of us—stemmed from the fact that Tzara was not as I had imagined him. He was a poet, to be sure, and even a great one when he felt like it. But around Paris he was rumored to be drugged, a dope addict. This statement is not colored by any polemical intentions: I'm only trying to describe my feelings of the period. He enjoyed himself, made witty remarks, reiterated stunts that had worked in the past, and exerted his personal charm as best he could—but in a domain that soon proved narrow. The "Dada Manifesto 1918" seemed to throw the doors wide open, but

* The "battle over *Hernani*" (*bataille d'Hernani*) refers to the tumultuous dispute between Romantics and Classicists that broke out at the premiere of Victor Hugo's play *Hernani* in February 1830. The expression "scarlet vest" (*gilet rouge*), which harkens back to poet Théophile Gautier's attire at the same premiere, once designated a partisan of Romanticism.

you discovered that these doors led to a corridor that turned around in circles.

AP: What marked the break between the two phases of Dada's evolution?

AB: The break between the first two phases I delineated was marked by the publication, in the August 1920 *Nouvelle Revue Française*, of a text of mine called "For Dada," which was answered by a text of Jacques Rivière's called "Reconnaissance à Dada" [Thanks Be to Dada]. The latter, whatever its reservations, struck Dada a heavy blow by placing it on the verge of literary acceptance.

AP: So we still need to examine your break from Dada, which heralded the birth of the Surrealist movement. This will be the subject of our next program.

I'm thinking of Marcel Duchamp showing friends a birdcage that, as far as they could see, contained no birds, but instead was half-filled with sugar cubes; and asking them to lift the cage, which they were astonished to find so heavy. What they had taken for sugar cubes were in fact little pieces of marble that Duchamp, at great expense, had had cut to his specifications. This trick, for me, is as good as any other—and even as good as nearly all the tricks of art put together . . .

—*Lecture at the Ateneo, Barcelona, November 17, 1922 (in* Les Pas perdus)

THE DISINTEGRATION OF DADA. THE BARRÈS TRIAL. BENJAMIN PERET. ON THE THRESHOLD OF SURREALISM STRICTLY SPEAKING.

ANDRE PARINAUD: What circumstances led you to break away from Dada? You were saying in our last interview that the article published by Jacques Rivière in *La Nouvelle Revue Française* was the first sign of a split that would continue to widen and . . .

ANDRE BRETON: Yes, you can easily imagine that the publication of a text signed by Jacques Rivière, then editor of the prestigious *Nouvelle Revue Française*, paying sympathetic attention to Dada's activities made us see things in a different light. Up until then Dada had benefited from widespread hostility, which it had done everything in its power to maintain. What could be more exhilarating, for the young men we were, than to be constantly faced with scorn, not to say actual fury? Our feelings about the value of our cause were fortified by the fact that public opinion was unanimously against us.

Indeed, public opinion had shown just how servile it could be in the preceding years, and to incur its wrath to such a point was enough to convince us we were on the right track. Rivière's study was, in short, the first text with wide repercussions that actually tried to delve deeply into our shared intentions. He at least granted us the merit of having attempted what he called "the experiment of absolute psychological reality," and of having raised language to a higher dignity by preferring to see it not as "a

means" but as "an entity." This account, rendered in serious and measured tones, entailed a certain unveiling of our objectives— and, as such, made ineffectual and pointless certain artifices and elementary means of defiance that we had used to excess until then, both in print and during Dada demonstrations.

AP: Why do you say "to excess"?

AB: Because, from that moment on, several of us became extremely tired of some of these forms of externalization: in the Dadaist periodicals, for instance, the overuse (to say the least) of more or less venomous remarks aimed at this or that person; or a marked self-indulgence toward rather debatable verbal humor. If the programs of our performances, which were patterned after cabaret shows, announced sensational "acts" with titles calculated to fill the hall, for some of us who acted in them their realization could not have been more paltry. The genuine scandal they provoked was the only benefit we reaped, but even this was increasingly unable to hide the poverty of the means used, which moreover were pretty much the same every time. False information: Charlie Chaplin has joined the Dada movement and will appear for the first time "in the flesh" at the Dada demonstration at the Salon des Indépendants; at the Salle Gaveau Festival, "the Dadas will shave their heads onstage"; etc. You didn't need any more than that to make people storm the box office. I've already said how laborious the elaboration of each program was. Its (quite fragmentary) execution was far worse. I'm speaking from experience, since I was the one—once the program had been fixed for better or worse, or at least once we had generally agreed upon it— who no doubt did most to ensure that its promises were minimally kept. Tzara, Picabia, and Ribemont-Dessaignes (the only true "Dadas," when you get down to it) were delighted by, or at least resigned to, the situation that had been created. The rest of us came away rather discontented, hardly proud of the pitiful carnival ruses we'd needed in order to attract the public. But the costs of renting an auditorium were high, for the most part we

were very poor, and the price of admission was calculated just to cover expenses, assuming every seat was filled.

AP: I don't know what our listeners will think . . . I'm grateful for these details, but it's clear that by placing these demonstrations in their true climate, you have singularly diminished their impact in our eyes—after we've lived with the legend for so long!

AB: I realize that the Dada demonstrations are seen quite differently by young people today. They'd rather prune away everything that might have made them pointless and boring. By definition, they want to retain only certain heroic aspects, a wholly exterior expression of the disagreement between so-called "Dada" ideas and those that continued to circulate in 1920. It probably wasn't a bad thing—perhaps it was even inevitable that this disagreement should take a spectacular form. I'll simply say that the Dada magazines and performances stagnated under Tzara's leadership. They stagnated, I believe, because they were cut from the same pattern, a pattern designed for Swiss audiences and, if I may say so, shaped by contact with those audiences. Seen from within and from without, they became stereotyped, ossified.

AP: Is this a retrospective judgment you're making, or was it your impression at the time?

AB: Aragon and I were the most sensitive to these symptoms of premature aging, perhaps because we'd had medical training. Not that we renounced the general goals of "Dada" activity, but we'd had enough—if not too much—of those supposedly breathtaking inanities that couldn't even boast freshness. We wanted a radical renewal of means; to pursue the same ends, but by markedly different paths. From that moment on, the movement's homogeneity was drastically compromised. Nothing shows this better than a kind of referendum we published in the March 1921 issue of *Littérature*. Using a scholastic "grading" system, which we'd set between −25 and +20, we proposed to illustrate the degree of

respect or disrespect we felt toward a wide variety of individuals, beginning with Antiquity (a grade of −25 meaning, of course, the depths of abomination; zero, utter indifference; and +20, unconditional devotion of heart and mind). Such a referendum was the fruit of one of our frequent meetings in a bar located in the old Passage de l'Opéra, which Aragon later described in *Paris Peasant*. Several of us would meet there two or three times a week; usually we spent the evening together, and a good part of the time was devoted to games of this kind, or of entirely different kinds. But this one, in retrospect, yields up some surprises. If you'll hand me the magazine . . . Let's see . . . Here's Baudelaire: Aragon 17, Breton 18, Eluard 12, Soupault 12, Tzara −25. Here's Foch (the marshal): Aragon −20, Breton −25, Eluard 16; Ribemont-Dessaignes, Soupault, and Tzara −25. Here's Hegel: Aragon 10, Breton 15, Eluard 6, Tzara −25. Here's Lenin: Aragon 13, Breton 12, Eluard −25, Soupault −25, Tzara −2. Here's Picasso: Aragon 19, Breton 15, Eluard −2, Tzara 3. Here's Rimbaud: Aragon, Breton, and Eluard 18; Tzara −1. Here's Sade: Aragon 17, Breton 19, Eluard 15, Soupault 16, Tzara −25. This −25 of Tzara's, moreover, extends to Dostoevsky, Aeschylus, Goethe, El Greco, and Homer, as well as to Matisse, Nerval, Poe, and Jean-Jacques . . . and Henri Rousseau. How could such profound divergences not give rise to an incompatibility of mood?

AP: Did this March 1921 issue mark the beginning of the break?

AB: Oh, the bonds weren't coming undone quite yet! The principle of Dada demonstrations hadn't been abandoned. We simply decided that they would happen differently. Toward that end, we planned a series of excursions around Paris, choosing the sites as gratuitously as possible: Saint-Julien le Pauvre, Buttes-Chaumont park, Gare Saint-Lazare, the Ourcq canal. It was also agreed that we would hand down indictments, followed by public trials.

But in reality, this new program was only barely put into practice. The meeting in the churchyard of Saint-Julien le Pauvre indeed took place, but it had against it the pouring rain and, still worse, the laborious nullity of the speeches, delivered in a tone

that strove to be provocative. Moving from auditoriums to the open air was not enough to get us away from the "Dada" cliché.

Another public demonstration, the "indictment and trial" of Maurice Barrès, which took place one month later, requires an almost total change of viewpoint if we are to see it accurately. Though on the posters and programs it was still "Dada" that led the dance, and though small concessions were made to Dada in the staging of the "trial" (a mannequin stood in for "Barrès," the "prosecution" and "defense" were curiously attired), in reality the impetus behind the event stood outside of Dada. This impetus actually came from Aragon and myself. The issues raised—which were of an ethical nature—might of course have interested several others among us, taken individually; but Dada, with its acknowledged bias toward indifference, had absolutely nothing to do with them. The problem was to determine the extent to which a man could be held accountable if his will to power led him to champion conformist values that diametrically opposed the ideas of his youth. Secondary questions: how did the author of *Un Homme libre* [A Free Man] become the propagandist for the right-wing *Echo de Paris?* If there was a betrayal, what were the stakes? And what recourse did one have against them? Above and beyond the Barrès case, these questions were to agitate Surrealism for quite some time.

AP: It would be interesting if you'd clarify the impact of this demonstration on your relations with Dada.

AB: On the whole, the evening kept to a rather serious level of discussion, the only discordant note being sounded by Tzara, who, as a "witness," contented himself with farcical statements and, to top it off, broke into an inept song. You need only refer to the write-up in *Littérature* to see just how little his attitude was appreciated under the circumstances, and how much it isolated him from the rest of us.

Despite this internal friction, the group that we continued to form took on some new elements of great importance. Benjamin Péret, who in the "Barrès Trial" played the very risky part of the

"unknown soldier," was, of all of us, the one who plunged the most recklessly into the poetic adventure. His book *Le Passager du Transatlantique* [The Transatlantic Passenger], which was about to be published, already demonstrated his greatest gift: an unprecedented freedom of expression. Just as Victor Hugo had abolished the distinction between "noble" and "nonnoble" words, so Péret abolished the distinction between "noble" and "nonnoble" objects. Jacques Rigaut found in our circle a necessary echo of his wide-ranging paradoxes, which were wrapped in the blackest of humor. A fundamental agreement was also reached with Max Ernst on the basis of his "collages," the first exhibit of which had opened in Paris several days earlier. We know that the collage process, which consists of juxtaposing visual elements borrowed from distinct wholes, such as photographs or engravings, was intended according to Max Ernst himself to realize "the union of two apparently incompatible realities on an apparently unsuitable scale." It's no exaggeration to say that we welcomed Max Ernst's first collages, with their extraordinary suggestive power, as a revelation.

This said, the summer vacation of 1921, which found Max Ernst, Tzara, and myself in the Tyrol, should have resulted in a lessening of hostilities; instead, hostilities began in earnest shortly after our return to Paris.

AP: How did the duel, if I may call it that, begin?

AB: For several more months, our disagreement remained latent. Picabia had left Dada and was sparing it none of his poisoned darts. The public demonstrations, which had become routine for some, naturally remained on the agenda; but because of the turn they'd taken, they had open adversaries within Dada itself. This engendered great confusion. Personally, I had come to the conclusion that Dada, in order to regain some of its vigor, would have to renounce its growing sectarianism and reinsert itself in a larger context; it was time to put an end to our isolationist policies. With this in mind, I tried to organize an "International Congress to Determine the Directives and Defense of the Modern Spirit," also

known as the "Congress of Paris." The steering committee was quickly assembled. It included four publishers or editors-in-chief of literary quarterlies: Amédée Ozenfant for *L'Esprit Nouveau*, Jean Paulhan for *La Nouvelle Revue Française*, Roger Vitrac for *Aventure*, and myself for *Littérature*; plus two painters, Robert Delaunay and Fernand Léger, and a composer, Georges Auric. We declared ourselves ready to proceed with the confrontation of new values, to establish the precise relationship among the opposing forces present, and to be as explicit as possible about the results of their interaction. But new disagreements soon arose: Tzara's inevitable obstruction and the tortuous paths it took led me—as I readily admit—to commit an imprudence. So as not to name Tzara, who was doing his best to block the project, and to deny him the opportunity for endless stalling tactics, I employed, in a communiqué from the Congress intended to warn others against his sabotage, an unfortunate circumlocution: "the promoter of a movement that comes from Zurich." It goes without saying that he immediately seized upon this to accuse me (in circles that largely surpassed Dada's, and included a number of elements that until then he had claimed to despise) of "nationalism" and "xenophobia." That round goes to him. Enough has happened since then to put the lie to those inane charges, but I've always granted that the expression I used was regrettably equivocal. The Congress of Paris never took place.

AP: But it would seem that from this point on, Dada was worse off than ever!

AB: Of course! Even in the minds of those who took part in it, the so-called "Dada Salon" was a fiasco, especially after Marcel Duchamp declined to participate—Duchamp, on whom the organizers had particularly counted, and who simply cabled from America the words "no dice" (*peau de balle*). But I won't linger on the stages of this collapse. By the spring of 1923, Dada, which for over two years had been gravely ill, was now in its death throes. Its last gasp was the "Gas Heart" evening in July. Let's not rehash the

incidents that marked it. The era of Surrealism properly speaking had begun.

AP: Wouldn't it be valuable to remind us of several events in this phase of . . . "rebirth"?

AB: In the time it took to do away with certain regrets, certain sentimental weaknesses, the new series of *Littérature* began reappearing under my sole editorship. Soupault had begun to distance himself. Ribemont-Dessaignes and Tzara kept to the sidelines. Picabia had come back among us. A staunch core, owing to its cohesion and solidity, was constituted by Aragon, Eluard, Ernst, Péret, and myself. At this point another core of activity, consisting of Jacques Baron, René Crevel, Robert Desnos, Max Morise, and Roger Vitrac, joined forces with us. With respect to the preceding period, we registered no loss of energy—quite the opposite. A lecture that I gave in Barcelona during a trip with Picabia describes the atmosphere of the times fairly well. It's called "Caractères de l'évolution moderne et ce qui en participe" [Characteristics of Modern Evolution and What It Consists Of], and it figures in my book *Les Pas perdus*.

At that moment, automatic writing experienced a great revival, and more than ever our attention was drawn to dreams. Everything that concerned any of us was daily put on the table and gave rise, for the most part, to very animated, very cordial discussions (rivalries arose only later). I believe I can say we put into practice a true collectivization of ideas, without individual reservations. If we can speak of Surrealism, as Jules Monnerot did in *La Poésie moderne et lê sacré* [Modern Poetry and the Sacred], as a "bund," in the sense of a "group whose members are joined only by bonds of choice," we have to recognize that it definitively aggregated there. No one sought to keep anything for himself. We all looked forward to enjoying the fruits of our mutual *gift*, of what we had *shared*. And indeed, nothing at the time was more fruitful. When today I see otherwise notable minds so intent upon maintaining their autonomy and so patently concerned about taking their little

secrets with them to the grave, I tell myself that we've regressed. No matter what they think, they're not out of the woods yet.

Games, too, were very popular with us: written games, spoken games, which we made up and tried out on the spot. It was perhaps in these games that our receptivity was constantly regenerated; at least they sustained the happy feeling of dependence we had on each other. You'd have to look as far back as the Saint-Simonians to find the equivalent.

I: "The fearless soul plunges into a land from which there is no escape, where one sees clearly without weeping. One goes there for no particular purpose; one obeys there without anger. There one can see behind oneself without turning around. At last I contemplate beauty without veils, the earth without stains, the medal without a reverse side. I am no longer at the stage of imploring pardon for nothing. No one can close a door without hinges. Why should those harmless traps be placed in the woods of the heart? No doubt, a day without bread will not be so long."

—"Introduction to the Discourse on the Paucity of Reality"

6.

EXPERIMENTAL ACTIVITY. THE *SYSTEMATIC* EXPLORATION OF "TRANCE-LIKE STATES." POWERS OF ROBERT DESNOS.

ANDRE PARINAUD: Mr. Breton, in order to recreate the atmosphere surrounding the events touched upon in this sixth broadcast, could you tell us whether, in the period that went from the end of Dada to the publication of the *Manifesto of Surrealism*, you already had well-defined goals?

ANDRE BRETON: "Well-defined" would be saying a lot. We all agreed at the time that great adventure was within our reach. "Leave everything . . . Take to the highways": that was the theme of my exhortations in those days. We hadn't forgotten Rimbaud, nor his friend Germain Nouveau, whose persistent wanderings were quite familiar to us (before he settled, dressed in beggar's clothing, in the doorway of Aix's cathedral). But what highways could we take? Physical highways? Not likely. Spiritual ones? Hard to imagine. Nonetheless, it occurred to us that we might combine these two types of roads. Out of this came a four-man stroll, undertaken at around that time by Aragon, Morise, Vitrac, and myself. We started out from Blois, a town we had picked at random on the map. It was agreed that we would head off haphazardly on foot, conversing all the while, and that our only planned detours would be for eating and sleeping. In actual practice, the project turned out to be quite peculiar, and even fraught with danger. The trip, which was scheduled to last for about ten days,

but which we finally cut short, immediately took an initiatory turn. The absence of any goal soon removed us from reality, gave rise beneath our feet to increasingly numerous and disturbing phantoms. We easily fell prey to irritation, and there was even a violent episode between Aragon and Vitrac. All things considered, the exploration was hardly disappointing, no matter how narrow its range, because it probed the boundaries between waking life and dream life. So it fell wholly within the scope of our concerns at that time.

AP: In other words, it was in line with your desire to explore the unconscious?

AB: Precisely. Moreover, the time had come when these concerns would find fertile ground for themselves: the induced or hypnotic slumbers, or "sleeping fits," with which we experimented every evening for several months. Although I'd once been a student of Joseph Babinsky—the main detractor of the theses of Charcot and the so-called "Nancy school"—at the time I retained a keen interest, albeit a skeptical one, in some of the psychological literature that was centered on or related to that teaching. I'm thinking in particular of F. W. H. Myers's beautiful work, *Human Personality and Its Survival of Bodily Death*; or Théodore Flournoy's exciting accounts of the medium Hélène Smith in *From India to the Planet Mars* and elsewhere; or even certain chapters of the *Traité de métapsychique* [Treatise on Metapsychics] by Charles Richet. All of this managed to fit together, to combine with my other ways of seeing, thanks to my enthusiastic admiration for Freud, which has never left me. Freud had agreed to see me in 1921 in Vienna and, although the account I published of my visit in *Littérature* was rather derogatory (out of a regrettable sacrifice to the Dada spirit), he had the good grace not to hold it against me and to keep up our correspondence.

Even though they predate the publication of the first *Manifesto*, the "sleeping fits" are an integral part of the history of Surrealism. The *Manifesto's* theoretical statements were derived from them no less than from the speculations that grew out of my increasingly

extensive return to automatic writing. These are its sole foundations.

AP: Nonetheless, it seems the *Manifesto's* importance was scarcely recognized at the time.

AB: Yes, or rather . . . The newspaper critics again reached for one of their favorite clichés: "Fewer manifestoes, more works." But no matter how much they affected to see this manifesto only as the birth announcement of a new literary school, they couldn't prevent it from having a much wider meaning and significance. The reason is that it sanctioned a way of seeing and feeling that had slowly been delineated and pondered, had gradually taken shape and formulated its demands over the preceding years. When the *Manifesto* was published in 1924, it already had behind it five years of uninterrupted experimental activity, involving a considerable number and variety of participants.

AP: There's no doubt that the *Manifesto of Surrealism* pinpoints a stage in the evolution of the mind. It's curious to note that the reactions it has elicited since its appearance rarely bespeak its importance. The articles written about it don't generally focus on its center of interest. Looking at them today, they seem rather like toothpicks trying to be banderillas . . .

AB: Even in retrospect, I have to say that those two fields of exploration—automatic writing and hypnotic slumber—are equally hard to define; that as soon as one tries to impose limits on them, a wide margin of uncertainty or vagueness becomes unavoidable. The ground is constantly shifting, and one is never entirely sure of gaining a foothold. Several incontrovertible documents, such as the first notebooks of automatic texts, the first transcripts of hypnotic sessions, still exist and can be consulted today. But they mark out a route that cannot be traced on any map. Whoever has not looked for himself on that path will have endless difficulty trying to imagine it with any accuracy. For the moment, it would be pointless to try to speak of this no doubt

mystic path in *rational* terms. We're dealing here with the systematic resumption of a *quest*, which the nineteenth century—
beginning with Novalis and Hölderlin in Germany, Blake and
Coleridge in England, Nerval and Baudelaire in France—placed
above all other so-called poetic concerns, and which was to take on
a truly summational character, possibly with Mallarmé, certainly
with Lautréamont and Rimbaud. Such passions are still being
aroused, incidentally. It was inevitable that the ambition—the
"Promethean" ambition, as they've since begun calling it—of the
poets I just cited, their will to force open the doors of mystery and
fearlessly advance over uncharted terrain despite every prohibition, would most offend those who had comfortably retreated
behind existing barriers: we know that these latter are legion.
Their fury is growing today because they cannot halt the history
of ideas, because regression is just as impossible in this domain as
it is in any other. Nothing can make poetic activity—which for
more than a century has been directed, then veritably aimed,
toward recuperating the mind's original powers—willingly return
to a subordinate position.

AP: In this regard, it would be interesting for you to analyze the
aspirations and ideas that determined your and your friends' research into the realm of the unconscious.

AB: First and foremost, we must understand that the processes
governing the practice of automatic writing and the study of the
outer manifestations of induced slumber were one and the same.
In both cases, what we were trying to reach and explore was none
other than so-called trance-like states. You asked me where our taste
for such states came from: it's very simple. What fascinated us was
the possibility they offered of escaping the constraints that weigh
on supervised thought. The most serious of these constraints is
the mind's subjection to immediate sensory perceptions, which to
a large extent makes it a plaything of the external world (I mean
that in normal conditions of ideation, we remove ourselves only
partially from what comes before our eyes, strikes our ears, etc.).
Because of their parasitic nature, the impressions resulting from

such perceptions cannot help but *falsify* the course of that ideation. Another, equally rigid constraint, which we felt an irresistible need to shake up, is the *critical spirit* imposed on language, and on means of expression in general. We felt—and personally, I still feel—that in order to save these means of expression from the increasing threat of sclerosis, and to restore the human verb to its original innocence and creative power, one had to clear away the obstacles that prevented it from making any new developments.

AP: And yet your goal, as we know, was not poetic. So what were these obstacles you wanted to remove, these limits that impeded your activities?

AB: There were *logical* obstacles (narrow rationalism not letting anything pass that hadn't received its stamp of approval), *moral* obstacles (in the form of sexual and social taboos), and, perhaps the worst of all, obstacles of *taste*, governed by sophistic conventions of "good manners." We noticed that in our day the role of this supposed critical sense, which willy-nilly we had inherited like everyone else, was to rein in all intellectual speculations of any breadth. We took it not as the voice of "good sense," but rather as that of the most hackneyed "common sense." We all agreed that this "critical sense," which we'd been taught to cultivate in school, was public enemy number one.

AP: And what did you set against this critical sense?

AB: Why, a hunger for the marvelous, as we could still revive it in childhood memories. Completely against the tide, in a violent reaction against the impoverishment and sterility of thought processes that resulted from centuries of rationalism, we turned toward the marvelous and advocated it unconditionally. In this regard, a sentence from the 1924 *Manifesto* is rather peremptory: "Let us not mince words: the marvelous is always beautiful, anything marvelous is beautiful, in fact only the marvelous is beautiful."

AP: Your hunger for the marvelous was not that of the common herd, however. You maintained certain distinctions. I have trouble imagining you lapsing into spiritualism, for example.

AB: Of course not, far from it. We were deeply suspicious of everything that came under the heading of spiritualism, which since the nineteenth century had claimed a large portion of the marvelous for itself. More specifically, we flatly denied the tenets of spiritualism (no possible communication between the living and the dead), all the while maintaining a keen interest in some of the phenomena it had helped bring to light. Despite its absurd and erroneous point of departure, it had detected certain powers of the mind, of singular character and no small importance. To give an idea of our qualified attitude toward spiritualism, I would place it midway between the attitudes held respectively, circa 1855, by Victor Hugo (see the transcripts of his sessions with the séance tables in Guernsey) and Robert Browning, as expressed in his poem "Mr. Sludge, 'the Medium.' " Between Hugo's and Browning's points of view, the (at least apparent) contradiction is total. Surrealism would resolve this contradiction by highlighting what remained of mediumistic communication once we had freed it from the insane metaphysical implications it otherwise entailed.

AP: This is without a doubt one of its essential contributions to science, and I hope you'll describe the methods and techniques you employed in exploring the unknown.

AB: I think you can see fairly clearly the state of mind we were in when we sought to approach these "trance-like states," which at the outset were Surrealism's ground of choice. Let me take the opportunity, in passing, to refute the accusation of *laziness* periodically brought against those who practice, or have practiced, with greater or lesser perseverance, automatic writing or any other form of automatic activity. For such writing to be truly automatic, the mind must in fact detach itself from the solicitations of the external world, as well as from individual cares of a utilitarian or sentimental nature, etc. Such detachment is tradi-

tionally held to fall much more within the sphere of Eastern rather than Western thought, and demands from the latter an extremely sustained tension or effort. I still think it's incomparably less difficult to satisfy the demands of reflection than it is to put one's mind in a state of total receptivity, to have ears only for "what the mouth of shadows says."

Today any number of books describe the circumstances in which the first automatic sentence, seemingly uttered to no one in particular, forced itself on my attention; and in the first *Manifesto* I told at length how Soupault and I managed to obtain a regular outflow of the same timbre. I'll simply repeat that, to guard against an undeniable monotony, we soon began to vary the speed of capturing that message, from an almost *calm* writing to one that was so fast we could hardly read it. This latter, by far, seemed to be richest in discoveries, which leads me to suspect that shorthand notation would give much better results—but I don't know if anyone's ever tried it.

AP: It also seems to me that automatic writing was used in different ways even within the Surrealist movement, and not always in the spirit of the initial experiments.

AB: I didn't fail to mention the vicissitudes that automatic writing had encountered in Surrealism. The main one came from the fact that, among those who practiced it, aesthetic competition could not entirely be avoided, and that a choice was made at least *a posteriori*, leaving in its wake only fragments of the message—those considered the most apposite. Actually, this was not so important as it might seem. The essential thing was that the *climate* of automatic productions made itself felt, that the mind got wind of a land whose flora and fauna were instantly recognizable, and especially whose *structure* (which was apparently the same for everyone) had only to be revealed. The hard part was to get people to try this recognition for themselves; to convince them that this land was not *elsewhere*, but *in themselves*; and to make them discard all their baggage so that their step would be light enough to cross the bridge leading there. It seemed to me that, sooner or later,

they'd find a way to cross to the other side at will, and return to this side equally at will, without any special discipline, as if they needed only push a button. Every idea in the world would be shattered, but I'm also convinced that the "real life" Rimbaud spoke about would begin.

AP: It was around 1922, I believe, that your activity and that of your friends entered a very important phase. Would you give us some details of the experiments performed at the time, which highlighted the talents of Crevel and Desnos?

AB: In an essay entitled "Entrée des médiums" [The Mediums Enter], reprinted in my book *Les Pas perdus*, I related how, at the end of 1922, during one of the many evenings that found us gathered in my studio, René Crevel induced us to elicit certain verbal or written manifestations from hypnotic slumber. Following Crevel's directions, we agreed to adopt the external apparatus of spiritualism—in other words, we sat in a circle around the table, the tip of each one's little finger touching the tip of someone else's so as to form the famous "chain." In the requisite conditions of silence and darkness, it was in fact not long before Crevel started banging his head against the wooden tabletop, and almost immediately he launched into a lengthy oral improvisation.

The subject of this rambling improvisation was similar to true crime stories. Extreme volubility, precluding any kind of hesitation. The emotional content must have been considerable, judging from the signs of agitation he gave. Irrational diction, alternating for no apparent reason between bombast and droning. Such a pity we weren't able to record it! In this speech—or in one of the similar ones he subsequently graced us with—we would have had an invaluable document, something like Crevel's *sentient specter*. Crevel, with his beautiful adolescent's gaze, which several photos have preserved; the way he so appealed to people; the fear and bravado that arose in him with equal suddenness . . . through all of this, what predominated was anxiety. He was, moreover, psychologically very complex, blocked by a sort of frenzy that

possessed him via his love of the eighteenth century, and particularly of Diderot.

That said, the one who would truly be in his element, in this
atmosphere of hypnotic slumber and the peculiar means of expression it bestowed, was not Crevel—no more than Péret, who
fell asleep during one of the following sessions and made rather
jovial remarks, whose tone and subject didn't substantially differ
from his written stories—but Robert Desnos. It was Desnos who
indelibly stamped his mark on this form of activity. Indeed, he
gave himself over to it passionately, bringing to it a romantic taste
for shipwrecks that is expressed in the title of one of his first
collections of poems, *Corps et biens* [Lost with All Hands]. No one
else ever rushed so headlong onto every path of the marvelous . . .

AP: It must indeed have been a marvelous adventure to join in
these sessions, the source of a new kind of poetry . . .

AB: In any case, we lived through them in a state of exaltation.
Everyone who witnessed Desnos's daily plunges into what was
truly the *unknown* was swept up into a kind of giddiness; we all
hung on what he might say, what he might feverishly scribble on a
scrap of paper. I'm thinking in particular of the "word games," of a
wholly new lyrical type, that he was able to string together for
extended periods, at a tempo that was nothing short of prodigious.
Desnos collected these "word games," which he claimed were the
products of telepathic communication with Marcel Duchamp
(who was then in New York), under the title "Rrose Sélavy" in
Corps et biens. I used the word "prodigious," by which I especially
meant Desnos's ability to transport himself, at will and instan-
taneously, from the mediocrities of daily life into a zone of illu-
mination and poetic effusion. The printed page is no doubt less
favorable to poems of this kind. When read silently, they are
marred by facilities, even trivialities; whereas when they spontaneously gushed forth, the very fact of their completely inspired,
irrepressible, inexhaustible nature provided no foothold for criticism. It goes without saying that "literature" and its criteria had
no business here.

Let us remember that the lowest actors of the period have had Anatole France as their accomplice and let us never forgive him for adorning the colors of the Revolution with his smiling inertia. To bury his corpse, let someone on the quays empty out a box of those old books "he loved so much" and put him in it and throw the whole thing into the Seine. Now that he's dead, this man no longer needs to make any more dust.

—A Corpse, *1924*

7.

PITFALLS OF HYPNOTIC SLUMBER: THE "HAZARDOUS LANDSCAPES." OFFENSIVE RETURN TO THE SURFACE. A "WHIPPING BOY": ANATOLE FRANCE.

ANDRE PARINAUD: In our preceding broadcast, Mr. Breton, you stressed the simultaneously scientific and poetic interest of your experiments with hypnotic slumber. But we also know that you were forced to interrupt your explorations of the unconscious, just when disagreements were arising between you and Robert Desnos. I believe this point deserves to be clarified at the start of the broadcast.

ANDRE BRETON: It would be a long story . . . . The striking thing is that the reasons we had had, in 1920, for pulling away from automatic writing were similar to the ones that made us guard against the frequent repetition of sleep sessions. Considerations of elementary mental hygiene were the deciding factor. As far as I was concerned, my initially immoderate use of automatic writing gave me a worrisome tendency toward hallucinations, which I had to counteract without delay. I talked about this in my book *Nadja*.

AP: What kind of distress did you feel, what was its nature?

AB: The "sleeping fits" not only provoked similar sensory disorders, but, in addition, they encouraged impulsive actions in cer-

tain sleeping subjects that boded the worst. I remember one session in particular that gathered some thirty guests at the house of a friend of Picabia's, Marie de la Hire. It was a huge house, with dim lighting: no matter how we tried to prevent it, about ten persons, men and women, who hardly knew each other, had fallen asleep at the same time. As they came and went, trying to outdo each other in prophecies and gesticulations, you can imagine that they did not look much different from the convulsionaries of Saint-Médard. At around two in the morning, concerned about the disappearance of several of them, I finally found them in the dimly lit anteroom, where, as if by common accord and provided with the necessary rope, they were trying to hang themselves from the coatrack. Crevel, who was with them, seemed to have been the instigator. I was forced to wake them with scant ceremony. Another time, after dinner at Eluard's house in the Paris suburbs, it took several of us to restrain a sleeping Desnos who was chasing Eluard across the lawn with a knife. As you can see, under these conditions the suicidal ideas that were latent in Crevel, the muffled hatred that Desnos harbored for Eluard, took an active turn that was extremely critical.

AP: Desnos is no doubt the measure by which we must judge the extraordinary power of the hypnotic slumbers' revelations. Could you tell us what dangers they exposed him to?

AB: Desnos, because of a strongly narcissistic side of his nature, soon wanted to be the sole center of attention. Although we had decided to interrupt our experiments midstream, for the reasons I just gave, Desnos could not resign himself to it. For several months, hardly an evening went by when he didn't show up at my door—even if more often than not it meant finding me home alone—and when he didn't drop off to sleep at some point, sometimes in the middle of dinner. On top of which, it was becoming more and more difficult to awaken him with the usual passes. One night when I was absolutely unable to bring him out of it, and when his frenzy had reached its peak—it must have been around three in the morning—I had to slip out to get a

doctor. Desnos greeted the man with insults, but nonetheless awoke before he was forced to intercede. That incident, and my worsening fears about damage to Desnos's mental equilibrium, convinced me to take all necessary steps to ensure that the same thing would never happen again. It goes without saying that our relationship was deeply affected by this. The experimental activity leading up to Surrealism marked a pause at this point. With the publication of the *Manifesto*, Surrealism entered its reasoning phase.

AP: Yes, in 1924, for those of us who have the benefit of hindsight, Surrealism drafted itself an official birth certificate. Was it also at this point that the period of scandals began?

AB: Our minds, indeed, were hardly in a state of calm. The years 1924 and 1925, when Surrealism was formulated and organized, were no doubt, along with 1930 and 1931, the ones when we rebelled the most violently against conformity and were the most resolutely "antisocial." The world we lived in seemed totally alien; by common accord, we rejected the principles that governed it. No need even to discuss it: every newcomer in our ranks had joined out of an exasperated refusal of these principles, out of disgust and hatred for what they engendered. We particularly hated every concept that by convention had been granted a sacred value, first and foremost those of "family," "country," and "religion." Nor did we exclude "work," or even "honor" in the most common use of the term. For us, such flags flew over a sordid lot of goods: very present in our minds were the human sacrifices that these gods had demanded, and were still demanding. Back then the press worshipped these values unequivocally, which didn't keep it from overflowing with stupidity, arrogance, and cynicism (times have changed only slightly). We felt that an outmoded world rushing to its doom could prolong itself only by reinforcing taboos and multiplying constraints, and we were radically in favor of escaping it. But this would still have been too passive: in truth, we were seized by a desire for widespread subversion. We must understand this, if the words "Surrealist revolution," which be-

came current a while later, are to have their full significance and not seem hyperbolic, as they did for those on the outside. In a sense, for a certain time, we simply responded in kind to a world that scandalized us.

AP: We still remember this revolt, which no doubt remains one of the major moments of the twentieth century. But what were you hoping for?

AB: Once again, we could share neither the imperatives of this world nor its values. What we set up in opposition, as I've had occasion to reiterate after the fact, was poetry, love, and liberty. *La Liberté ou l'Amour* [Give Me Liberty or Give Me Love]* was the title of a work by Desnos. *L'Amour la Poésie* [Love/Poetry] was a title of Eluard's.

I've already mentioned the figures from the past with whom we felt a bond of kinship. Our selection was already quite significant, as it brought to the fore Sade, Lautréamont, Rimbaud, and Jarry—in other words, those who offered the greatest leeway for protest. Let's not forget that when we were adolescents, Baudelaire was still widely considered a corrupter of youth. We were a long way from the "enormous" irony that so delighted Flaubert when he dreamed of his "dictionary of accepted ideas," a compendium of everything that was generally admitted, which would have been, as he said, an "apology for human baseness in all its forms." The effectiveness of such ruses struck us as dubious, and in any case too remote. We were on an aggressive tack. Moreover, certain imperious statements of Lautréamont's or Rimbaud's stood out from their overall message as if they had been written in letters of fire. For us they constituted veritable watchwords, and we intended to carry them out without delay.

AP: Lautréamont and Rimbaud, of course, but your filiation was not limited to them . . . ?

---

* The title is an untranslatable homophonic pun between *l'amour* (love) and *la mort* (death).

AB: Naturally, there were many others toward whom we felt indebted to a greater or lesser extent. The *Manifesto of Surrealism* lists some of them, such as Young (the author of *Night Thoughts*), Swift, Chateaubriand, Hugo, Aloysius Bertrand, Germain Nouveau, Raymond Roussel; a little later, I filled in a few gaps in that first roster by adding Heraclitus, Raymond Lully, Nicolas Flamel, Paolo Ucello, Achim von Arnim, Gérard de Nerval, and several others. Moreover, to my mind, this is strictly indicative and should not be taken as a limitation. I mention it only to establish once and for all that Surrealism has never tried to conceal what nourished its roots. And, too, to show that its extreme irreverence toward those whose reputations it considered odiously overblown or usurped was always counterbalanced by the passionate exaltation of many works and human attitudes that, it's true, usually lacked official consacration. The role of our generation was to show that the sap was flowing there, and nowhere else . . .

AP: Was this sap already sustaining a much greater number of poets than at the beginning?

AB: Indeed, new elements had come to join us in the meantime. It's striking that people rarely joined Surrealism alone. In almost every instance several personalities, who had discovered prior affinities among themselves, approached us at the same time. This had been the case with Baron, Crevel, Desnos, Morise, and Vitrac. A little later, with Antonin Artaud, Michel Leiris, and André Masson; then with Francis Gérard and Pierre Naville; then with Georges Sadoul and André Thirion; and still later with Marcel Duhamel, Jacques Prévert, and Yves Tanguy. Each time, these new elements jointly contributed knowledge, personal reactions, and very beneficial suggestions to the life of the group. What constituted what I call their prior affinities influenced our overall activity, but no one questioned the fundamental validity of the Surrealist procedure.

AP: Can you give us an idea of the Surrealist climate in 1924?

AB: There's no shortage of indicators: Aragon gave us *The Libertine*; under my signature appeared *Las Pas perdus* and the *Manifesto*, followed by the automatic texts of *Soluble Fish*; Eluard published *Mourir de ne pas mourir* [Dying of Not Dying]; Peret *Immortelle maladie* [Immortal Malady]; and Artaud *The Umbilicus of Limbo*.

It was also in 1924 that Aragon and I unveiled an important unknown work of Rimbaud's, *A Heart under a Cassock*, whose disclosure Claudel had managed to block up until then. From that point on, Catholicism's confiscation of Rimbaud became much more problematic. But the ire that this publication aroused was nonetheless limited to intellectual circles: these were still banderillas. It was a far different matter, upon the death of Anatole France, with the appearance of a pamphlet called *A Corpse*, which flew in the face of public opinion almost in its entirety. This time the bull was being seized by the horns: we had no doubt it was going to give us a rude toss . . .

AP: We have to remember Anatole France's status at the time, in order to understand the violence of the reactions against your pamphlet.

AB: France represented the prototype of everything we despised. If, in our eyes, there was one usurped reputation above all others, it was his. We were completely insensitive to the supposed limpidity of his style, and his celebrated scepticism particularly revolted us. He was the one who'd said that Rimbaud's sonnet "Vowels" made "no sense," but that its verses were "amusing." On the human level, we considered his attitude the shadiest and most despicable of all: he had done everything possible to win the approval of both Right and Left. He was bloated with honors and self-satisfaction, etc. We felt exempted from any need for restraint.

That windbag has so completely been deflated since then that today it's difficult to imagine the furies unleashed by our four pages, which included texts by Aragon, Joseph Delteil, Pierre Drieu la Rochelle, Eluard, and myself. According to Camille Mauclair, Aragon and I belonged to the "race of raving lunatics."

He exclaimed, "These are not the manners of upstarts and hood-lums, but of jackals . . ." Others went so far as to demand repri-sals.

AP: This pamphlet is also remembered for a phrase that greatly embarrassed Aragon, its author, several years later . . .

AB: I have to say that Aragon never came up with a less fortunate circumlocution than the one by which he meant to do justice to France: "the *littérateur* hailed simultaneously today by the imbe-cile Maurras and doddering Moscow." And yet, this statement was very much in the frenetic style (as one might say of Pétrus Borel) that he'd adopted as of about 1922. Although it had quite an impact on the crowd—by which I mean it stirred things up considerably and provoked some delightful indignations—such a style did not have our unqualified support. In 1923, in *Littérature*, we had already seen Aragon preach "scandal for scandal's sake." Within Surrealism itself, such an assertion seemed indefensible and was harshly criticized. However much influence he exerted at the time, not even his friends failed to detect a tendency in him toward *verbal* overstatement. We have to see Aragon as he was then, split between his natural gifts on the one hand, which made him stand out and which he made use of; and on the other, his efforts to conform to the—fundamentally darker—mood and perspectives of Surrealism. Small wonder this caused a certain excitability on his part . . .

AP: I believe, Mr. Breton, that much of the ground has been prepared. But before starting in on the period of *La Révolution Surréaliste*, could you document one important point, which is your and your friends' financial situation at that time?

AB: Back then, the precariousness of our means of material existence certainly added to the other causes of our instability; it accentuated our feeling of dissent, our dissociation from a world we found absurd. This instability took several forms: it led Elu-ard, for example, to disappear without warning in the spring of

1924. We learned only several months later that he had gone on a trip around the world. The paintings and primitive objects he had so lovingly collected were sold off for practically nothing. Most of us lived, if not hand-to-mouth, at least without any thought to planning for the future. Given this, it might seem surprising that so many Surrealist or pre-Surrealist publications managed to see the light of day without a publisher's help; and yet, for years, we raised the necessary funds by taking collections among ourselves, with varying degrees of difficulty. But in this regard, life back then was more accommodating than it is today . . . You can imagine that the Surrealist refusal to come to terms with any accepted practice resulted in every door being slammed shut, including ones that had been open to some of us before our dissidence took such an absolute and public turn.

AP: More specifically, what was *your* source of income back then, and what was your professional activity?

AB: For several years I had worked as librarian for the couturier and collector Jacques Doucet. It was also my job to select the paintings and sculptures that should figure in his collection of modern art. I believe I was up to the task, since the acquisitions I engineered included *The Snake Charmer* by Henri Rousseau, the sketch for Seurat's *The Circus*, the *Demoiselles d'Avignon* and the so-called woman "with sherbet" by Picasso, De Chirico's *The Disquieting Muses*, Duchamp's *Glider* and *Rotary Glass Plate*, and important works by Picabia and Miró. When I think about it, that Jacques Doucet was an odd fellow. Already in his seventies, he sometimes gave proof of unimpeachable taste, and he passed, not unjustifiably, for a generous sponsor. He had already given the City of Paris a library of art and archaeology; and he was preparing to bequeath it the collection of books and manuscripts for which I was then responsible, which one can consult today at the Bibliothèque Sainte-Geneviève. Convincing him to buy a painting was nonetheless an extremely laborious process. Not only did I need to extoll its exceptional qualities in person, and many times

over, but I had to continue doing so in several letters. Needless to say, this very quickly turned into pure verbiage . . .

AP: But at least you had the satisfaction of getting the modern works you deemed most important into a reputable collection.

AB: Since I don't believe it's a professional secret, and since it could be of interest to elucidate the relations between artist and collector, let me mention that purse strings such as his did not loosen very readily for young painters. After interminable negotiations, whose aim, on my part, was to have him buy a canvas of Max Ernst's exhibited at the Salon des Indépendants (I forget its title,* but it was five identical vases on a black background, *into* which grew five identical bouquets; Max Ernst was asking 500 francs for it), I was authorized to offer 200 francs for a replica of the painting reduced to two vases, which to Doucet seemed quite sufficient. Another time, having turned hoops to interest Doucet in acquiring a large work by André Masson, all I managed to obtain was that he purchased, from the gallery where Masson exhibited, the smallest canvas he could find—a landscape— which was also the least elaborate and, naturally, the least expensive. Satisfied as he seemed to be when he showed it to me, he nonetheless asked me if I didn't think something was missing. And as I naturally remained perplexed: "Yes, I think it could use a little bird. We're going to ask that good Masson to add one . . ." Such characteristics might very well make one think of an "Ubu, patron of the arts." They would not be out of place among the traits that Ambroise Vollard made famous.

AP: All this is rather painful, and seems ill-suited to modifying your position of revolt.

AB: Like me, Aragon owed Doucet the better part of his means of subsistence, for which he wrote two letters per week on literary

* *The Interior of Sight.*

subjects. This earned him between 500 and 800 francs monthly. My own salary was 1,000 francs.

But the publication of the pamphlet against Anatole France was to deprive us of these resources. Doucet immediately sent for us. He first indulged in a long preamble about everything and nothing, then ended by asking if we didn't think brevity was indeed the soul of wit. As we had no particular opinion on the subject, he launched into a tirade over what was so odious and ill-mannered about what we'd just done, and, after having given free rein to his indignation, informed us that his relations with us were terminated. The last thread by which we still, despite our reservations, hung onto a crumbling world had just snapped.

Several days later the *Manifesto of Surrealism* appeared, which must be situated in that atmosphere of tension. All those on whom the movement's development would depend for at least the next several years had given up trying to fit into the social structure they condemned. Whatever personal difficulties this might have entailed, you could tell who they were by the fact that they were free.

All of our hands together will be needed to grip the rope of fire that runs up the black mountain. Who dares speak of using us to improve our horrid earthly lot? We demand, and will have, the "beyond" in our time.

—*"Pourquoi je prends la direction de* La Révolution Surréaliste,*"* *in* La Révolution Surréaliste *no. 4*

8.

ANDRE PARINAUD: Today we're going to touch on one of the essential phases of your movement, marked by the publication of the magazine *La Révolution Surréaliste*. We know about your position of revolt—what we might call at once a poetic, moral, and political revolt. The first issue of your magazine attests to your resolutions, which are contained in this peremptory statement: "We must formulate a new declaration of the rights of man." I believe the best way to explain your thought at the time is to clarify exactly what meaning you attached to these words.

ANDRE BRETON: When the first issue of *La Révolution Surréaliste* appeared—at the end of 1924—its contributors unanimously agreed on the following point: that the so-called Cartesian world around them was indefensible, a humorless prankster, against which all forms of insurrection were justified. The whole psychology of understanding was put in doubt. We categorically refused to accept anything that derived from what we considered a purely "cortical" view of the mind. Our friend Ferdinand Alquié, in an extremely well-informed text on "Surrealist and Existentialist humanism," reprinted in *Les Cahiers du Collège Philosophique* in

1948, stated the problem as well as anyone could: "To claim that reason is man's essence is already to cut man in two, and the classical tradition has never failed to do so. It has drawn a distinction between what is rational in man, which by that sole fact is considered truly human; and what is not rational (instincts and feelings), which consequently appears unworthy of man." All the teachings of Freud, who increasingly in that domain had emerged as our intellectual guide, pointed out the mortal danger incurred for man by this split, this schism between the "forces of reason" and deep-seated passions, which seemed destined to remain unaware of each other. Naturally, our only recourse was to counter the exorbitant pretensions of this "reason" that, as we saw it, had usurped the place of true reason; and also to save impulses and desires from the grip of repression, which only made them more harmful. To the extent that we stripped old "reason" of the omnipotence it had assumed over the centuries, it is also understandable that the moral "duties" it helped foist on man lost almost all justification in our eyes. I don't mean to say that we considered ourselves "above the law," only that we had serious doubts about that very law. We seized every opportunity to point out its failings, until another law, founded on true principles, could take its place. This is the meaning we should ascribe to the statement on the cover of the first issue of *La Révolution Surréaliste*: "We must formulate a new declaration of the rights of man."

AP: Could you clarify an important point: was the Surrealist group unanimous in its revolutionary ambitions?

AB: When it came to the firm intention to break open closed rationalism; or the absolute rejection of reigning moral laws; or the attempt to liberate man using poetry, dreams, and the marvelous; or our concern with promoting a new order of values—on these various points, we were in total agreement. But we could not avoid certain differences about the means of realizing these goals, given each one's psychological makeup.

AP: At that time, Mr. Breton, what was Aragon's status in your group?

AB: Aragon? He was as I've already described him: ever fond of acrobats. No one knew which way the wind was blowing so well as he. You had no sooner made up your mind to climb a hill, even against his wishes, than he was already at the top . . . Most of us felt that he remained very much the "writer": even while walking with you in the street, he rarely spared you the recital of a text, finished or not. Inevitably, these texts came to be increasingly *affected*; just as he loved, while talking in cafes, to watch his poses in the mirrors. At the time, this was considered only a minor flaw and had little negative impact on his contributions, which were always remarkably intelligent and nimble.

AP: Eluard's attitude also stood somewhat apart from your conception of the "Surrealist revolution," wouldn't you say?

AB: Eluard's participation in the group's activities, steadfast as it was, was no doubt accompanied by a certain reticence. Between Surrealism and poetry in the traditional sense, it was very likely the latter that seemed an end to him—something that, from the Surrealist point of view, constituted major heresy. (It goes without saying that aesthetics, which we meant to prohibit, passes through that door with the greatest of ease.) That Eluard's intentions always fell short of the *Manifesto's* objectives was clearly shown by the "blurb" to his book *Les Dessous d'une vie ou La Pyramide humaine* [The Underside of a Life, or The Human Pyramid], published in 1926, in which he labored to establish a formal distinction between dreams, the automatic text, and the poem—one that in his case always privileged the latter. This division by *genres*, with a marked predilection for the poem "as the consequence of a well-defined will," immediately struck me as reactionary and in direct violation of the spirit of Surrealism. Of course, that in no way diminished the sensitive qualities that distinguished Eluard's personality.

AP: What was the magazine's first issue like? What would you say were the centers of interest?

AB: In the beginning, the stress was placed on pure Surrealism—Surrealism, let's say, in its native state—and that's why the editorship was entrusted to Pierre Naville and Benjamin Péret, who at the time seemed the most completely driven by the new spirit and the most resistant to compromise. It should be noted that the first issues of *La Révolution Surréaliste* contained no poems, while automatic texts and dream narratives abounded. If I think back to our situation then, as it resulted from the interaction of the currents I mentioned, here's how it appeared in broad outline:

The lyrical current remained very strong, as much with Desnos's prolongation of Romanticism, as with Jacques Baron's kind of expression—"buffoonish and strange as possible," as Rimbaud advocated—or with Eluard's poetry particularly modeled after Baudelaire's. Michel Leiris and Desnos shared a taste for altering language, operating on its very matter, by forcing words to lay bare their hidden life and reveal the mysterious trade they indulge in, independent of their meaning. From this viewpoint, their master and ours was of course Raymond Roussel. Repeated requests for contributions from the latter went unanswered, to our great disappointment. We came to understand that Roussel was engaged in a wholly individual opus that brooked no vista onto the outside world; even today, hardly any light has been shed on the meaning and scope of such a project. Our admiration for Roussel nevertheless remained untarnished: with the same enthusiasm that prompted us, and us alone, to applaud the performance of his play *The Star on the Forehead* in early 1924, we were again alone, in 1926, in acclaiming *The Dust of Suns.*

AP: Apart from Roussel, didn't you also approach other possible contributors? This choice could enlighten us further about your intent.

AB: I can think of only one other contribution that we desired but didn't obtain: René Guénon's. True, we had no reason to expect it, and yet it was also a disappointment. In any case, it was

very symptomatic that we should turn to Guénon. It shows that, even then, we were attracted by so-called "traditional" thought, and ready to honor it in him. I believe that those of us who were most inclined in that direction were Artaud, Leiris, and myself, even though it was Naville who had suggested writing to Guénon. It's curious to imagine how different the evolution of Surrealism might have been, if by some impossible chance he hadn't refused his support . . .

AP: Since you've mentioned the name of Antonin Artaud, I think our listeners would never forgive me if I didn't ask you to talk about that lofty figure, and to describe his contribution to the Surrealist movement.

AB: Very little time had passed since Antonin Artaud had joined us, but no one had put all his abilities, which were considerable, so spontaneously in the service of the Surrealist cause as he had. In the past, his great reference—in this he would have agreed with Eluard—was Baudelaire; but if Eluard took his inspiration from "The Fine Ship," Artaud much more darkly savored "The Murderer's Wine." Perhaps he was at even greater odds with life than the rest of us were. He was very handsome back then, and when he moved he dragged behind him a gothic landscape pierced throughout by lightning. He was possessed by a kind of fury that spared no human institution, but that occasionally dissolved into laughter containing all the defiance of youth. Be that as it may, his fury, by its astonishing power of contagion, profoundly affected the Surrealist procedure. It enjoined the lot of us truly to take every risk, to attack, *without restraint*, what we couldn't abide.

AP: And how was this will to combat expressed? Were you in complete agreement over it?

AB: The tone of various individual or collective texts published during the year 1925 bears witness to a hardening in our positions. A "Bureau of Surrealist Research" was opened at 15 Rue de Grenelle, its initial aim being to collect every communication

touching on the forms that the mind's unconscious activity was liable to take. Given the number of busybodies and intruders who besieged it, we were soon forced to close its doors to the public. Artaud, who took over running the bureau from Francis Gérard, strove to make it a center for "rehabilitating" life. On the walls hung several of De Chirico's early paintings, which enjoyed an unparalleled prestige in our eyes, along with casts of women's bodies. It wasn't rare to see Valéry and Léon-Paul Fargue in that room, among others who weren't scared away by subversive activities.

Under Artaud's influence, collective texts of great violence were published at the time. Whereas the "Surrealist stickers" [*papillons*: literally, butterflies] that had flown two or three months earlier from the Bureau of Research still seemed to hesitate as to the best route to take (poetry, dreams, humor) and, all things considered, were highly inoffensive, these collective texts were suddenly filled with an insurrectional ardor. This was the case with the "Declaration of January 27, 1925," with the one called "Open the Prisons! Disband the Army!" with addresses "to the Pope" and "to the Dalai Lama," and with letters "to the rectors of European universities," "to the Buddhist schools," or "to the heads of insane asylums." Their language had been stripped of all ornaments; it eschewed the "wave of dreams" that Aragon had spoken of;* it meant to be sharp and gleaming, but gleaming like a weapon. I love these texts, in particular the ones that most strongly bear Artaud's imprint. Once again, I'm judging by his eventual destiny, the large measure of suffering behind his almost total refusal—which was also ours, but which he formulated more aptly and more heatedly than anyone.

Still . . . if I completely shared in the spirit behind these texts— moreover, they were the fruit of long discussions between several of us—and if I had few reservations as to their content, I soon began to worry about the atmosphere they were creating. The very fact of their rapid succession, and the fact that this highly

* *Une Vague de rêves* [A Wave of Dreams] was the title of a 1924 Surrealist manifesto by Aragon.

polemical activity necessarily tended to subordinate all the others, gave me the impression that, without our quite realizing it, we had been seized by frenzy, and that the air had rarefied around us. Looking at the situation more closely today, I better understand my resistance, which at the time remained obscure. That half-libertarian, half-mystical path was not really mine, and I came to see it as more of a dead end (I wasn't the only one). The space that Artaud led me into always strikes me as abstract, a hall of mirrors. For me, there's always something "verbal" about it, even if that verb is very noble, very beautiful. It's a place of lacunae and ellipses in which, personally, I lose all my means of communication with the innumerable things that, despite everything, give me pleasure and bind me to this earth. We forget too easily that Surrealism has had an enormous capacity for *love*, and that what it violently condemned were precisely the things that impaired love.

Finally, I distrusted a certain fever pitch that Artaud was definitely trying to reach—just as Desnos must have been trying to reach it on another level. I felt it entailed an expenditure of energy that we would not subsequently be able to offset. In other words, I saw all too clearly how the machine was running full steam ahead, but not how it could keep fueling itself . . .

AP: This no doubt explains the abrupt change in course of *La Révolution Surréaliste*, which you took over at that moment.

AB: Yes, it was for those reasons—and a few others—that, not without great misgivings, I put a stop to the experiments Artaud was initiating and decided to assume the editorship of *La Révolution Surréaliste* myself. In the rather confused text in which I announced this—where it's clear that I was holding back from saying certain things—I tried with uneven success to explain that we still wanted very much to "do away with the ancien régime of the mind," but that, in order to do this, it was not enough to try to "intimidate the world by banging it over the head with brutal demands." I recommended returning to earlier positions—in other words, essentially and above all, that we restore language's

effervescence, as we had done with automatic writing and the sleeping fits—and counting blindly on the eventual results.

AP: So your attitude implied no renunciation. It seems, moreover, that the movement was entering a particularly active phase.

AB: We hadn't abandoned our social concerns, but only sought to express them less lyrically, more rigorously. Our political turning point was not far away. The introductory text of the issue we're speaking about, number 4, contains a sentence in which I still recognize myself fairly easily. If I may quote it: "In the current state of European society, we remain faithful to the principle of any revolutionary action, even when it takes class struggle as its point of departure, on condition that it goes far enough."

A period of scandals "came full circle" at that very moment, with a literary banquet in honor of Saint-Pol Roux. Since the disciplines to which some of us would soon bend were not yet defined—remember, we're still in mid-1925—the Surrealists constituted a homogeneous and extremely tight-knit group. We shared the same fundamental convictions and nurtured some of the same outer irritations (which, of course, were hardly in short supply). The very morning of the banquet, our signatures had appeared on a petition drafted by intellectuals against the Moroccan war, which had just broken out. And closer to home, we had another reason for exasperation. In an interview with an Italian newspaper that *Comoedia* reprinted, French ambassador Claudel, after having stated that Surrealism, like Dadaism, had "only one meaning: pederastic," had boasted about his patriotic activity during the First World War, which consisted of buying lard for the army in South America. This time it was too much. If we subsequently hurled invectives, let's at least recognize that in this case we weren't the ones who started it . . .

But the Saint-Pol Roux banquet nonetheless began under unfortunate auspices. Just as we were heading over to it, our famous "Open Letter to Paul Claudel" arrived from the printer's, printed on blood-red stock. We decided to get to the Closerie des Lilas a little early, so as to slip a copy under everyone's plate.

AP: What was, *a priori*, the Surrealists' attitude toward this event?

AB: Such a banquet was not at all to our taste. Even as we honored Saint-Pol Roux as one of the great creative minds of Symbolism—I myself had celebrated him as "the master of the image," and had been so bold as to dedicate a book of poems, *Clair de terre* [Earthlight], "to those who, like him, offer themselves the *magnificent* pleasure of letting themselves be forgotten"—we unanimously deplored that his visit to Paris had occasioned these outmoded and ridiculous feasts. If he had all too readily agreed to them, it was because, in the solitude of Brittany, he had lost any true contact with the companions of his youth, most of whom were woefully decrepit. He didn't doubt for a moment that, if only for one evening, he could bridge the gap between them and the Surrealists . . .

AP: I'd like you to give us your version of the evening's main events, since there have already been several others.

AB: The banquet, or rather what went on in its stead, did not happen exactly as people have described. From the outset, the terms of the letter to Claudel stupefied and infuriated a large number of the guests and, because they didn't know how to react to it, created extreme tension between them and us. For several of the ladies in the room it translated into such a feeling of suffocation that one of them demanded I open the window behind me. I must have complied rather violently, or else the façade of that second floor facing Boulevard de Montparnasse was pretty delapidated, since the two doors of the casement came off their hinges in my hands. Those sitting next to me quickly grabbed them and helped me set them on the floor, thus keeping the glass from breaking.

It's true that the presence at the table of honor (the very term put us beside ourselves) of Mme. Rachilde and Aurélien-Marie Lugné-Poe, against whom we had serious grievances, was enough to poison everything. Rachilde, in I don't remember which news-

paper, had just made various Germanophobic statements (a Frenchman could never marry a German woman, etc.) that we found odious. Lugné-Poe we pardoned still less for having worked in counterintelligence during the war (the "Deuxième Bureau"). Their meeting with us that evening constituted an explosive mix. We know that the remarks the Surrealists made aloud about them triggered the start of the fight. The waiters were just serving a rather sorry "hake in white sauce" when several of us got up on the tables. Things turned irremediably nasty when three of the guests left, only to return shortly afterward with the police. But as humor would have it, in the general confusion it was Rachilde, then at the height of her agitation, who was arrested. It was too late for Saint-Pol Roux's exhortations to restore calm. We also know that Leiris narrowly escaped being lynched for having yelled intentionally seditious statements out the window, then down on the boulevard itself. The reason that this episode—the Saint-Pol Roux banquet—is important is that it marks Surrealism's final break with all the conformist elements of the time. The newspapers, *Action Française* at the helm, joined by professional groups such as the "Société des Gens de Lettres" and the "Association des Ecrivains Combattants," demanded retaliations (they would no longer print our names; they even wanted us deported from France—although I wonder under what statutes). At that instant, the bridges had been burned between Surrealism and all the rest. We managed quite nicely without them. Nevertheless, from that point on, our shared revolt focused much more on the political sphere.

In the realm of facts, as we see it, no ambiguity is possible: all of us seek to shift power from the hands of the bourgeoisie to those of the proletariat. Meanwhile, it is nonetheless necessary that the experiments of the inner life continue, and do so, of course, without external or even Marxist control.

—Legitimate Defense, 1926

9.

A MAJOR DOUBT: DOESN'T THE EMANCIPATION OF THE
MIND FIRST REQUIRE MAN'S SOCIAL LIBERATION? THE
COMMUNIST PARTY'S WELCOME.

ANDRÉ PARINAUD: Today we'll discuss the specifically political
phase of Surrealism, which was marked by your rapprochement
with the *Clarté* group, followed by your and several of your
friends' attempts to join the Communist party. A host of documents trace this evolution, but would you nonetheless pinpoint
the beginning of your political period, touch on the salient elements, and name the significant figures?

ANDRÉ BRETON: Surrealism's turn toward politics can be situated precisely in the summer of 1925. I was spending my vacation
with André Masson and a few other friends in Thorenc
(Provence), where, although we spent most of the day watching
insects and catching crayfish, our discussions went briskly from
dusk until well into the night. "Self-criticism," even though the
term was not in our vocabulary, was taken to great lengths in
Surrealism. The preceding months had been the most electrically
charged, as well as the most devoted to frequently contradictory
impulses. We had in no way erased from the Surrealist blackboard
the polemic surrounding Aragon's famous wisecrack about "doddering Moscow." Jean Bernier had responded rather sharply in
Clarté, a paracommunist periodical that in many respects had our
support, even though we hated the fact that so tainted an intellectual as Henri Barbusse had control over it. For his troubles,

Bernier incurred a livid response from Aragon that made some of us feel he was *tangling himself up in knots*: "The Russian Revolution?" he insisted. "Forgive me for shrugging my shoulders. On the scale of ideas, it is, at best, a vague ministerial crisis . . . The problems raised by human existence do not derive from the miserable little revolutionary activity that has occurred in the East during the course of the last few years. I shall add that it is only by a real abuse of language that this latter activity can be characterized as revolutionary." Even those of us most removed from politics considered this an indefensible piece of hubris.

AP: And as such, you felt that some explanation was called for?

AB: Well, it evidently continued to weigh on my mind, since I was to reopen the debate shortly afterward. The opportunity was provided by a review of Trotsky's book on Lenin that I published in issue number 5 of *La Révolution Surréaliste*. This text has never been picked up in Surrealist anthologies, which is a shame, because it undoubtedly marked the first step, and a decisive one (even though it's often been said that it was a false step, on my part and Surrealism's), toward a better understanding of the ideas and ideals that had triggered the Russian Revolution. It's true that I've resisted reprinting this text in my own books of essays because of its unsatisfactory formulation, especially in retrospect; but how could it have been otherwise? At the time I was practically groping my way forward. In order to be understood by those around me, I had to buttress my call for a reconsideration of the problem with arguments of a purely sentimental nature. Furthermore, none of us had yet felt the need to go beyond the rudiments of Marxism. I was nonetheless quick to distance myself from "one or another of my friends to the extent that he [had] believed it possible to attack communism in the name of some principle or other." For us, I said, "the general spirit we maintain . . . can rest only on revolutionary reality, carrying us forward by any means and at any price." And, as if that allusion to Aragon's recent behavior still struck me as insufficient, I directly challenged him by adding: "Free in such conditions as Louis Aragon may be to

inform Drieu la Rochelle, through an open letter, that he has never shouted 'Long live Lenin!' but that he will *howl* it (sic) the moment it is banned, I am no less free to find this . . . a surrender to our worst detractors . . . by letting them suppose that we would only take up a challenge. On the contrary: 'Long live Lenin!' only *because he was Lenin!*"

Dare I say that I exerted enough influence at the time for this position to be immediately adopted by the majority of Surrealists, and that Aragon did not raise the slightest objection—indeed, was the first to be won over?

AP: Why did reading Trotsky's *Lenin* have such a particularly revelatory effect on you?

AB: I can't deny that, if reading such a work sent me into raptures, it was especially because of the personal aspect. Something very engaging emerged from a certain relation between the *human* (the personality of Lenin himself as the author had known him) and the *superhuman* (the task he'd accomplished), which, by the same token, made his ideas enormously attractive . . . The thought police in France must really have been vigilant for these ideas to have taken so long—almost eight years—to reach us! It's striking that, until 1925, our understanding of the word *Revolution*, what we found exhilarating about it, extended only to the Convention and the Paris Commune. Our way of speaking about it back then shows that we were more attuned to the accents it took on in the mouths of Saint-Just or Robespierre than to its doctrinal content. This doesn't mean that the causes espoused by the revolutionaries of 1793 or 1871 were not completely espoused by us. Surrealism's demands, no matter how absolute these demands might at first seem, have never completely overshadowed the urgent need for an economic and social upheaval that would put an end to certain glaring inequities. But until that moment, we had barely given a thought to the *means* of effecting such a transformation. I'm stressing this, because people have often claimed not to understand the processes that abruptly tilted us to that

side—that regrettably misled us, some would say, into limiting our field of action.

AP: In your view, what were the texts and activities that marked the principle stages of that period?

AB: Today an entire body of critical literature retraces the path—quite a bumpy one, to tell the truth—of Surrealism's political evolution. Its principle stages were marked by the publication of the tract *Revolution Now and Forever!* in 1925, foreshadowing the creation of a kind of joint committee that united the active elements of the periodical *Clarté*, the Belgian paper *Correspondance*, the magazine *Philosophies*, the Surrealists, and several independents—a committee whose goal it was to standardize its vocabulary as much as possible and to pour into the common pot the most precious contributions of each of its constituent groups. Let me just mention our abortive attempt to found a joint magazine, which was to be called *La Guerre Civile*; the publication in 1926 of my pamphlet *Legitimate Defense*, which I pulled from circulation and destroyed out of loyalty to the Communist party when I decided to join in 1927; and the publication, also in 1927, of the pamphlet *Au grand jour* [In Broad Daylight], a collection of open letters collectively addressed by Aragon, Eluard, Péret, Unik, and myself, both to the Communists and to those of our friends with whom there were lingering or newly arisen disagreements. This kind of activity reached, if not a conclusion, at least a resolution in the text *A suivre* [To Be Continued: A Small Contribution to the Files of Certain Intellectuals with Revolutionary Tendencies], which Aragon and I co-authored in 1929.

AP: Let's come back, if you would, to the period when the Surrealists made contact with the *Clarté* group. What was the nature of your relations in the beginning?

AB: Our friend Victor Crastre, in magazine articles for *Les Temps Modernes* and elsewhere, has best evoked the atmosphere of the times. He himself belonged to the *Clarté* group, along with Marcel

Fourrier, Jean Bernier, and Georges Altman: he therefore had a political education that far surpassed the Surrealists'. He was of a less argumentative temperament than his comrades, more open and attentive than they to the foundations of Surrealist thought. Whereas Fourrier and Bernier, deliberately stressing their Marxist training, went to great lengths to make us recant on several of our earlier positions so as to make us join them in the voice of militantism, Crastre showed himself to be more circumspect and sympathetically informed about our particular resolutions. In his recent articles, he has ably recounted certain paradoxical exchanges that took place between his group and ours, in which the Surrealists effected (no doubt too hastily) their conversion to dialectical materialism, while the *Clarté* elements—including Fourrier and Bernier—clumsily denied a certain inclination toward Surrealism.

AP: It seems that all the good intentions and efforts at mutual understanding still didn't lead to cohesion.

AB: No, and it was perhaps inevitable: the gathering of various groups toward the accomplishment of a single task—in this case, the building of a common platform that would have allowed us to act—raises a psychological problem, which until now has barely been touched upon. Each of these groups, within its very heart, behaved like an *"egregore,"* in the sense of a "collective psychic being" driven by a life of its own.* Even if the constituent elements of these *egregores* had temporarily managed to fuse, no *egregore* had renounced its autonomy in any deep way, and each one jealously defended this autonomy as soon as it was threatened. This explains the not very homogeneous character of many of our texts and resolutions of the time, typified by *Revolution Now and Forever!* It also explains the hidden resentments, with variably

* Breton borrowed the term from *Egrégores ou la vie des civilisations* by Pierre Mabille, who himself took it from the ancient hermeticists. Mabille defined *egregore* as a "human group" of any size, "endowed with a personality different from that of the individuals who constitute it" and bound together by "a powerful emotional shock" (such as love, patriotism, etc.).

long-standing consequences, entailed by the examination—and sometimes the exclusion—of a member of this or that group who had been accused of failing our collective commitment.

AP: That *is* an explanation; but is it complete, in your view?

AB: Another cause of our relative failure was the fact that not everyone trying to orchestrate this action had reached the same stage in his evolution. The details of our personal lives did not allow for equal availability on everyone's part. The sanctions required by the life of the joint committee against a few of its members did not fail to cause some serious traumas, nor to create some strong grudges and, in certain cases, to trigger a most unexpected evolution.

AP: Such as?

AB: I can't think of a better example than Henri Lefebvre. A member of the *Philosophies* group, he was asked to justify several of his writings that attested to his deistic stance, which was obviously incompatible with the Marxism we had all adopted. Lefebvre admitted that he hadn't renounced the faith of his youth, and tendered his resignation. He was to resurface several years later as the appointed theoretician of official Marxism, by which I mean Stalinism, being most notably empowered to denounce the slightest deviation from the head-office line. His departure, which we had unanimously turned into an exclusion, entailed that of the two other leaders of *Philosophies*, Pierre Morhange and Georges Politzer, who, although hardly Marxist at the outset, underwent an evolution similar to Lefebvre's. That's also a good example of a threatened *egregore* reconstituting itself, against all odds.

AP: That's quite a curious situation, and fairly difficult to understand, given (as you say) that these men were not Marxists, or hardly so, and that their sole ambition seems to have been to act like Marxists . . . And what was happening with the Surrealists, in this regard?

AB: I admit it looked very much like a mass conversion. If this were religion, the fervor of our intentions alone would have been enough. The Surrealists in particular gave much of themselves. They had adhered to the view that what was still—and by far—most shocking about the world around them was the subservience in which a minuscule part of the human race held the rest, without any justification whatsoever. Of all the evils this was the most intolerable, since it was entirely within man's power to remedy. In reality, eliminating this state of affairs hardly struck us as a cure-all; I mean that, even if it *were* eliminated, we hardly thought that everything would be "for the best in the best of all possible worlds." As Surrealism has never stopped looking toward Lautréamont and Rimbaud, it's clear to us that the world's real torment lies in *the human condition*, even more than in *the social condition* of individuals. Be that as it may, this social condition, which was totally arbitrary and inequitous (in twentieth-century France, for example), acted as a screen between man and his true problems—a screen that we therefore needed first and foremost to pierce. Throughout history, plans had been drawn up with this in view, but one of these plans dominated all the others, and that was the Marxist plan. We might have deciphered it too rapidly, or at least very eagerly. This doesn't mean that we had read every volume of *Capital* to great benefit (we weren't very gifted for political economy), but we were fairly familiar with Marx's *The Holy Family*, *The Poverty of Philosophy*, and major philosophical writings; Engels's *Anti-Dühring*; and Lenin's *Materialism and Empirio-Criticism*, to list only the fundamental works. The surest thing we deduced from them was that, in order to help "transform the world," we had to start by thinking of it in ways other than we had done until then, and particularly by subscribing without reservation to the famous "primacy of matter over mind." We were resigned to this necessity, even though it meant considerable sacrifice for some of us.

AP: No doubt . . . It's difficult to imagine how your concept of the world could accommodate such a postulate. Did you adhere to it simply out of discipline?

AB: Still today, I think that a principle such as "the primacy of matter over mind" can claim to be no more than an "article of faith": it presupposes a dualism that even then I found hard to accept, except for the needs of a cause whose main objective—the social transformation of the world—had to be accomplished at any price. Like it or not, we had to take that path. I'm expressing this naively, but I believe this is how we Surrealists generally felt about it. Personally, and despite all my efforts, I couldn't hew to that line for long. Others clung to it with all their might, come what may.

AP: On another subject, is it true that Pierre Naville had a determining influence on Surrealism's political orientation?

AB: Naville's influence on decisions the group made at the time has been highly exaggerated. Remember that Naville, along with Péret, had edited the first issues of *La Révolution Surréaliste*. Our disagreement over an article in the third issue, in which he stated that there was no such thing—letting it be understood that there never could be—as Surrealist painting, was not unrelated to my decision to take over editorship of the magazine (which in his eyes meant taking it away from him). I don't believe it was in his nature or temperament to take such things lightly. The absence of his name in the next five issues, covering a period of two years, is rather significant in this regard. Moreover, his military service kept him away from Paris. When he returned, he had liquidated his Surrealist past and decided to pursue a purely political course of action. For a long time after that, I reproached him not only for not helping his friends with the difficult task of trying to be true both to the revolution and to themselves, but also for doing his utmost to widen the breach between us and those we wanted to join. The debate between Naville and the Surrealists began in his pamphlet *La Révolution et les intellectuels* [Revolution and the Intellectuals], to which I responded in *Legitimate Defense*. He answered in turn in a text entitled "Mieux et moins bien" [Better and Not So Well]. It came to an end with the letter we addressed to him in *Au grand jour*.

This said, and contrary to what has been printed with, at very least, his consent, there was never a "Naville crisis" in Surrealism.* There was a Naville *defection*, of a particular type, and that's all.

AP: So the arguments that Naville used against you had nothing to do with the contemporaneous objections raised by your entering the Communist party, which came from within the Party itself?

AB: Nothing at all. These latter objections were of an extremely simplistic nature, which didn't stop them from quickly becoming insurmountable obstacles. Naturally, they were addressed especially to me, insofar as I was editor of *La Révolution Surréaliste*, in other words of a magazine whose title alone, obscure and at first glance heretical, aroused all kinds of suspicions. Neither my good will, which was total, nor the ardor of the conviction that urged me to join the Party were entirely able to overcome the fears that this title awakened in the Party "heads"—fears compounded by the contents of the magazine, which, stupefied and soon offended, they passed around among themselves. Considering what all that has become, I won't bother suppressing a certain sarcasm in recalling those sessions: summoned to appear very early in the morning before a succession of "supervisory committees," either in a school on Rue Duhesme or at the Union Hall on Avenue Mathurin-Moreau, I tried to defend Surrealism's actions and give proof of my intended loyalty.

AP: What were these committees like? What kinds of investigations did they conduct?

* Breton is referring to Maurice Nadeau's *The History of Surrealism*, an entire chapter of which is devoted to "the Naville crisis." Naville and Nadeau, as fellow members of the Trotskyist opposition, were in close touch at around the time Nadeau wrote his history. Breton disliked Nadeau's book on a number of accounts, not the least of which being its inference that Surrealism could be encapsulated into a finite (and therefore finished) history. Cf. his remarks in interview 15.

AB: These committees were composed of three members, never known to me personally, who used only their first names. Usually they were foreigners with a very sketchy command of French. Apart from that, nothing seemed more like a police interrogation, when you think about it. It sometimes happened, moreover, that these sessions spilled over into the afternoon, with a strictly regulated time allotted me for lunch. My explanations were deemed satisfactory soon enough, but there was always a moment when one of the inquisitors would brandish a copy of *La Révolution Surréaliste* and put everything back in question. At a distance (so to speak), the most amusing part of all this is that what inevitably sent them into a rage were some of the illustrations—above all, the reproductions of Picasso's work.* Seeing these, they egged each other on as best they could, each trying to be more caustic than the others: which way was right-side-up, could I tell them what that "meant," so I felt I could waste my time with this petty-bourgeois nonsense, did I really find this compatible with the Revolution, etc. I felt I'd gotten through it reasonably well: in the end, each committee was in favor of ratifying my membership. But for some unknown reason, a new committee always decided to meet shortly afterward to hear my comments and, to everyone's consternation, the orange-covered magazine was once again thrown on the table . . .

AP: Your stretch of road toward the Communist party seems to have been rather arid . . .

AB: All the more so in that this tiring gauntlet was nowhere near run, nor the investigation closed, when I was finally assigned to a cell. Before the persistant hostility that I was shown, not to say actual provocation, I was forced to abandon all hope of advancing any further on that road. Those of my Surrealist friends— notably Aragon and Eluard—who had acted on the same impulse as I, were also forced to turn back.

---

* As is well known, Picasso was a leading figure in the French Communist party by the time these interviews were taped. He and Breton had severed relations over precisely this issue several years earlier.

Who were we, confronting reality, that reality which I know now was lying at Nadja's feet like a lapdog? By what latitude could we, abandoned thus to the fury of symbols, be occasionally a prey to the demon of analogy, seeing ourselves the object of extreme overtures, of singular, special attentions? How does it happen that thrown together, once and for all, so far from the earth, we have been able to exchange a few incredibly concordant views above the smoking debris of old ideas and sempiternal life? I have taken Nadja, from the first day to the last, for a free genius, something like one of those spirits of the air which certain magical practices momentarily permit us to entertain but which we can never overcome.

—Nadja

10.

THE INTERNAL ADVENTURE AND PERSONAL CREATION
COMPETE WITH SOCIAL DISCIPLINE. THE NEW SPIRIT IN
THE FORM OF "OBJECTIVE CHANCE." ELECTIVE LOVE
AND SEXUALITY. A GLIMPSE OF RUE DU CHÂTEAU.

ANDRE PARINAUD: In retrospect, Mr. Breton, it seems that the
Surrealists joining the Communist party was a misunderstanding
from the start. Still, you and some of your friends tried, for
several years running, to maintain that dialogue. What were the
major milestones in the evolution of the Surrealist movement
from 1927 to 1932, the year when the break from, let's say at least,
official Communism became final?

ANDRE BRETON: The obstacles that a certain number of Surrealists encountered in 1927 when trying to join the Communist
party, which forced them to turn away from it almost immediately, were to engender a fairly tense situation within the group
itself. Certainly, it had been a failure; but those of us who had
suffered it in no way considered it final. We believed the hostility
we had encountered—I in particular, as editor of *La Révolution
Surréaliste*—arose from a misunderstanding that would be resolved sooner or later. This misunderstanding seemed to us to
result solely from the inability (quite natural, all things considered) of men involved in completely different kinds of problems to
understand even slightly our intellectual position and to justify in
their own minds the general orientation of our activities. We

harbored this illusion—that their distrust would eventually subside—from 1928 to 1932. Nonetheless, for the moment, this failure seemed to vindicate those Surrealists who had abstained from political commitment, whom the others had reproached for their more or less avowed indifference to social action. The admission of this indifference, or its flagrant demonstration, had furthermore entailed several exclusions by a vast majority of votes, as in the cases of Artaud, Soupault, and Vitrac. Everything happened as if, in Surrealism at that time, it was vitally necessary that we not backslide into the literary and artistic sphere and be stuck there forever. So we can say that, for years, the deviation we hunted down above all others was the one that led someone to see art as a refuge and to deny or put in doubt, for any reason whatsoever, that man's social liberation concerned us *any less* than did the liberation of the mind.*

AP: But I imagine the attraction to art was not the only deviation you feared, since the moral and political pressures the Communist party exerted on your movement constituted equally serious threats!

AB: Of course. So there were two sides to this stiffening of our views: we sought on the one hand to guard against a return to our initial position, which stated that Surrealism was sufficient unto itself; and on the other, to counter any tendency toward putting an end to Surrealism as such, as a way of eliminating the frictions that kept its members from joining the political revolutionaries. I believe we never would have envisioned this latter extreme, not even to dismiss it, if Naville hadn't done his utmost at that moment to try to catch us in a dilemma. Having readily agreed with everyone's opinion—by which I mean: constantly supplying the political side with arguments that stressed Surrealism's incompatibility with communism; and not breathing a word of these

---

* Breton seems to have gotten entangled in his own sentence, which no doubt should read: ". . . concerned us *just as much* as did the liberation of the mind."

arguments to the Surrealists, some of whom had remained his friends—Naville did his best to make this reconciliation impossible. Nor did he change his attitude toward us in the years 1930 to 1939, when he became one of the heads of the French section of the Fourth (Trotskyist) International.

AP: Did the Communist party's opposition to your activity, as well as its—soon apparent—intent not to allow the existence of an independent, autonomous group within its ranks, lead you to question the very principle of communism, I mean the fundamental concepts of Marxism?

AB: Whatever setbacks we experienced while trying to fit into a militant political framework, it is certain that, for several of us, the premises of this activity remained and would long remain beyond doubt. In an interview published in 1935 and reprinted in my book *Political Position of Surrealism*, I confirmed that we had never stopped embracing all the theses of dialectical materialism, and I listed them to make it very clear that I exempted none. My first doubts didn't occur until after the Spanish Civil War . . . but no point in getting ahead of myself.

AP: So the actual theses of Marxism were not being questioned, granted, but was this because there was a logical bond or internal affinity between Surrealism and Marxism, or because you were anxious not to challenge the largest organized revolutionary force?

AB: In this regard, the main thing is to understand that, even if Surrealist activity properly speaking continued to develop on its own terrain—that of *inner* experience and adventure—it nonetheless remained subtended by our concern with avoiding a fundamental conflict with Marxism. Not because the workings of our minds inevitably led us to meet up with and confirm Marxist theses on our own, but because there was no doubt, at least until the period in question, that Marxism bore the greatest hope for the liberation of oppressed classes and peoples.

Whoever has already said, or has yet to say, that Surrealism proved deficient in this regard, that it was up to Surrealism to suggest its own political agenda instead of trying to adapt to an existing one, is perhaps right on the intellectual level, but (to my mind) wrong on the human level. When it came to the social transformation of the world, several urgent considerations prevailed over all the others. The tool needed for this transformation existed and had proven itself: it was called Marxism-Leninism. We had no reason as yet to suspect that its tip had been coated with poison.

AP: It doesn't seem that the difficulties involved in trying simultaneously to pursue internal (Surrealist) activities and external (political) ones ended up paralyzing your means of expression . . .

AB: No—perhaps just the opposite. The period that ran from 1926 to 1929 saw a flowering of Surrealist works that is often considered the most dazzling. Aragon published *Paris Peasant* and *Treatise on Style*, Artaud *The Nerve Meter*, Crevel *L'Esprit contre la raison* [The Mind against Reason], Desnos *Deuil pour deuil* [Mourning for Mourning] and *La Liberté ou l'amour*, Eluard *Capital of Pain* and *L'Amour la Poésie*, Ernst *The Hundred Headless Woman*, Peret *Le Grand jeu* [The Big Game], and myself *Nadja* and *Surrealism and Painting*. From the Surrealist perspective, it was also one of the most outstanding periods visually, being one of extraordinary inventiveness for Arp, Ernst, Masson, Miró, Man Ray, and Tanguy. Picasso, too, took great strides toward us at that time.

AP: Mr. Breton, do you think that in a more favorable climate, it would have been possible for the Surrealist group to become more deeply involved in political action?

AB: Even if we'd decided to put our combined resources in the service of political action (we called it "revolutionary action" without a second thought), I don't believe we could have. Sooner or later we would once again have succumbed to the appeal of Surrealism, which as these works demonstrate was quite strong at the

time and, no doubt, of an irrepressible nature. Either because we were still very young and had in no way restrained our playful tendencies, or because it was not in our power to turn away from those horizons that had previously captivated us, in spite of ourselves we were not prepared to devote more than a portion of our minds to rationalistic and disciplined activities. Our taste for adventure in every sphere had never died—I'm speaking of adventures in language as well as in the street or in dreams. Works such as *Paris Peasant* or *Nadja* give a good idea of this mental climate, in which our penchant for wandering was taken to its furthest limits. An uninterrupted quest was given free rein: its purpose was to behold and disclose what lay hidden under appearances. Unexpected encounters, which explicitly or not always tend to assume female traits, marked the culmination of this quest.

AP: Can you detail the origin of this taste for chance, this expectation, this pursuit of the unforseen in all its forms, which characterized a period in the history of the Surrealist movement?

AB: For several of us, this attitude predated the birth of the Surrealist movement. It was already expressed in a "play" written jointly by Soupault and myself: *If You Please*, acted by us at the Théâtre de l'Oeuvre during a Dada demonstration and published in 1920 in *Littérature*. The hero of the play, Mr. Létoile, is fairly clear on this point: "It happens from time to time," he says, "that I pace up and down for hours between two houses or four trees in a square. The passersby smile at my impatience, but I'm not waiting for anyone." It's positively true that he's not waiting for anyone, since he hasn't made any dates. But, by the very fact of adopting this ultrareceptive posture, he intends to help chance— how should I say it—he means to put himself in a state of grace with chance, in such a way that something *will* happen, that someone *will* show up. In *Littérature*, at the beginning of 1922, Aragon and I published an account of the very fugitive encounter we had had, separately, on the same afternoon, with a young woman whose appearance struck us as extremely unconventional, and of our vain attempts to find her again. The title given to this

text, "L'Esprit nouveau" [The New Spirit], indicates fairly well the kind of importance we attached to it (it was later reprinted in *Les Pas perdus*). We were stalking that "objective chance" (to use Hegel's term) whose manifestations I'd never stop watching out for, not only in *Nadja*, but later in *The Communicating Vessels* and *Mad Love* as well.

AP: I have a rather naive question, and I hope your answer will justify it: why did you attach such special importance to what the common herd calls coincidence?

AB: Because, philosophically, objective chance—which is nothing more than the geometric locus of these coincidences—seemed to constitute the knot of what for me was *the problem of problems*. I was trying to clarify the relations between "natural necessity" and "human necessity," and correlatively between necessity and freedom. I don't see how I can speak of it any less abstractly. The problem must be posited this way: how can phenomena that the human mind perceives only as belonging to separate causal series come so close together that they actually merge into one another (although, to tell the truth, they rarely do)? Why is the glow resulting from such a fusion so bright, albeit so ephemeral? Only ignorance could make us see these concerns as mystical. When we think that Engels himself said, "Causality cannot be understood except as it is linked with the category of objective chance, a form of the manifestation of necessity," we might as well try to pass even Engels off as a mystic. Whoever wishes to pursue the question further might consult my introductory remarks to the survey that Eluard and I launched in *Minotaure* in 1933. The survey went like this: "What do you consider the most important encounter of your life? To what extent did this encounter strike you as being fortuitous, or preordained?" Other surveys to have come out of Surrealism have been granted retrospective success: "Why do you write?," "Is suicide a solution?," "What do you do when you're alone?" (interestingly, not a single person responded to this last one). But it was by far the survey on encounters that was closest to my heart.

AP: It seems that you endowed the encounter, at least in the current state of knowledge, with a kind of magical power. Doesn't a work such as *Nadja* constitute the best illustration of your thinking on the subject?

AB: A kind of magical power, yes, all the more so in that, for me, the highest point this idea of encounters could reach, and the chance of its supreme accomplishment, naturally resided in love. No revelation on any other plane could even compare to it. Perhaps the object of that quest I mentioned was love and love alone, although sometimes in disguise. It seems to me, in fact, that a work such as *Nadja* clearly establishes this. The book's heroine possessed every charm one could want; we could truly say that her role was to focus the entire appetite for the marvelous upon herself. And yet, all the seductions she exerted on me remained on an intellectual level, were not resolved in love. She was a sorceress, but all of her magic thrown into the balance weighed little against the pure and simple love that a woman like the one we see passing at the end of the book inspired in me. It's possible, furthermore, that the magic Nadja surrounded herself with was the mind's compensation for the heart's defeat. We see something similar in the case of the celebrated medium Hélène Smith, whose marvelous peregrinations from planet to planet, recorded in *From India to the Planet Mars* and *Nouvelles observations sur un cas de somnambulisme* [New Observations Regarding a Case of Somnambulism], seem to be aimed mainly at capturing the attentions of Théodore Flournoy, who was caring for her, and whose love she had not managed to win.

AP: So at that time, Surrealism's great source of inspiration was love?

AB: Yes: independently of our profound desire for revolutionary action, all the subjects of exaltation proper to Surrealism at that time converged toward love. "Hands Off Love" was the title of a Surrealist broadside that aimed to counter the accusations of "immorality" brought against Charlie Chaplin, in whom we

honored above all "the defender of love." The most beautiful poems that Eluard, Desnos, or Baron published at the time were love poems. This kind of love that we glorified to the maximum was strong enough to break down every barrier. A young priest, Ernst Gengenbach, who had written to *La Révolution Surréaliste* that he'd tried to commit suicide out of amorous despair, was welcomed by most of us with open arms. And what did Aragon and I celebrate in "The 50th Anniversary of Hysteria," in 1928? It was the "passionate attitudes," veritable *tableaux vivants* of a woman in love, that the archives of the Salpêtrière hospital had brought to light. *La Révolution Surréaliste* ceased publication at the end of 1929, but the crowning glory of its penultimate issue consisted in an extremely liberal survey "on sexuality," conducted by the Surrealists in order to establish the "share of objectivity," the "individual determinations," and the "degree of awareness" that might exist in this domain. The last issue closed on a synthetic survey, which was still more significant. This survey is still ongoing; it could just as well be addressed this evening to our listeners. This was the questionnaire:

"What kind of hope do you place in love? How do you envision the passage from the *idea of love to the fact of love*? Would you sacrifice your freedom for love? Have you already? If such a step seemed necessary, in order not to be unworthy of love, would you sacrifice a cause that up until then you considered it your duty to defend? Would you accept not becoming the person you might have been if this were the price you had to pay for fully enjoying the certainty of loving? How would you judge someone who would even betray his convictions in order to please the woman he loved? Can such a token be asked for? Can it be obtained?

"Do you feel you have the right to deprive yourself temporarily of your loved one's presence, knowing how exhilarating absence is for love, but realizing the mediocrity of such an ulterior motive?

"Do you believe in the victory of admirable love over sordid life, or of sordid life over admirable love?"

What remains unspoken—and what, to my mind, is endlessly fascinating—is the fact that if, at the time, the Surrealists as a whole theoretically (and lyrically) agreed that the highest human

aspiration, the one that transcended all others, resided in *elective love*, it could hardly be said that some of them did not prove unworthy of this idea every single day . . .

AP: Why did you use the word "unworthy"? Do you attach a moral meaning to it, and if so, which?

AB: I use the word "unworthy" today, in other words *at my age*, because of certain confidences that were subsequently made to me, but without giving it the conventional moral definition. Be that as it may, debauchery is the worst enemy of this elective love; it precludes the sublimation that is a necessary ingredient. Whoever, contemplating this aspect of his memories, suddenly sees in an anonymous crush the hundreds, even thousands of women with whom he has "made love" cannot—and here I rely on accounts by the parties concerned—have anything but a very vague and very brief nostalgia for elective love. This love has turned irrevocably away, and he knows it. I came back to this problem in 1947, in the "Ajours" [Openwork] section of the second edition of my book *Arcane 17* [Arcanum 17], where I said: "I've opted for the passionate and exclusive form of love, to the detriment of anything that can be attributed to accommodation, whim, or deviation. I know this view might seem narrow and arbitrarily limiting, and I've long been hard pressed to make valid arguments in its defense when it ran up against the viewpoint of skeptics, or of self-avowed libertines. The striking thing is, I was able to verify *a posteriori* that the majority of disputes within Surrealism, which took political divergences as a pretext, were overdetermined—not, as has been insinuated, by personal issues, but by an insurmountable disagreement on this point."

Whether I still have long to live or not, I'm sure that I'll never retract that statement.

AP: For those who know you, there's no doubt about it! And yet, there exists an apparent contradiction between your concept of elective love and the Surrealists' admiration for someone like Sade. I think you could easily clarify this ambiguity . . .

AB: Though the Surrealists elevated to the zenith the meaning of that "courtly" love that is generally thought to derive from the Cathari tradition, just as often they anxiously studied its nadir, and it's this dialectical process that made Sade's genius shine for them like a black sun. Wasn't it Valéry who said that "the truth sayers are never strangers to eroticism"? Were it to remain in the very elevated spheres where poems such as Baudelaire's "Hymn," Germain Nouveau's "Aimez," Eluard's "Amoureuses" [Women in Love], and almost the entirety of Péret's collection *Je sublime* [I Sublime] place it, this love, which such works bring to the point of incandescence, would soon become rarefied. Such a flame's admirable, blinding light must not be allowed to conceal what it feeds on, the deep mine shafts criss-crossed by hellish currents, which nonetheless permit us to extract its substance—a substance that must continue to fuel this flame if we don't want it to go out. It's because Surrealism started from this viewpoint that it has made such an effort to lift the taboos that bar us from freely treating the sexual world, and *all* of the sexual world, perversions included—a world about which I later said that, "despite the memorable explorations made by Sade and Freud," it "has never, as far as I know, stopped countering our will to penetrate the universe with its unshatterable knot of *darkness*."

On a wholly different plane, which in retrospect seems to me to belong to the realm of . . . mental choreography (it's hardly within everyone's reach), Aragon showed his mettle, and even outdid himself, in *Treatise on Style*. He worked on the manuscript during the summer of 1927 in Varengeville, Normandy, not far from the beautiful pirate's lair, the Manoir d'Ango, where I was endeavoring to set the tone of *Nadja*. The ten or so manuscript pages that he set as his daily goal cost him scarcely more than a half-hour's work, if we can even call those effortless acrobatic feats "work." He never failed to read them to me, every afternoon, sitting with an "Alexandra" cocktail beside the seashore at Pourville. I remember that he took great pride in the collection of ties (some two thousand of them) that he brought on vacation. Always the whole rainbow . . .

AP: So we might think that Surrealism, during this period,

wasn't suffering overly from internal upheavals, even though they resulted in several exclusions.

AB: If some drastic cuts had to be made in Surrealism at the time as a precaution against relatively serious deviations—I mentioned the exclusion of Artaud, Soupault, and Vitrac, and many others were to follow—our ranks were still a long way from depletion. Among the most notable new members that I haven't yet had a chance to discuss (this brings us back to 1925) were Yves Tanguy, Jacques Prévert, and Raymond Queneau. Actually, the last two ended up taking part only rarely in Surrealism's public activities, unwittingly saving themselves for the period to come when they would both be put in the spotlight. By that time they had made a noisy break from Surrealism's ranks, all the while remaining faithful to the spirit of the movement on a large number of points.

Be that as it may, never had Surrealism shown such an organic unity, nor known greater effervescence than during that time, when our evening meetings were most often held in the old house (since demolished) at 54 Rue du Château. It was there, in the heart of a neighborhood unforgettably depicted by Huysmans in *Les Soeurs Vatard*, that Marcel Duhamel, long before he thought of launching the *"série noire"* and the *"série blême,"** lodged his friends Prévert and Tanguy. Péret and Queneau also enjoyed long stays in that house, at his expense. Absolute nonconformism, total irreverence, and the most wonderful humor held sway there. In a corner papered with movie posters—vampish looks and drawn pistols—stood a small but always well-stocked bar. There were seven or eight cats, upon whom they lavished attention. And frogs behind green-tinted glass. I know of no easier gestation than the one that later gave birth to Prévert's "Attempt to Describe a Dinner of Heads in Paris-France," or Péret's *Je ne mange pas de ce pain-là* [I'll Have None of It], or Queneau's *Exercises in Style*. That was the veritable alembic of humor, in the Surrealist sense of the word.

---

* The *série noire* (literally, "black series") was a line of mass-market paperback mysteries that Duhamel created for Editions Gallimard in the 1940s. The *série blême* ("pallid series") is Breton's little joke.

The poet to come will surmount the depressing idea of the irreparable divorce between action and dream. He will hold out the magnificent fruit of the tree with those entwined roots and will know how to persuade those who taste of it that it has nothing bitter about it. Carried along on the wave of his epoch, he will assume for the first time, free from anguish, the reception and transmission of all the appeals pressing toward him from the depth of ages. He will hold together, whatever the cost, these two terms of human relationship upon whose destruction the most precious conquests would become instantly redundant: the objective consciousness of realities and their interior development, since this relationship, through individual feeling on the one hand and universal feeling on the other, contains something magical for the time being.

—The Communicating Vessels

11.

THE CENTENNIAL OF 1830 IS MARKED WITHIN SURREALISM
BY VIOLENCE. A NEW WAVE ENGULFS THE OLD ONE.
SURREALISM "IN THE SERVICE OF THE REVOLUTION."

ANDRE PARINAUD: The years 1929 to 1933 were the time of
Surrealism's greatest agitation, in both the active and passive
senses of the word. Since then, many have said that this agitation
was the inevitable product of a serious internal contradiction—
and even, if we are to believe a number of those who have studied
the problem, that this contradiction was insurmountable, and
that Surrealism's reaction to it was necessarily overheated. What
are your own thoughts on this critical period?

ANDRE BRETON: Nothing could be further from my own view,
even today. Such a contradiction did not exist *in the mind*. Just
because we felt "called upon" to carry out a particular task in the
realm of expression—and, subsequently, to explore the issues it
raised—it didn't mean that we could ignore social ills or remain
indifferent to the available remedies. And these remedies existed;
they had been found and had proven themselves, at least in a
negative sense: the abolition of the so-called "bourgeois" regime,
with its proliferation of monstrous inequities. If we were already
worried about how the new machine was running (it had been
years since Trotsky had joined the opposition and had had to go
into exile), we did not yet consider these remedies compromised *in
their essence*.

AP: Still, Surrealism hardly dismissed the upheavals at the head of the Communist International as unimportant?

AB: Of course not! And in this regard, it's still rather significant that the summons to the general meeting of March 11, 1929—the so-called "Rue du Château meeting"—proposed as its topic of discussion a "critical examination of the recent treatment of Leon Trotsky." In reality, this subject was never even broached, as too many preliminary questions, raised by the individual behavior of various participants, had immediately created an extremely tense situation. In retrospect, I don't see how it could have been otherwise. It was necessary for the assembly to begin by verifying each member's "moral qualifications," if we wanted to keep some of these members from confining themselves (as had already been the case) to a purely verbal commitment, which they could revoke at the first opportunity. You mustn't believe we were too stringent. What should we think, for example, of an editor of *Le Grand Jeu*,* present at that meeting and thus making a show of pursuing the same goals as we, who shortly before had penned an article in praise of Jean Chiappe, the fascist police commissioner, for *Paris-Midi*? Really, could that be tolerated? Not long ago—in 1947, I believe—the same individual, now a Stalinist, published a lampoon called *Le Surréalisme contre la Révolution* [Surrealism versus the Revolution]. His initials are Roger Vailland. He sent me written death threats because my only public response was to mention that earlier episode—one of the most brilliant of his career . . .

AP: Various texts of yours from that time clearly show the tension and fever that reigned in Surrealism. Don't you now think that the vehemence of certain expressions exceeded the errors or deviations that you meant to castigate back then?

* *Le Grand Jeu* was a magazine published by a group of younger Surrealist sympathizers, including poet and essayist René Daumal (best known for the allegorical novel *Mount Analogue*), poet Roger Gilbert-Lecomte, novelist Roger Vailland, painter Josef Sima, poet and critic André Rolland de Renéville, and cartoonist Maurice Henry. Their often stormy relations with the Surrealist group proper lasted from 1928 through 1930.

AB: I won't claim that the sustained effort—particularly on the part of Aragon, Fourrier, Péret, Queneau, and myself—to heighten the intellectuals' *revolutionary awareness* was pursued with all due calm. There's no denying that this effort bore fruit (even if these fruits have become bitter and suspect); but, as it encountered all kinds of self-conscious dodges and resistances, it ended up being expressed in terms in which exasperation played too great a role. Reflecting on the situation fifteen years later, I showed some regret at having let myself fall at the time into useless polemical violence. This regret was stated in the "Preface" to the *Second Manifesto of Surrealism*, which was published in the collected edition of the *Manifestoes* in 1946.

In the same preface, I pointed out, as extenuating circumstances, that those who were treated worst were necessarily those from whom Surrealism expected the most—such as Artaud and Desnos. In order to avoid weakening our *active element*, we had to ensure, whatever the cost, that individual problems not interfere with the group solution we were after. I also added that, if in Surrealism at that time the violence of expression might sometimes seem out of all proportion to the deviation, the error, or the "sin" being castigated, the blame for it must be placed on the period itself, on the one hand, and on the other—this is of no small importance—the formal influence of a good portion of Marxist literature, in which every weapon was used to put the enemy out of commission.

AP: Yes, but isn't it also true that various latent conflicts within Surrealism seemed to take on the proportions of a life-or-death struggle in 1929?

AB: That's true. And yet, it was certainly not with a light heart that I attacked, in the *Second Manifesto*, a number of those on whom I had counted, with whom I'd shared a common stretch of road for a fairly long time. One of the worst drawbacks of committed intellectual activity in the collective sense is the need to subordinate personal sympathies to that activity, come what may. At that moment, I felt a pressing need to react against various kinds of

deviations. One of these was stagnation, as can result from too much self-satisfaction (which is essentially what I held against Desnos). Another is the one that leads to social abstentionism, and by that very path brings one back to the literary or artistic plane (as was apparently the case with Artaud and Masson, for example). Still another, the one that leads to abandoning Surrealist demands, in their unconditional specificity, for political action (which is what Gérard and Naville were trying to incite). All the while putting these tendencies on trial, I did not hesitate to attack certain individual behaviors that seemed to engender them. Admittedly, other parts of the *Second Manifesto* are less episodic or perishable. If only for the benefit of ideas, perhaps it was necessary to cut certain ties in order to move forward. It's also possible that, on my part, some excessive rigors in judgment, some extremes of expression can be ascribed to a nervous tension that stemmed not only from the critical situation of Surrealist ideas, but also from a certain upheaval in my personal life, which I alluded to in *The Communicating Vessels*.

AP: Moreover, if I may say so, you've been made to pay rather dearly for that intransigence! Could you remind us what reactions your position provoked at the time?

AB: The majority of those I had mistreated, and a few others who had joined them, devoted a pamphlet to me, whose title—*A Corpse*—was taken from the old lampoon against Anatole France, published right after his death. I was not spared a single insult. Its authors, furthermore, didn't stop there. With great obstinacy they tried to reach me more seriously through the person with whom I was living, and anonymously to boot: telephone calls in the middle of the night, funeral wreaths delivered in the morning . . .

AP: But there's a large portion of the *Second Manifesto* that transcends these various polemical asides. One that has been especially noted, and often cited, is the passage in which you assign as Surrealism's motivation to find and fix the "point of the mind at

which life and death, the real and the imagined, past and future, the communicable and the incommunicable, high and low, cease to be perceived as contradictions." Moreover, diverse and prolonged reactions greeted the sentence: "I ask for the profound, the veritable occultation of Surrealism." I believe these two statements could bear a few words of comment, if you wouldn't mind?

AB: Of course. It goes without saying that this "point," in which we sought to resolve all the antinomies that gnawed at us and drove us to despair, and which in my book *Mad Love* I named the "supreme point" in memory of an admirable site in the Basses-Alpes, can in no way be situated on the mystic plane. I hardly need stress the "Hegelian" aspect of the idea of surpassing all antinomies. It was undeniably Hegel—and no one else—who put me in the condition necessary to perceive this point, to strain toward it with all my might, and to make this very tension my life's goal. No doubt there are others whose knowledge of Hegel's works far surpasses mine: any specialist could teach me a thing or two when it comes to interpreting his writings. Be that as it may, since I came to know Hegel—or even since I had my first inklings of him through the sarcasms with which my philosophy professor, a positivist named André Cresson, taxed him in around 1912—I have become imbued with his views. To my mind, his method has bankrupted all others. When Hegelian dialectic ceases to function, for me there is no thought, no hope of truth. Only when the floodgates of that dialectic opened in me did I realize that the distance between the *place* where Hegelian thought emerged and the *place* where so-called "traditional" thought rose to the surface was not so great. For me, both of them tended to become a single place . . .

As far as my request for the occultation of Surrealism is concerned, we're dealing here with an intentionally ambiguous expression, and the context says as much: on the one hand, a prohibition against exhibiting oneself or "appearing onstage"; and on the other an invitation to compare the evolution of the Surrealist message with the message of esotericism. In the *Second Manifesto*, there are numerous references to astrology, alchemy, and

magic. They show that, despite what current detractors of Surrealism maintain, preoccupations of that order are not new, and that
it is totally inaccurate to claim that they demonstrate a recent
change in my thinking.

AP: In 1930 you founded a new magazine, called *Le Surréalisme
au Service de la Révolution*. This suggests to me that the very violent
attacks you'd just suffered had not caused excessive damage, and
that you retained many supporters . . .

AB: There was no shortage of them. If the publication of the
1930 *Corpse* consecrated my break with numerous Surrealists of
the first or second wave, from the standpoint of collective activity
it entailed no loss of energy. A lot of mud was slung at me—no one
will ever do better, nor even as well, by a long shot: that much can
be said, at least!—but in return, I still had the support of my old
companions Aragon, Crevel, Eluard, Ernst, Péret, and Tanguy.
They banded together to declare publicly that "the *Second Manifesto* is the surest way to appreciate what is dead and what is more
living than ever in Surrealism," and that in this book "the rights
and duties of the mind" were added up. If I was very sensitive to
the loss of certain collaborations and friendships, particularly
Prevert's and Queneau's, this loss was compensated to some degree by the arrival on the scene of very active new elements, such
as Buñuel and Dali, René Char, Georges Sadoul and André
Thirion, who, along with a few others, joined in the statement on
my behalf. I also reconciled with Tzara, which was no doubt
strategically motivated on his part. In any case, it was with the
confidence of the above-mentioned vested in me, and duly mandated by them, that I took control of the magazine *Le Surréalisme
au Service de la Révolution* in 1930.

AP: What was this new periodical meant to be? To what extent
did it accept Communist party discipline, and to what extent did
it remain independent?

AB: The magazine's title alone represented an appreciable politi-

cal concession, further underscored by the publication, on page one of the first issue, of a telegram addressed to the International Bureau of Revolutionary Literature in Moscow. In this telegram, the Surrealists pledged, in the event of "imperialist aggression" against the USSR (you see that the slogan is hardly new), to obey the directives of the Third International. But despite our desire to give such assurances, to affirm our absolute and unconditional solidarity with the proletarian cause, the Surrealist experience nonetheless continued with total independence; one could even say that it attained its highest point at that moment, that never before had it been carried out so brilliantly. Of all the Surrealist magazines, I think that *Le Surréalisme au Service de la Révolution*, whose six issues ran from 1930 to 1933, was by far the richest, in the sense that mattered to us: the most balanced, the best put together, as well as the most fully alive (with a thrilling and dangerous life). It was in this magazine that Surrealism burned with the most intense flame. For a time, we all saw nothing but this flame, and were not afraid to be consumed by it.

AP: Did this flame, at that moment, have a radiance to match the intensity you ascribe to it?

AB: One would have to say that its light was bright and rather dazzling, since Surrealist groups, or groups strongly related to Surrealism, were formed at that time outside of France, and maintained increasingly close contact with us. This was the case in Belgium, under the leadership of Paul Nougé, E. L. T. Mesens, and René Magritte; in Yugoslavia under Marco Ristich; in Czechoslovakia under Karel Teige, Vitezslav Nezval, and Toyen; as well as in the Canary Islands, Peru, and Japan. Because of this phenomenon, a wealth of Surrealist publications spread throughout the world. It was also on the appearance of a pro-Surrealist magazine with West Indian contributors that we entered into long-standing relations with Jules Monnerot.

Surrealism during that period strikes me as a superb and dismasted ship, which from one moment to the next might sink to the bottom, just as easily as it might triumphantly approach a shore

that would finally reveal the "real life" Rimbaud spoke of. The tempest was all around, but it was also *within*. It was completely outside the circuits in which adventure had hitherto been sought. The lives of those who participated in it were all the more impassioned in that they were terribly *exposed*.

AP: What do you mean by "exposed"?

AB: Our ties had been cut not only with the "literary" world, but also with "civilized" conformism, in whatever insidious form it might take. Nothing gives a better example of that frame of mind than a film such as *L'Age d'or* by Buñuel and Dali, which today you can see in the revival houses, if only to reassure yourself that it's lost none of its virulence. What does this film *respect*, if not, as always, love in its most carnal aspects, freedom pushed to the point of delirium, and, in the context of a morality without obligation or penalty, a worship for the pathos that might enter into certain of life's moments? I can still see (it was on the morning of December 4, 1930) the "Studio 28" cinema where *L'Age d'or* was being shown, and the state in which protesters from the day before had left it: the screen spattered with ink; the seats furiously smashed; the Surrealist paintings, which were on exhibit in the lobby, lacerated one by one with a knife. These exploits were the doing of two groups that called themselves the "Patriots' League" and the "Anti-Jewish League." In that theater, one could visually measure the depth of the abyss that separated us from the "right thinkers," or those who claimed to be such.

AP: So it was in that period of violence that Salvador Dali appeared. Wasn't he at once its product and its exemplary expression?

AB: Dali? Surely, his first Surrealist canvases—*Accommodations of Desire, Illumined Pleasures, The Lugubrious Game*—were shattering. Whatever reservations we might subsequently have had about his academic technique, which he justified by saying that he had taken as his task the "trompe-l'oeil photography of dream im-

ages," it is undeniable that the poetic, visionary content of these canvases has exceptional density and explosive force. Nothing, in any case, had been so laden with *revelation* since Max Ernst's work from 1923 and 1924, *The Revolution by Night* or *Two Children Are Threatened by a Nightingale*, for example; or Joan Miró's work from 1924, such as *The Tilled Field* and *The Harlequin's Carnival*. Nor was anything more carefully worked out, more rigorously perfected, than the "paranoia-critical method," to which Dali claimed exclusive allegiance, and which he beautifully defined as "a spontaneous method of *irrational knowledge* based on the critical and systematic objectification of delirious associations and interpretations."

AP: Can we say that Salvador Dali "invented" his method?

AB: He was not so much its inventor as its popularizer: we know, in fact, that this method takes root in Da Vinci's lesson, where he asks his students to stare fixedly at the stains on old walls, ashes, clouds, and streams, until battles, landscapes, and fantastic scenes emerge from their textures. As early as 1925, Max Ernst had been the first to give a very lively push in this direction, and even to rejuvenate the ancient method with his *frottage* technique. Nonetheless, Dali, by deciding to build his capital *strictly* on this means of visualization, for a time had triumph after triumph. Paintings that are worth far more than the oh-so-American fame they enjoy today were not the only trophies from that exploration that permits no return: it also gave us, as we saw, *Un Chien andalou* and *L'Age d'or*, which I still consider the two most accomplished Surrealist films; as well as lyrical works of the first water: *La Femme visible* [Visible Woman], *L'Amour et la mémoire* [Love and Memory], and *Babaouo*.

And I want to bring thee to the astrakhan shore that is being built on two horizons for thine eyes of gasoline to wage war I will lead thee by paths of diamonds paved with primroses with emeralds and the cloak of ermine that I want to cover thee with is a bird of prey the diamonds that thy feet shall tread I got them cut in the shape of a butterfly. . . .

      —*"Simulation of General Paralysis," in* The Immaculate
        Conception

12.

SALVADOR DALI AND PARANOIA-CRITICAL ACTIVITY. TWO ROUND TRIPS TO MOSCOW. FROM *THE POVERTY OF POETRY* TO *THE COMMUNICATING VESSELS*.

ANDRE PARINAUD: To complete the portrait of Salvador Dali that you began during our last broadcast, Mr. Breton, could you please introduce the man himself, situate his influence and his limits, and describe the peculiarities of his artistic nature, which, I believe, in his way of living, would soon destroy what he supposedly loved?

ANDRE BRETON: For three or four years, Dali would incarnate the Surrealist spirit and make it shine as brilliantly as ever, as only someone who hadn't participated in the sometimes thankless episodes of its gestation could hope to do. It's in this sense that he could already be considered a "cultural product." He who shortly afterward would enjoy introducing himself as the "colossally wealthy prince of the Catalan intelligentsia," only to make the feverish pursuit of such wealth his complete agenda (before long I would refer to him only by the now-famous anagram "Avida Dollars"), intended more than anyone else to take advantage of his—admittedly very peculiar—temperament. Physiologically, he was rather pleased to still have some of his baby teeth, and he boasted of never having known a woman before the age of twenty-five. Mentally, no one was more passionate about psychoanalysis; but if he used it, it was so he could jealously maintain his complexes, raise them to the level of exuberance. Leaving my apart-

ment to meet his friends in a cafe in Place Blanche (about a hundred yards away), he regularly hailed a cab in front of my door; having reached his destination, he'd throw a hundred-franc bill at the driver and flee so as not to have to take his change. If, as Arthur Cravan claimed, "every great artist has a sense of provocation," we must admit that no one ever took such a taste further than Dali, both in art and in his person. At the time he liked to appear in public in very elegant suits, onto which he had quite prominently sewn seven or eight artificial flies, which perfectly simulated the real thing . . .

AP: In some ways, your book *The Immaculate Conception* seems to come under the heading of paranoia-critical activity. Was that intentional?

AB: No, there was nothing deliberate about it; but it was in close convergence with paranoia-critical activity, as Dali had recently defined it, that Eluard and I ended up coauthoring *The Immaculate Conception*. Independently of an old score we wanted to settle with psychiatrists—at least those of the old school (over long-standing quarrels, traces of which can be found in *Nadja*, in the epigraph to the *Second Manifesto*, and in various texts signed by Artaud, Crevel, and myself)—it in fact concerned, once again, "the critical and systematic objectification of delirious assocations and interpretations." Whence the large amount of space devoted, in the book, to the verbal simulation of various "forms of certifiable madness." We began with the totality of symptoms that allow one to catalogue mental illness—for example, for acute mania, "flight of ideas," volubility, euphoria, erotomania, and so on. At the same time, what fundamentally distinguishes such an undertaking from Dali's is that our overriding intentions go much further. In the preamble I wrote to the chapter called "The Possessions," you can easily see that our main concern was to reduce the antinomy between reason and unreason—which was one of Surrealism's permanent ambitions.

AP: It seems that, in Surrealism, nonconformism was then at its

peak. Did poetry and art manage to convey it all? In other words, did this nonconformism still use them as its outlet?

AB: This nonconformism hardly limited itself to poetic or visual works. Within those confines, however, we should reserve a special place for "Surrealist objects," which mark the convergence of several distinct processes. The first of these can certainly be traced back to Marcel Duchamp, who—after having signed manufactured objects in around 1916, such as a bicycle wheel, a snow shovel, or a coatrack, with the intent of raising them to the status of "art objects" by sole virtue of his choice—had resorted in 1921 to filling a birdcage with lumps of white marble, cut to imitate lumps of sugar, in which he had planted a thermometer and which he had presented under the irrational title, "Why Not Sneeze?" A second process, related to the first, had been my own in 1923, when I suggested the fabrication and mass circulation of objects seen only in dreams, such as the book I describe in the "Introduction to the Discourse on the Paucity of Reality." A third, still more decisive process was due to Alberto Giacometti and his astonishing constructions, which began in 1930 with the "suspended ball" in impossible equilibrium over an inclined crescent. A fourth, finally—Dali's—leaned toward the creation of objects "with symbolic functions" (of the automatic type). Numerous "Surrealist objects" appeared at that moment, very diverse in nature and intent: the most remarkable were by Dali, Valentine Hugo, Miró, Meret Oppenheim, and Man Ray. In my view, it's a great shame that most of these objects, made of fragile materials and often assembled with the means at hand, have since disappeared. My own, assiduous, contribution to this activity consisted in "poem-objects."

AP: Could you remind us of your definition of the "poem-object"?

AB: I defined the poem-object as "a composition that tends to combine the resources of poetry and the plastic arts, by speculating on their reciprocal power of exaltation." Magritte, for his part,

taking his cue from the visual arts as I took mine from poetry, glimpsed what could result from juxtaposing concrete words with great resonance (such as the words "mountain," "pipe," or "child's head") with forms that negated them or, at the very least, did not rationally match them.

AP: But you were saying that your nonconformism was not always expressed in books, paintings, sculptures, or the "creation" of this kind of object?

AB: Far from it. Some of our young friends at the time made do, if I may put it that way, with nonconformism in its raw state, which incited them to great turbulence. "Black humor"—inherited from Swift, Jarry, Vaché, even Alphonse Allais and Sapeck; humor that, if the truth be told, was not always very discriminating—was their principle medium. This humor was given free rein during that period . . .

AP: If we didn't know that, we'd have a hard time understanding some rather feverish demonstrations by certain individuals . . .

AB: It would be impossible. Here's an example: in many respects, the most dubious of these demonstrations (but one, nonetheless, that would have considerable consequences) was a letter full of seditious statements that Georges Sadoul and another of our friends—one day when they were traveling together, and after copious libations—sent to the student who had placed first at the Saint-Cyr military academy, whose name they had read in the newspaper. The student deemed it wise to show the letter to the school's head, and legal proceedings brought against Sadoul led to his being sentenced to three months in prison.

AP: I imagine Sadoul's decision to accompany Aragon to Russia, where the latter was about to go, was a way of trying to delay facing that sentence?

AB: Exactly. Note that this trip, which was to be full of

surprises—and consequences—was in no way Aragon's idea, but that of Elsa Triolet, whom he had just met and who urged him to join her. In retrospect, and given her subsequent profile, there's every reason to believe that she made known and obtained what she wanted once they got there. Be that as it may, if Sadoul hadn't followed them to escape the police, everything might have turned out differently. It was the exchange of views between Aragon and Sadoul, who were cut off from the rest of us—exchanges over which hung the desperate situation in which Sadoul had put himself—that led them to make a series of decisions whose effects would overflow the context of Surrealism, and be felt even today and beyond.

Without this combination of circumstances, which I'm consciously stressing in order to underscore the glaring disproportion of effects and causes, Aragon, as I knew him then, would never have taken it upon himself to do anything that would risk his separation from us. I don't believe Sadoul was any more inclined toward this separation than he was, but I repeat that he was under the influence of his recent conviction, ready if need be to make concessions toward a regime in which he saw the negation of the one that had just sentenced him. I'm stressing this only to show a progression of facts that started from the most insignificant thing in the world: *a drunken practical joke* . . . Conflicting developments would stem from it; an unbridgeable gap would open between individuals who only yesterday had been in complete agreement. Because of the prominence of some of the protagonists, the conflict would become an open debate in intellectual circles.

AP: What happened during the voyage in question?

AB: It's fairly painful to tell. Aragon, who kept me informed of what he was doing over there, even up to the telegram announcing his return, showed great optimism. He had forged relations with the literary circles of Moscow and Leningrad, had explained our common viewpoint, and believed he had dissipated certain apprehensions about the Surrealist concept of poetry and art. His claims seemed to be corroborated by the facts: he was invited to

participate as a consultant in the Second International Congress of Revolutionary Writers, which was held in November 1930 in Kharkov; and—an undeniable coup—he managed to make them adopt a resolution (which we'd previously formulated in case the opportunity arose) condemning Henri Barbusse's newspaper, *Monde*, with which we were engaged in open conflict in Paris. A discussion of the literary situation in France—which, despite some reservations, engendered another resolution—seemed to place great faith in Surrealism.

AP: Then suddenly everything went wrong.

AB: Very suddenly. I can still see the more than anxious expression Sadoul wore on his return, and the painful embarrassment my questions caused him (Aragon had stopped off in Brussels, and would not arrive for two or three more days). Yes, everything had gone smoothly; yes, our goals had been met; but . . . There was, in fact, a very large "but." An hour or two before their departure, they had been asked to sign a document that implied the abandonment, not to say the repudiation, of practically every position we had held until then: rejection of the *Second Manifesto* "to the extent"—I'm quoting verbatim—"that it contradicts dialectical materialism"; denunciation of Freudianism as an "idealist ideology," of Trotskyism as a "social-democratic and counter-revolutionary ideology." To top it off, they had to agree to submit their literary activity "to the discipline and control of the Communist party." "So?" I asked bluntly. And, as Sadoul didn't say anything: "I assume you refused?" "No," he said, "Aragon thought it best to agree if we wanted—you and we two—to be able to work in the Party's cultural organizations." This was the first time that I saw open at my feet the abyss that since then has taken vertiginous proportions, growing as fast as the impudent idea that truth must take a back seat to expediency, or that neither conscience nor individual personality are worthy of consideration, or that the end justifies the means.

AP: And how did you greet Aragon? What was his attitude?

AB: Two tracts published in 1932, one called *Certificat* [Certificate] and signed by Eluard, the other called *Paillasse!* [Clown!] and bearing various signatures, give sufficient idea of the welcome Aragon received on his return. The sentimental chord, which was the only one he had left to play, swearing (as these tracts attest) that his agreement with his oldest friends was for him "a matter of life and death," nonetheless managed to provoke a response, especially on my part. After agreeing to some minimal public retractions, in the form of a letter "To Revolutionary Intellectuals"—an extremely ambiguous letter, to tell the truth—he again took his place among us, although not without lingering afterthoughts.

AP: But didn't the break with Aragon follow only several months later?

AB: Yes. New elements arose that made it inevitable. Aragon and the Surrealists who were then members of the Communist party found themselves in an extremely difficult position. On the one hand they had agreed, as I said, to submit their literary activity to Party control and discipline—and it goes without saying that the Party continued to look very unfavorably upon Surrealist activity. On the other, as Surrealists, they could not restrict the kind of adventure that Surrealism needed to run with complete freedom. Dali in particular had chosen to push that adventure further and further, and to shake off all constraints. In this regard, Aragon occasionally gave signs of overheated agitation. One day, for example, Dali had just described and sketched his latest "Surrealist object," which consisted of a dinner jacket studded all over with shot glasses full of milk. To the amazement of everyone present, Aragon vehemently protested the waste of this milk, and even went so far as to say that children might go hungry . . .

AP: This seems to be a new order of concern for him.

AB: We couldn't believe our ears! An even more significant episode arose from the publication, in the fourth issue of *Le*

Surréalisme au Service de la Révolution, of a very liberal "Daydream" by Dali . . . But here, I have to take a few steps backward.

Aragon, owing to the publication of a long poem called "Red Front," which he had composed in Russia and which had been published in the magazine *Littérature de la Révolution Mondiale*, had recently been indicted for "inciting soldiers to disobey orders" and "incitement to murder for purposes of anarchist propaganda." He stood to spend several years in prison. "Red Front" is a poem of political agitation, full of the verbal violence and excess to which we'd already seen Aragon resort in other circumstances. Whatever my reservations about both the spirit and the form of this poem, it goes without saying that one issue took precedence in my view: at all costs we had to save Aragon from legal proceedings and, to do that, to sway public opinion to his side. This is what I tried to do, with his full consent, by writing *The Poverty of Poetry*.

The galleys of this text had just come back from the printer when Aragon told me how he and four of our friends in the Party had been ordered to appear before a supervisory committee to justify the contents of the fourth issue of the magazine I edited, and to formally disavow Dali's contributions. The session had just ended: it had begun with their being left standing for a very long time, ignored by everyone there, after which the criticisms leveled against them had turned so hostile, so disdainful, that they had hardly been able to reply. I especially recall a sentence about Dali's text, which utterly infuriated me: "All you want," they had been told, "is to complicate the simple, healthy relations between men and women." Who dared maintain that, in bourgeois society, these relations were simple, or healthy?

I felt I needed to mention this statement in *The Poverty of Poetry*, to illustrate just how much bad faith or mental indigence we were up against. Aragon was strongly opposed: the statement had been made within the Party, and therefore was not to be made public. As I persisted in my intention, having no obligations in this regard, he warned me that my inserting this sentence in *The Poverty of Poetry* would inevitably mean the end of our relations. Paradoxically, our break became final the moment

my pamphlet saw daylight, even though its object had been to defend him.

AP: But despite this resounding breakup, you hadn't cut all your ties to the Communist party, since you continued to be involved in the activities of the Association of Revolutionary Writers and Artists.

AB: Indeed, one shouldn't think that this break, which was painful on both sides—some tender souls are still weeping over it—removed our last illusions about the compatibility of Surrealist and communist aspirations, in the doctrinal meaning of the word, any more than it did about the possibility of a political and cultural redress of the Party. The complaint against Aragon and several others was that he had surrendered without a fight, had espoused (with greater or lesser repentance) the official *line*, instead of trying to rectify it from within the organization, which still seemed possible to us. This is why, in the two years that followed, we would see a fair number of Surrealists struggle to remain in the Association of Revolutionary Writers and Artists (Association des Écrivains et Artistes Révolutionnaires, or A.E.A.R.), over which Paul Vaillant-Couturier then presided. In passing, I'd like to point out that I first had the idea for such an association, which André Thirion and I had tried to set up while Aragon was still in Russia: it was to be called the Association of Revolutionary Artists and Writers (Association des Artistes et Écrivains Revolutionnaires, or A.A.E.R.). If the A.A.E.R. never got past the planning stage, it was because Aragon asked us by telegram to postpone its foundation until he'd returned.

AP: What was your activity within the A.E.A.R.?

AB: In Vaillant-Couturier's A.E.A.R., our attitude at the time was basically modeled on that of the leftist opposition (the Trotskyites)—which means that, although I was one of the four or five "officers," my "vote" was almost always in the minority. Whoever wants a truly evocative image of that period would find it

in a brochure published in 1934 by Claude Cahun under the title *Les Paris sont ouverts* [Anyone's Bet]. The first one to be excluded from the A.E.A.R. was me. The reason was that the fifth issue of *Le Surréalisme au Service de la Révolution* contained a letter that Ferdinand Alquié had written me—libertarian in spirit, and moreover quite moving—in which he violently attacked the civic and moral concepts that had governed the Russian film *Road of Life*. Independent of the opinions he expressed, not all of which I shared, the intensity of life and revolt that ran through that letter seemed to me to warrant its publication. So there was no question of my granting them the repudiation they demanded.

I've dwelled on this external side of our activity between 1930 and 1934 only because I believe I needed to in order to explain certain convulsive movements in Surrealism during that period. If I wanted to account for my innermost thoughts in the same period, by which I mean the subterranean progression of my mind, I could only refer you to my book *The Communicating Vessels*, for which I confess I've retained a special fondness. Not that I still agree with everything it says (far from it), but I like the will it demonstrates to take the reins again, and even—how can I say it?—hold them from then on in a single hand. It's true that in this book I still insist upon materialist theses, even in the realm of dreams, which I grant is rather arbitrary; but as we've seen, I was more or less obligated by the need for practical action that I expressed in other domains.

AP: In your view, what still constitutes the work's interest and importance today?

AB: In my eyes, still today, *The Communicating Vessels* marks the point where I managed to surpass, to overcome certain contradictions that initially were the principle of my own evolution; as well as certain extremely perturbing trials in my private life. It took me until I was thirty-six to reach that point. I'm not a man who likes books for their own sakes. What saves this particular one for me, and what spawned its existence, was the discovery I believed I'd made, and the description I attempted, of a *capillary tissue* permit-

ting "the constant exchange in thought that must exist between the exterior and interior worlds, an exchange that requires the continuous interpenetration of the activity of waking and that of sleeping." It still seems to me that on this *level*, which human reflection will someday manage to attain, the outmoded opposition between materialism and idealism loses all its meaning.

I mentioned earlier the "sublime peak" of a mountain. There was never any question of my settling permanently on this peak. In fact, from then on, it would have ceased to be sublime, and I should have ceased to be a man. However, although unable to settle there, at least I never have gone so far from it as to lose sight of it, or to be unable to point it out to others. I chose to be the guide, in consequence of which I forced myself to be worthy of that power which, in the direction of eternal love, made me see *and granted me the rarer privilege of* making others see. *I never have been unworthy of this trust; I never have ceased to identify the flesh of the being I love with the snow on the heights at sunrise.*

—Letter to *"Chipnut of Munkhazel," in* Mad Love

13.

THE "CONGRESS OF WRITERS FOR THE DEFENSE OF CULTURE." THE SPANISH CIVIL WAR. A MONSTROUS INIQUITY: THE MOSCOW TRIALS. THE INTERNATIONALIZATION OF SURREALISM.

ANDRE PARINAUD: From 1933 until the war, Surrealist activity was necessarily subtended, and in part governed, by events whose increasingly disturbing and rapid development would lead to the last worldwide catastrophe. The principle stages of this march toward the abyss were marked by Hitler's coming to power; the fascist riots in 1934, in Paris; the declarations by Stalin and Laval in 1935, inviting France to accelerate its arms development; the Spanish Civil War and the French government's decision, under the Popular Front, not to intervene; the hazards, by turns exciting and shattering, of the struggle up until its final outcome; and finally, the succession of Moscow Trials in 1936, 1937, and 1938. All these events motivated you to take an extremely clear stand, which was recorded in a series of tracts and pamphlets. Without listing them all, could you briefly outline their general significance?

ANDRE BRETON: I can try . . . but it will be possible only if I can elaborate a bit on certain side events, and underline the sometimes tragic implications of our various stands.
 It was on the evening of February 6, 1934, in other words in the three or four hours following the fascist putsch, which some of us

had observed up close—some on the boulevards, others near Place de la Madeleine—that at my instigation we called an immediate meeting of as many intellectuals as we could gather, of every tendency, who were determined to face the situation. Our immediate task was to define possible means of resistance. This meeting, which lasted all night, led to our drafting a text entitled "Appel à la lutte" [Call to Battle], which exhorted the unionist and political organizations of the working class to take united action and called for a general strike. This call appeared on February 10, bearing almost ninety signatures. Among those least related to Surrealism were Alain, Michel Alexandre, Jean-Richard Bloch, Elie Faure, Jean Guéhenno, Henri Jeanson, Maximilien Luce, André Malraux, Marcel Martinet, Pierre Monatte, Henri Poulaille, Paul Signac, and others. A survey concerning the practical means of carrying out this unity of action followed shortly afterward. The "Intellectuals' Vigilance Committee," presided over by Paul Rivet, was not formed until later.

AP: I believe that as part of this will to struggle, you met Léon Blum. Can you tell us about the circumstances?

AB: In hopes of hastening this unity of action, I was indeed mandated to make contact with Léon Blum and to explain what many of us still expected of him. I have to say that my mission was a complete failure. All morning long, in his office on Ile Saint-Louis, I labored in vain to turn the conversation away from the literary track onto which he had steered it, moreover with extreme ease and finesse. Unfortunately, that wasn't what I had come for. Blum showered me with kindness, but every time I tried to bring him back to the object of my visit, he confined himself to dilatory statements.

AP: Another determinant event of the time, I believe, was the "Congress of Writers for the Defense of Culture," which was held in Paris, and in which you tried to participate.

AB: That's what I was thinking of when I spoke of the tragic

implications of some of our stands, which in retrospect have become indissociably linked. We have to keep in mind that in those days, a congress of that order could not muffle (as it would shamelessly do today) opinions that could still be more or less freely debated from the revolutionary standpoint, even if they didn't "toe the line." It was therefore understood from the start that I'd be able to state my views without constraint.

AP: But this is where the so-called "Ehrenburg incident" came into play.

AB: Yes. Fate, which several evenings earlier had made me run into the false witness Ilya Ehrenburg on Boulevard du Montparnasse, decided otherwise. I had not forgotten a certain passage in his book *Vus par un écrivain de l'U.R.S.S.* [As Seen by a Writer from the USSR], published several months earlier, where among other things he had said that the Surrealists "go in for Hegel and Marx, but work is something to which they are not adapted. They are too busy studying pederasty and dreams . . . Their time is taken up with spending their inheritances or their wives' dowries," etc. After having introduced myself, I slapped him several times over, while he pitifully tried to bargain without even raising a hand to protect his face. I don't see what other revenge I could have taken on this professional slanderer, who several years later would say that Vercors's *The Silence of the Sea* was a poison that could only have emanated from the offices of the German secret service. I was unaware that our insulter was part of the Soviet delegation to the Congress, which I certainly had no intention of offending through his person. It was nonetheless on this pretext that they informed me, via third parties, that my right to speak was being denied.

AP: From that moment on—once again because of an entirely chance incident—there was no further possibility of letting the Surrealist voice be heard from within cultural organizations inspired or controlled by the Communist party.

AB: Yes. And I have to say that this finally toppled the hopes that for years, despite everything, we'd had for reconciling Surrealist ideas with practical revolutionary action. That some of us were deeply affected by this is shown by the fact that, on the night before the Congress opened, our friend René Crevel killed himself, following an exhausting argument he'd had with the Congress organizers in vain hopes of winning back my right to speak. With him, we lost one of our best friends from the earliest days, or almost; one whose emotions and reactions had truly helped determine our common state of mind; the author of such works as *L'Espirit contre la Raison* and *Le Clavecin de Diderot* [Diderot's Harpsichord], without whom Surrealism would have lacked one of its most beautiful volutes. It is quite certain that Crevel's desperate action could only have been "overdetermined," and that other latent causes had been brewing for some time. Still, you can imagine the mood we were in when the Congress opened.

AP: And what finally happened during the Congress itself?

AB: Owing to Crevel's express wishes, it was finally agreed that my speech would be read by Paul Eluard; but he was given the floor only after midnight, when the hall was already emptying out and the lights were being switched off. Other statements from the opposition were similarly stifled.

This speech, along with the joint conclusions imposed by various recent events, was published under the title "On the Time When the Surrealists Were Right." In this text, the modes of enforcement of the Franco-Soviet pact, which was engineered by Laval and Stalin, were viewed in the darkest possible way. We firmly stated our mistrust of what the Russian regime had become over the preceding several years, and of its chief.

AP: What was the influence of this break on Surrealist activity, and what was Surrealism's attitude toward the declaration of war in Spain?

AB: From that point on, whether we liked it or not (or rather

whether we accepted it or not), our situation, with respect to what had previously been the twin poles of our activity, was profoundly altered. When it came to the expression and publication of our ideas about the world's social transformation, we were forced to rely on our own resources—which of course were laughable compared to those set against us. But it definitely wasn't possible to compromise any longer.

And indeed, the Spanish Civil War broke out in the middle of all this. Its echoes are still so vivid today that you can easily see how it crystallized our aspirations toward a *better human condition*. Never had a battle been more circumscribed—from the start—between the forces of obscurantism and oppression on the one hand, and on the other every will toward man's liberation— emancipation in its native state, so to speak. At that moment, when Stalinism had not yet had time to put its stamp on the Spanish and Catalan proletariat, the situation was admirably clear. We could unreservedly, indiscriminately applaud the victories of the F.A.I. [Federation of Spanish Anarchists] or the P.O.U.M. [Unified Marxist Workers' Party], and daily calculate their chances of bringing about the third great revolution of modern times—perhaps the first one not to have its Thermidor. We know all too well what Stalinist intervention made of these illusions, of all these hopes. But it is still alive; against all expectation it even raised its head again in March 1951, and it is far from having said its last word.* As to the mental imagery of the Spanish revolution, from its early days we have retained the vision of Benjamin Péret sitting in a Barcelona doorway, holding a rifle with one hand and petting a cat on his knees with the other. In my book *Mad Love*, which came out in 1937, I explained why I wasn't physically with him: it was because of a child, my own, who had recently been born and who could not have survived without me.

AP: But the blows that the Spanish Civil War subsequently dealt

---

* Breton is referring to widespread strikes by Catalan workers, which were soon quelled by Franco's army. The Surrealists had published a tract supporting the Catalans.

you were soon joined by those—still more cruel, if possible—dealt in 1936, 1937, and 1938 by the infamous "Moscow Trials"!

AB: There's no comparison between them. I cannot understand how, today, every last scrap of conscience does not rebel against the affront—I won't only say to any conception of justice, but also to the most elementary common sense—that the staging of these trials, and the reasons adduced for the sentences, constituted. I persist in thinking that they opened, and inevitably let fester, the most horrific scourge of modern times. We have accepted once and for all that "reasons of state" have thrown innocence and honor to the winds, and along with them the exemplary claims of certain men to universal gratitude. I know we've been through a war, which swelled our forgetfulness out of all proportion. But I'm still astonished and horrified to observe that this monstrous iniquity is generally ignored; that those who committed it have not been discredited and tarnished forever in the eyes of the world. I have no revisions to make to the protest I raised against the fate of Lenin's former companions and the absolutely unbelievable accusations that set the stage long in advance for the pickax in Trotsky's skull.

AP: What form did your protest take?

AB: At the time, this protest had no vehicle other than tracts, and I must say that the French leaders of the International Workers' Party (the Trotskyites), headed by our old friend Naville, did nothing to facilitate matters. In September 1936, at the meeting on "The Truth about the Moscow Trial," I was able to state my and my friends' opinions only thanks to the intercession of Victor Serge, who had just escaped from a Russian prison and, although detained in Brussels, insisted by telegram that they let me speak.

AP: And as for Surrealist activity in general, how and where was that expressed?

AB: It had been some time since the last autonomous Surrealist magazine. The movement was reduced to splitting its activity into two parts: one expressed in tracts, as I just said, the other seeking the widest possible development in the sumptuously produced magazine *Minotaure*. The contributions that set this magazine apart came from Dali, Eluard, Maurice Heine, Pierre Mabille, Péret, and myself. The Surrealist painters and sculptors— Bellmer, Brauner, Arp, Dali, Dominguez, Ernst, Giacometti, Magritte, Masson, Matta, Miró, Paalen, Man Ray, Seligmann, Tanguy, and others—were amply represented in its pages. At first the magazine was rather eclectic, but Surrealism gained territory with every issue, until finally it took over completely. From this viewpoint, and because of its external splendor, it gave Surrealism a dimension that we hadn't had before this. It's a shame the magazine can't be consulted today, but the collection of the thirteen published issues fetches prohibitive prices . . .

AP: Still, it seems that the hardships you faced in the years before the war did not prevent Surrealist activity from taking on an increasingly international character.

AB: Yes, Surrealist groups came together and were constantly gathering force in various countries. International Surrealist exhibits, with a growing number of participants, were held in Tokyo, Copenhagen, Teneriffe, London, and Paris. The most spectacular was the latter one, which opened at the beginning of 1938. Its principal organizer and director was Marcel Duchamp, who had always enjoyed an unmatched prestige in the Surrealists' eyes, particularly my own, owing both to the genius that all his artistic and antiartistic interventions demonstrated, and to his exemplary emancipation from every servitude and every misery that are the price of artistic activities properly speaking.

AP: I don't think the 1938 exhibit will soon be forgotten.

AB: In these blasé times, it's hard to imagine the fury and torrents of abuse that this exhibit earned us in the press! After a

long corridor, where they were greeted by mannequins decorated by the Surrealist painters, visitors reached a large room whose ceiling was hung with twelve hundred sacks of coal, still covered with dust. In the center of this room burned a brazier. One corner of the room was filled by a pond (a real pond, not a simulation), bordered by real plants and reflecting an unmade bed . . .

AP: Did any new prospects come from your actions at the time?

AB: It would seem so. The desire to accelerate Surrealism's internationalization showed in the frequent trips some of us took. Prague, where I went with Eluard; the Canary Islands, with Péret; London, where a number of us joined up, saw an uninterrupted series of lectures, interviews, and exchanges of ideas toward a more complete unification of our efforts. Following each of our trips abroad, moreover, an *International Bulletin of Surrealism* was published, usually in two languages, which measured the depth of the understanding reached and precisely delineated the possibilities of joint action between us and our friends.

At that very moment, serious ideological differences arose with Dali. He had already flirted with exclusion on several occasions, either for having presented a gratuitously indecent image of Lenin in one of his paintings, or for stating to all and sundry that train derailments delighted him no end, provided the first-class cars were spared . . . His sympathies, which led him more and more openly toward fascism, would soon entail our break from him. On the other hand, we had reconciled with several earlier dissidents and, against my wildest expectation, I had renewed some great friendships. Particularly with Artaud and Prévert, in human terms it was as if we'd never parted company.

AP: What was your personal situation at the time?

AB: Around 1936 and 1937, my material situation had been extremely critical. The new problems raised by the needs of a small child sometimes made it seem quite bleak. I made sufficient

allusion to these problems in a letter to my daughter, who was eight months old at the time—the letter that ends my book *Mad Love*, which I meant for her to read in the spring of 1952. Try as I might to obtain a visiting professorship or other position abroad from the appropriate authorities, notably through the offices of Jean Giraudoux, I was regretfully informed that my request could not be granted, as I lacked the necessary university diplomas. Luckily, for the few months that threatened to be the worst, a friend's generosity allowed me to run (as best I could) a small art gallery on Rue de Seine, which I opened under the name "Gradiva." The word means "She who walks," and it was the title of the admirable novella by Wilhelm Jensen that Freud superbly analyzed. You entered the shop through a glass door that had been designed and executed by Marcel Duchamp, whose opening silhouetted, as their shadows might, a rather large man and a noticeably smaller and very slim woman, standing side by side . . .

AP: How did your trip to Mexico at around that time come about?

AB: The adventure of the Gradiva gallery came to an end the day I was told that, for lack of anything better, the cultural services of the Ministry of Foreign Affairs had decided to offer me an assignment in Mexico, during which I'd have to give a certain number of lectures on literature and art, from the Encyclopedists to the present. And so one of the great aspirations of my life was realized. No matter how little I tend by nature to like travel, Mexico—perhaps because of some childhood memories—was the one country that attracted me. I hasten to add that I was not disappointed, even though some people did everything in their power to try to ensure me the worst possible reception. The Stalinist organization—a spin-off of the A.E.A.R. called the "International Association of Writers for the Defense of Culture," whose organ in Paris was the periodical *Commune*—had in fact taken pains to precede my arrival with a circular sent by airmail to the top Mexican writers and artists. I've kept a copy. Above the signature of René Blech, "for the international bureau," it said in

particular: "Mr. André Breton has always taken a stand against the Popular Front and toward this end (sic) has allied himself with the most suspect political factions. His action against the Spanish Republic has taken the most insidious forms. . . ." One of the addressees showed me the letter the moment I arrived. Luckily, I was carrying all the documents I needed to thwart my accusers.

Lovely loaded dice
Fortune and misfortune
In the three-card trick all those wide-eyed stares
around an open umbrella
What revenge the flea-figurine of the bohemian
My hand closes on her
If I were to escape from my fate

—Fata Morgana, *1940*

14.

IN MEXICO. TROTSKY UP CLOSE. FOR AN INDEPENDENT
REVOLUTIONARY ART. THE SECOND WORLD WAR, THEN
EXILE. THE "VOICE OF AMERICA" AND *VVV*.

ANDRE PARINAUD: Mr. Breton, I'd like you to give us some
details on your relations with Trotsky, a topic you broached in our
last broadcast, and to underscore some of the difficulties you had
to surmount in order to meet the great revolutionary. Could you
tell us the circumstances of your encounter, highlighting your
impressions?

ANDRE BRETON: I did not even have to request this meeting.
The painter Diego Rivera, who had taken me into his home the
moment I arrived in Mexico, lost no time in arranging it. Moreover, Trotsky knew that on several occasions I'd raised my voice in
his defense and wanted to see me. While he had wandered
throughout the world without a visa, it was Rivera who had found
him safe haven in Mexico and had swayed President Cardenas in
his favor. From that moment on, he was Rivera's guest; but he
lived in another house with his wife, secretaries, and bodyguards.
An assassination attempt was considered so likely that his house
was flanked by two outposts, about fifty yards away, manned at all
times by five or six men whose mission it was to stop all cars for
inspection. In a speech delivered at a meeting of the International
Workers' party after my return, and published in the magazine
Quatrième Internationale, I related my impressions from my first
meeting with Trotsky, which was followed by many others. I

didn't stress strongly enough his prodigious mental organization, which allowed him, for example, to dictate three texts simultaneously. But that day, I was speaking to men well versed in his thought, who were not likely to underestimate his capabilities. It seemed more important to show them Trotsky's *human* side, in the most elevated sense of the word; and in order to do that, to underscore his ability (which I'd admired during our trips together through Mexico) to relate every small observation to a larger fact, to bend it—without this ever seeming forced or artificial—toward the hope of redefining worldly values, which further reinforced the sense that revolutionary struggle was necessary.

AP: What was the "climate" of your meetings with Trotsky?

AB: I won't pretend that vast educational and other differences between Trotsky and his usual interlocutors—Rivera, his wife,* and myself—did not occasionally lead to some flare-ups in our daily relations. No matter how great our deference, and despite the care we took to contradict him as little as possible, we couldn't entirely avoid banding together out of an "artistic" temperament that was fundamentally alien to him. It's not the least striking aspect of the man's life that he won the sympathy of artists, whereas his own understanding of artistic problems was average at best. He was visibly pained when one of us paused to handle a piece of pre-Colombian pottery. I can still see the reproachful look he gave Rivera when the latter maintained (which was hardly extravagant) that drawing had been in decline since the cave period; and how he exploded one evening when we casually remarked in his presence that once a classless society was established, new causes of bloody conflict—that is, causes other than economic—would surely arise. But these were fleeting disagreements, which could not damage the basic harmony of our relations.

* Painter Frida Kahlo.

AP: Could you present Trotsky from within, if I may put it that way, highlighting the most original aspects of his personality?

AB: From within would be beyond my powers, but I've never known anyone less distant, more attentive to others' ways of thinking and feeling. Although Trotsky believed through and through in a system, and above all wanted to be the instrument of its practical realization, I admired the way he had managed to keep in contact with nature, either when we went fishing together, or when he very animatedly described one of his old wolf hunts in Siberia. I'll skip over what constituted his great personal attractiveness: it goes without saying that a large part of it came from the prestige conferred by his role in 1905 and 1917, but also from the eminent intellectual gifts that were revealed in works such as *My Life* and *History of the Russian Revolution*. It was of course something else entirely when one witnessed the workings of this thought, which was expressed in the liveliest possible manner, without excessive dogmatism; or which relaxed in rambling conversations that he gave a playful, teasing tone all his own. I don't believe anyone ever scorned more loftily, resisted more imperturbably the persecutions that, even then, had attacked him through his children and his old comrades in arms, and that he knew would not end there. He confined himself to joking about it, sometimes . . .

AP: In your eyes, what remains of that important figure today?

AB: There's no denying that the Second World War and its aftermath have lowered a veil of shadows over him. I'm sure the new generations no longer feel what was so electrifying about the name "Trotsky," which for a long time was charged with the highest revolutionary potential. But for some, myself included, that name permanently bars me from being drawn toward a regime that stopped at nothing to silence him. For me, his assassination is far more significant than the assassination of the Duc

d'Enghien . . .* In Surrealism, we have often cited Lautréamont's phrase, "All the water in the sea would not suffice to wash away one intellectual bloodstain." But in this case, there's no question of taking it figuratively . . .

AP: What was the outcome of your meetings with Trotsky?

AB: I reached an agreement with him about the conditions that, from a revolutionary standpoint, should be established for art and poetry so that they might participate in the struggle for liberation, while remaining completely free to follow their own paths. We stated this agreement in a text published under the title "For an Independent Revolutionary Art." It concluded with the foundation of an "International Federation of Independent Revolutionary Art" (Fédération Internationale de l'Art Révolutionnaire Indépendant, or F.I.A.R.I.). Although Trotsky requested, for tactical reasons, that the printed version of the tract bear Diego Rivera's signature instead of his own, the latter had no hand in writing it.

AP: It seems that at that moment several new crises arose in Surrealism . . .

AB: The reflections inspired by my stay in Mexico made these crises inevitable. The magazine *Clé*, house organ of the F.I.A.R.I., allowed us to discriminate very precisely between those who adopted the position of the Mexican manifesto and those who, most often for opportunistic reasons, tried to prevaricate. But nothing could affect Surrealism so deeply as the rift that occurred at that moment with Eluard.

AP: How did this rift occur?

* Executed by Napoleon Bonaparte in 1804, on unproven charges of conspiracy. The brutality of the procedure lost Napoleon much of his support, and is sometimes credited with spurring his downfall.

AB: In precisely the following way: having learned while in Mexico City that some poems of Eluard's had just appeared in *Commune*, which was published by the "House of Culture," I had naturally written him about the unspeakable measures this organization had taken against me, and I had no doubt that he would immediately sever relations with it. But I received no answer and, on my return, I was dumbfounded to hear him maintain that such a contribution entailed no particular solidarity on his part, that he'd come to believe his poems held their own in any setting, by virtue of their intrinsic qualities—so much so that during these last months, no less willingly than with *Commune*, he'd contributed to fascist publications (those were his words) in Germany and Italy. I simply pointed out to him that such an attitude implied the repudiation of every understanding he and I had ever shared, and made any further contact pointless. We have not seen each other since. Suddenly, just like that, a friendship ended that had been growing for years, to the point of making us like brothers.

AP: How do you explain Eluard's attitude?

AB: The sudden eruption of a kind of "Olympian" sentiment in him, based on an overblown confidence in his own worth: I believe that's what our complicity had just run up against. I've often wondered how he'd reached that point. It's true that Eluard was the only one of us for whom the critics, for some time, had had only praise. His occasional moments of violence were not imputed to him personally, but attributed to contagion and blamed on his friends. All anyone seemed to want to know of him were his poems, which were utterly devoid of aggression and, unlike the majority of Surrealist poems, were inspired by strictly aesthetic criteria. Surrealism pulled him back from this downward slope, reined in his need for expansion. I hadn't yet realized that he had limited tolerance for Surrealist prohibitions in literature and elsewhere. In this regard, the titles of some of his books (*La Rose publique* [The Public Rose], *Facile* [Easy]) mark a very clear protest . . .

AP: Can we say that the F.I.A.R.I.'s activity was ultimately a failure?

AB: Yes, but let's not forget the causes of this failure. If the F.I.A.R.I.'s activity was not more rousing even at the start, we must look toward the increasing gloominess of the international situation after Munich. It was one thing for our organization's national committee to gather representatives of the various non-Stalinist revolutionary movements, but quite another to achieve an indispensable organic unity between these movements, with the result that *Clé* ended after its second issue. This particular failure was one among many at the time. It was as if intellectual activity, whatever its direction, had marked a pause; as if the mind already knew that nothing was powerful enough to turn back the coming plague.

AP: What forms did Surrealist activity take in the years 1937 to 1939?

AB: In the three years before the new war, Surrealism reaffirmed its will not to make peace with the entire value system promoted by bourgeois society. This will was expressed with maximum intransigence and audacity in Benjamin Péret's collection of poems, *Je ne mange pas de ce pain-là*. It also shone through Jacques Prévert's poems "Flag of Surrender" (La Crosse en l'air) and "Hard Times" (Le Temps des noyaux), which were utterly faithful to the Surrealist spirit, even if their author had chosen to follow a separate path. In this sense, Prévert's method—as well as Queneau's, which found its way around then—drew its principal energy from humor. This humor, inherited from Swift, Jarry, and Vaché, was more relevant than ever. It took on the status of a last resort, a supreme refuge, and this is what encouraged me to try to define it (in what would become the *Anthologie de l'humour noir* [Anthology of Black Humor]), via a certain number of works that contained it to varying degrees. The other, ever more pressing call that Surrealism responded to came from love in its most exalted form, the kind that infuses *Je sublime* by Péret and *Mad Love*; as well as

from the marvels that Pierre Mabille prospected throughout the ages in *Le Miroir du merveilleux* [The Mirror of Marvels], and that Julien Gracq, imbued with the Grail romances, set off to find in *The Castle of Argol.*

AP: What was Surrealism's attitude at the onset of the war? To what extent did it consider itself involved?

AB: Overnight, the war would toss our hopes to the winds. Free speech was once again put on a shelf. Many days would pass before we knew what had happened to given individuals, before we could get back in touch with each other. The Surrealists, of course, harbored no illusions about the justification of the Allied cause in absolute terms, and they explained their position again, at the end of September 1938, in a tract entitled *Neither Your War, Nor Your Peace.* But it also goes without saying that racism and totalitarianism had no adversaries more sworn than they. The signing of the Nazi-Soviet nonaggression pact and the reactions it inspired made the situation even more inextricable, coloring reality—for the first time—in an atmosphere from Kafka's fictions.

AP: What did you do from 1939 to June 1940?

AB: I tried . . . to build myself, as much as possible, a raft on which to float. War—this or any other war—means the eclipse of all things of the mind. Once in uniform, everyone is sent back to a relatively precarious individual existence. For my part, I performed as best as I could (but a little as if in a dream) my job as doctor for the flying school in Poitiers. After the school was evacuated, the national demobilization found me in the unoccupied zone, a mile or two from the demarcation line.

AP: From June 1940 until your departure for the United States, what did you think of the military defeat and the resulting situation?

AB: It seemed to me that what was most incumbent upon intellectuals at that time was not to let this defeat—which was in no way the intellectuals' doing—remain purely military, but instead to try to turn it into a debacle of the mind. I hardly need add that, at the end of 1940, the intellectual situation was extremely somber. The nauseating concepts that substituted a "French State" for the Third Republic, hiding behind so-called patriarchal authority, were too obviously the kind that the Surrealist spirit was least able to accept. Certain courtesans of the new regime, moreover, even went so far as to accuse Surrealism in the press of having had a hand in the military defeat. The immediate prospects were quite alarming. The vise was squeezing harder every day. It was in the middle of all this that I heard the wrenching news of Trotsky's assassination.

AP: But by that time, you'd managed to regain contact with some of your friends?

AB: Yes. In the winter of 1940, in Marseille, Victor Serge and I were the guests of the Emergency Rescue Committee, living with its directors in a spacious villa, the "Air-Bel," on the outskirts of town. A number of Surrealists gathered there daily, and we did our best to forget the anxieties of the moment. Those who came were Bellmer, Brauner, Char, Dominguez, Max Ernst, Jacques Hérold, Sylvain Itkine, Wilfredo Lam, Masson, and Péret. A certain tendency toward games sometimes got the better of us: most notably, that period saw the joint creation of a deck of cards, designed to incorporate new symbols representing love, dreams, revolution, and knowledge. I mention it only because it shows what, by common consent, we took as our orientation at the time.

AP: What were the circumstances of your departure for America?

AB: If I and others of us need to justify the steps we took to gain asylum in a foreign country, I would point out that the situation of certain Surrealists vis-à-vis the Vichy regime was exceptionally

critical, and in any case that it brooked no comparison with the situation of other intellectuals—particularly of ex-Surrealists who collaborated on magazines and newspapers that were at least tolerated by the government, or who were even heard regularly on the radio. Pétain's trip to Marseille was the signal for my arrest, along with that of the members of the Emergency Rescue Committee. The long interrogations that followed had no object other than to sound out Surrealism's true attitudes, but I believe I can say that the inquisitors were not up to their task. The censorship board refused to grant a permit to my poem *Fata Morgana* or to the *Anthologie de l'humour noir* . . . The publisher of the latter work, inquiring about the reasons for this interdiction, was advised not to draw any more attention to an author who—I'm quoting verbatim—was "the negation of the spirit of the National Revolution." It's clear that I was being denied any right to speak, and the future promised only more of the same. It would be too easy for me to remind one of the persons who later attacked me for my departure to America—I mean Tzara—of his own application to the Rescue Committee for a visa, an application that he even asked me to support. Perhaps he doesn't know that I did so with great insistence, and wholeheartedly . . .

AP: You spent five years in the United States, Mr. Breton. What parts of your stay deserve special mention?

AB: As far as public activity is concerned, the five years I spent in New York do not seem to warrant any more space than I gave my participation in the two armed conflicts. Where my freedom is limited, I *am* not, and my temptation is to move on very quickly. But I must admit that it was I who limited this freedom, rather than it being limited by American institutions. Amidst numerous causes for despair, I encountered brief but intense joys in New York, such as the ones afforded by my occasional lunches, far removed from anything I might find unpleasant, with my admirable friend Marcel Duchamp. And I will add in hushed tones, as befits the topic, that against all hope I also encountered happiness. I would hate to be unjust toward the safe haven America granted

me, almost without my asking, or toward those joys and—as if this were possible—that happiness. Given the place that circumstances had allotted me, I pride myself on not having betrayed the spirit of the French Resistance, by agreeing to commit the messages of the "Voice of America" to the airwaves each day, which nonetheless implied great servitude on my part—but at least, freely and deliberately accepted.

AP: So you considered your job as a radio announcer compatible with the Surrealist activity you continued to lead in New York?

AB: Better than that: the former seemed to me to be the price of the latter. In those years, Surrealist activity in New York mainly took the form of an international exhibit, which Duchamp and I organized in 1942 at the request and on behalf of a prisoners' aid organization; and of a magazine called *VVV*, whose editorial board consisted of Duchamp, Max Ernst, David Hare, and myself. Let me simply say that the title *VVV*, which I had explained this way: "VVV: that is, V + V + V" (you remember that the letter *V*, which had come to mean victory, was formed by spreading two fingers), *triple V*, "that is, not only V as a vow—and energy—to return to a habitable and conceivable world, Victory over the forces of regression and of death unloosed at present on the earth, but also double V, that is, V beyond this first Victory, V over that which tends to perpetuate the enslavement of man by man, and beyond this VV of that double Victory, V again over all that is opposed to the emancipation of the spirit, of which the first indispensable condition is the liberation of man." This to show that there was no contradiction between my activities as a radio "announcer" in New York and as editor of the magazine *VVV*. In both cases, liberation from the Nazi yoke took precedence over everything else. It's only when the outcome of the struggle was no longer in doubt that I allowed myself to take some distance from it, to pull back. Word of the liberation of Paris reached me in Canada, by the sea. The feelings it stirred are expressed in the opening pages of the book I had just begun writing, which was to be called *Arcane 17*.

Melusina at the instant of the second cry: it surged from her globeless haunches; her belly is the entire August harvest; her torso thrusts forward like fireworks from her arched waist, modeled after two swallows' wings; her breasts are ermines caught in their own cry, blinding with the light of burning coal in their screaming throats. And her arms are the soul of the streams that sing and perfume. And beneath the collapse of her tarnished hair, all the distinctive features of the child-woman forever come together—that special kind of child-woman who has always enthralled poets, because time has no hold over her.

—Arcane 17

15.

ON SOME MISPLACED HOPES. IN PARIS, SURREALISM MUST OVERCOME VARIOUS OBSTACLES. PROOF OF ITS VITALITY.

ANDRE PARINAUD: Before starting in on the main part of this interview—Surrealism's positions since the Liberation—I'd like you to tell me what symbolic and personal reasons induced you to choose the title of the book that bridged two periods: *Arcane 17*.

ANDRE BRETON: The title *Arcane 17* is a direct reference to the traditional meaning of the tarot card called "the Star," symbol of hope and resurrection. As I was saying at the end of our last interview, the new dawn promised by the liberation of Paris, as it seemed from the extremely excited news I had of it, would alone have inclined me to place my book under this sign. But it is certain that, in my mind, it was overdetermined by the presence of an infinitely dear person by my side, whom I knew had lost all reason for living shortly before we met—and whom I therefore wanted more than anything to "bring back to life."* It was to this exceptional conjunction of such distinct emotions that I appealed for an elucidation of the other meaning of that "Arcanum 17," which, for occultists, is none other than sensitivity as the seed of intellectual life. As to the intellectual life that was soon to be reborn—free of constraints, or so we hoped—we had to know what renewed sensibility was liable to carry it forward, once its

* This was Elisa Bindhoff, who became Breton's third wife in 1945.

original powers were restored. At the end of summer in 1944, when my eyes opened on the coast of the Gaspé peninsula—with its island, so invitingly named Bonaventure, in the distance—circumstances favored my exploring the outermost bounds of those lands of desire that had been devastated for so long, but that were suddenly allowed to flower again, and that had never stopped calling to me, even when they seemed most out of reach: poetry, love, freedom.

AP: What were your hopes and emotions on the eve of your return to France? Did you still feel the enthusiasm and the will to struggle that had driven you twenty-five years earlier?

AB: At the end of the last war, which in many ways had been the most demoralizing of all, I believed (and I'm sure I wasn't alone) that the world could now make a jump that would put it back in its orbit—an orbit from which centuries of so-called "civilization" seemed to have removed it more and more. In any case, it seemed impossible that certain all-too-costly illusions, which had managed to sustain themselves right up to the outbreak of the war, would not be refuted. The devil take me if we could reasonably have expected, even knowing how short human memories are, that the old political parties, all of them more or less bankrupt—through either their acceptance of the Nazi-Soviet Pact or their deference to the Vichy government, if not through out-and-out collaboration with the occupier—would be called upon at war's end to rebuild themselves, bringing to power the same men who had already proven so unequal to their task.

AP: More specifically, what did you hope to see from human government, for example?

AB: One could at least hope for the systems to be recast, and for men of *character*—which at the time only the so-called Resistance movement seemed to include—to be elected. My recent disputes with him notwithstanding, I'd like to say how right the articles that Albert Camus was then publishing in *Combat* sounded from

afar, and how they went to the heart of the matter. In one stroke, the air seemed to have become breathable again. We told ourselves that the time was perhaps not far off when we would begin hearing proposals as audacious as they were generous. We know all too well what became of such hopes.

AP: Were you interested in a particular form of government?

AB: Of government? No, but let's say in a less unreasonable *management* of human interests. It seemed to me that one could, at least for a large part of the world, have called for the constitution of a new kind of States-General, in which the three old orders would have made way for three new ones, such as (pending a deeper study of the problem): technicians and scientists, educators and artists, and urban and agricultural workers. I have in fact become convinced, notably by reading Saint-Yves d'Alveydre, that the States-General, even in their original way of functioning, had the enormous advantage of promoting the social over the political; that, by their own means—keeping a daily "record of grievances," and, in certain cases, addressing "remonstrances" to the constituent powers—they were the only ones able to surmount the *mortal* dualism of governors and governed. I also favored returning to the *source* of aspirations toward a balanced and harmonious world; and I favored people taking the time to study, without prejudice, Fourier's *Théorie des attractions* and Father Enfantin's theses on the emancipation of women.

AP: In any case, it was at this time that you composed your *Ode to Charles Fourier.* What were the circumstances?

AB: I wrote the *Ode to Charles Fourier* during a trip to the western United States, which allowed me to visit Nevada, Arizona, and New Mexico. I spent a long time contemplating such ghost towns as Silver City and Virginia City, vestiges of the "gold rush," with their abandoned houses and banging doors, their theaters still showing posters from the last century. Most of all, I was able to satisfy one of my greatest and oldest desires, which was to meet

the Indians—particularly the Pueblo Indians (Hopi and Zuni), whose mythology and art held a special attraction for me. I haven't abandoned the idea of relating the very vivid impressions I experienced in their villages (Shungopavi, Wolpi, Zuni, Acoma), where I became utterly convinced of their inalienable dignity and genius, which contrasted so sharply and movingly with their miserable living conditions. I don't understand how the streak of justice and reparation that sometimes carries the white man toward the black and the yellow, more and more often neglects the Indian, who has given so many proofs of his creative power and has been, by far, the most despoiled.

AP: Before returning to France, you spent several months on a lecture tour in Haiti and Martinique. What were the notable events of this trip?

AB: Thanks to my friend Pierre Mabille, who at the time was the cultural attaché in Port-au-Prince and who had good contacts there, I was able to witness a number of voodoo ceremonies and observe up close the phenomenon of "possession," which has always constituted one of Surrealism's poles of interest. It's worth noting that this phenomenon is considered, by Haitian specialists in the matter, to be the syncretistic product of certain Dahomean and Guinean traditions on the one hand, and on the other of mesmeric practices that were imported to Port-au-Prince by Martinez de Pasqually in the eighteenth century.

AP: What were your prognostics at the time for the state of intellectual life following the Liberation?

AB: When I left America in the spring of 1946, I didn't have a very clear idea of the intellectual situation in Paris. For a long time, in fact, I'd believed that everything that had been upheld between the two wars would be gone over with a fine-toothed comb, and that even Surrealism would not be spared. Whence the tone, which some consider reticent, of my 1942 speech to the

students of Yale;* whence also a title—from the same period—such as "Prolegomena to a Third Manifesto of Surrealism *or Not*." Of course, since the Liberation, the letters I've received and various works I've been sent make me clearly understand that, intellectually speaking, the winds hadn't changed all that much. In New York, I also had long conversations with Camus, then with Sartre, who gave me a glimpse of the state of mind here. I remember that Sartre particularly stressed the "terror" that the Stalinists waged over the literary world. As he told it, it was extremely unwise to openly dispute the poetic merits of the Aragon who had written *Le Crève-coeur* [Heartbreak]: you ran the risk of not waking up the next morning . . .

AP: What emerged from the events you then witnessed?

AB: In Paris, I soon realized that if Sartre had employed somewhat romantic terms, what he was describing was nonetheless real. The Stalinists, the only group that had been powerfully organized during the clandestine period, had managed to occupy almost every key post in publishing, the press, radio, the art galleries, etc. They were quite determined to stay there, using methods they had adopted long before, but which they had just had an opportunity to perfect experimentally. Even though I had long been aware of these methods, I admit that their application constantly surpassed my expectations. One heard the staunchest antimilitarists upholding the most chauvinistic viewpoints, brandishing "black lists," howling for sanctions, while secretly agreeing to overlook certain things in exchange for solid guarantees: the technique called "clearing someone's name." Naturally it was of the utmost importance for them to neutralize, stifle those intellectuals who might denounce such an operation and penetrate its true motives. Via countless infiltrations into every organization liable to influence public opinion, the Stalinist apparatus managed, at least to a large extent, to muffle the voices of such men,

* An English version was published in *Yale French Studies*, Fall/Winter 1948, as "The Situation of Surrealism Between the Two Wars."

even as it tried to discredit them in its own press by repeated slander.

AP: Did this sort of threat affect Surrealism?

AB: Surrealism, of course, was one of the troublesome obstacles. First of all, we knew too much about some of the intellectuals that the Stalinist party had promoted to stardom. Secondly, they had at all costs to keep Surrealism from appearing as an ongoing movement, faithful to its original precepts, which would have ruined the spurious argument that events had passed it by. This was all the more difficult in that part of the younger generation continued to support us, and that we were constantly gaining new members. Were it not for a subtle network of influence, which deprives them of their means of expression (notably a regular, collective periodical), figures such as Jean-Louis Bédouin, Adrien Dax, Jean-Pierre Duprey, Jindrich Heisler, Gérard Legrand, Gherasim Luca, Nora Mitrani, Jean Schuster, Dolfi Trost, and Michel Zimbacca (but I won't list all my friends) would long ago have become prominent. Luckily, the signs are that this situation is nearing an end.

AP: How did Surrealism continue to develop?

AB: Because of hidden obstructions placed in its path, Surrealism these last six years has affirmed the continuity of its message only in individual works. It's quite obvious, moreover, that after some thirty years of existence, and precisely because of the influence it has exerted in fairly distinct waves, Surrealism cannot be limited to those who willingly fill its current ranks. Today any number of works, without being strictly Surrealist, share more or less deeply in its spirit. To my mind, there is no intrinsic difference between what might inspire the lyricism of Jean-Pierre Duprey and that of Malcolm de Chazal. In the theatre, two recent works of very high caliber, Julien Gracq's *Le Roi pêcheur* [The Fisher King] and *Monsieur Bob'le* by Georges Schehadé, must by the same token be considered fully Surrealist.

AP: Couldn't you just as well include some recent films?

AB: I could indeed: in this domain, even if Luis Buñuel's *Los Olvidados* demonstrates a formal break with *Un Chien andalou* and *L'Age d'or*, such a film, when compared with the earlier two, nonetheless shows the continuity of Buñuel's spirit—which, like it or not, is a constituent part of Surrealism. Furthermore, what we're saying about theater or film could be applied to other forms of expression. The poems of Georges Schehadé and Octavio Paz, Jean Ferry's *Le Mécanicien* [The Mechanic], and Maurice Fourré's *La Nuit du Rose-Hôtel* [A Night in Rose-Hotel] are Surrealist in the same way, and destined to take the elevated place reserved for them in the history of the movement. A choice will no doubt be made, moreover, among many other works in which the Surrealist spirit comes through in diffuse form.

AP: And in the sphere of visual arts, how would you characterize the situation?

AB: It's obviously more complicated. During the same period, all kinds of plots were hatched against Surrealism's expansion in the visual domain. Some people, on Moscow's orders, tried to kill imaginative art once and for all, and to substitute a kind of painting and sculpture called "Socialist realism," which simply means putting a few academic rudiments in the service of state propaganda and agitation. Others—and this mainly concerns American interests—tried to depreciate Surrealist visual art to the benefit of so-called "nonfigurative" art, whose authenticity, through its successive demonstrations, has proven to be more dubious with each passing day.

As to that, money was apparently no object, since a large Parisian gallery offered to stage an international Surrealist exhibit, featuring a "rain room" and a "maze" designed by Marcel Duchamp; a "superstitions room" entrusted to architect Frederick Kiesler, whom they had purposely brought over from New York; as well as twelve "altars," each of which was to be devoted to "a

creature, a category of creatures, or an object liable to be endowed with mythic life." But the organizers' good will ended there. What am I saying! As if it had been planned in advance, the gallery's owner seemed to want to join the ranks of his worst detractors, since he allowed tracts, signed by his main partner at the time and attacking the exhibit, to be handed out at the entrance. With him, we were as far as we could be from the constant affability with which Georges Wildenstein had put his "Beaux-Arts" gallery at our disposal for an exhibit of the same type, in 1938.

AP: Two important Surrealist works—whose tone was not unlike the manifestoes of the early years—stirred some comment shortly afterward: I'm speaking of *A la niche les glapisseurs de dieu* [Back to Your Kennels, You Curs of god] and *Flagrant délit* [Caught Red-Handed]. Could you explain what was so interesting about them?

AB: In point of fact, during the same period Surrealism also had to defend itself against a bold attempt at monopolization and confiscation by religion's henchmen: their goal was no less than to show that Surrealism's aspirations were, if not shared by, at least compatible with certain Christian views. The same operation had already been led against Baudelaire and Rimbaud, and would be continued against Sade and Lautréamont. With the collective pamphlet entitled *A la niche les glapisseurs de dieu*, my friends and I think we've thwarted that siege tactic for some time to come.

A final assault, which I was forced to confront, was launched surreptitiously (I suppose in the name of hackneyed rationalism) by the author of a certain *History of Surrealism*, which was not devoid of merit but was often based on unreliable information, and which furthermore contained a certain number of inaccuracies and some rather alarming gaps. Where the fundamentally malevolent spirit of . . . this makeshift historian shows through is at the end of the book, where, after having tried—he

wouldn't be the last—to set my oldest and dearest comrade-in-arms, Benjamin Péret, against me, he decrees on his own authority that "all that remains is to draw up the death certificate of the Surrealist movement."* You've never seen such a rushed biographer. As I was still in New York when the book came out, he'd taken the liberty of following this declaration with a venomous postscript about me, founded on the basest hearsay. Nonetheless, I was perfectly willing to believe that he'd simply been misled, and didn't hold it against him on my return. I was finally moved to react only after he seized upon the pretext of Antonin Artaud's death to incriminate me for still being alive, which according to him conclusively proved my lack of authenticity. The profound ties that had bound me to Artaud, the unforgettable signs of attachment that he himself had shown me (as the publication of his correspondence will attest), and the effect his shattering and gruesome end had on his friends made such an expedient particularly grotesque. The man who had resorted to it, moreover, was soon laughing out of the other side of his mouth. Shortly after that I was given the best possible opportunity for rebuttal when he endorsed a text attributed to Rimbaud, the falseness and poverty of which were glaring. I related the ins and outs of that episode in *Flagrant délit*, which gives some idea of the rout he suffered. In earlier times, such a rebuke would have kept a critic from ever taking up his pen again.

AP: So all things considered, you feel that Surrealism has not exhausted its historical necessity or lost any of its spirit?

AB: None at all. That's why I insisted, for this last session, not only on underscoring the new strengths that Surrealism has acquired, but also on showing who it has run up against. If it were truly dead, as those who take their desires for realities have re-

---

* This sentence, which figured in the 1945 edition of *Histoire du surréalisme* by Maurice Nadeau, was deleted from subsequent versions; it does not appear in the English translation of the work.

peated every year since its foundation, I'd have trouble understanding why the offensives launched against it have only intensified in recent years. Far from saddening us, these constantly reiterated offensives are our surest sign of Surrealism's deep penetration into the ground on which we walk, and of its hardy nature.

Poetry is made in bed like love
Its unmade sheets are the dawn of things
Poetry is made in the forest

*   *   *

Don't shout that from the rooftops
It's not fitting to leave the doors open
Or go around calling for witnesses

*   *   *

The act of love and the act of poetry
Are incompatible
With reading newspapers at the top of one's voice

*   *   *

The room of marvels
No gentlemen not the forbidden chamber
Nor the fumes of the barracks room on Sunday evenings

*   *   *

The embrace of poetry like the embrace of the naked body
Protects while it lasts
Against all access by the misery of the world

—"On the Road to San Romano"

16.

SOME FINAL BACKWARD GLANCES. HAPPINESS? THE MAIN THING IS NOT TO HAVE "GIVEN IN." THE FLOWER OF THE MOORS.

ANDRE PARINAUD: Having reached the end of these broadcasts, Mr. Breton, I'd like you to answer one question: do you feel that what you've told us has really let us gain some specific knowledge of André Breton as a human being?

ANDRE BRETON: I'd say I'm the last person who could judge that . . . From the first questions you asked me, I naturally understood that the subject of these interviews was Surrealism and not myself. Given that I was invited to describe the chronological development of a spiritual adventure that was and remains collective by nature, I was forced to erase myself somewhat. Above all, I had to be as objective as possible. By definition, I was not free to skate over any of the facts that profoundly concerned the history of the movement, and I was also bound by the need to show how events were linked together. In this regard at least, I had to strive to be impartial and, up to a certain point, leave the stage. But I don't believe I completely avoided making judgments and comments that would allow someone to pinpoint my distinctive features, if he so desired. I've often regretted that people generally expect me to make the sort of statement that pushes me into the shadows rather than into the light—which frankly, especially in the long run, goes against my personal desire and inclination. But what can I say? This

must be the price of any life that has largely been absorbed by the affirmation of a certain ideal.

AP: Allow me to push further ahead with my question. By deliberately refusing to adopt a formula for these interviews that would have consisted in asking you about your attitudes toward life (such as my colleague Robert Mallet, for example, so brilliantly did with Paul Léautaud), and by preferring to approach you via the history of Surrealism, to which every day of your life adds a page, I believed that objectively we would gain a deeper, more complete sense of you. But haven't I left out equally essential, albeit less apparent, aspects of yourself? Do you feel that these interviews missed their target, which was above all to show who you are?

AB: Not at all. The way the interviews with Paul Léautaud were conducted, while quite appropriate to the person he is, would hardly have been suitable for me. For one thing, Léautaud is a wit, which I'm not. Also, his adventure has been purely individual, and he can therefore indulge every whim, take any detour, and say whatever comes into his head. I can't claim to have the detachment that his age and natural skepticism grant him. I can admire the outward freedom conferred by this skepticism, without sharing it in the slightest degree. As far as your interviews with me are concerned, the alternative was the following: either they would be about me alone, or they would be about Surrealism via my life. You opted for the second possibility, and it would have been presumptuous of me to find fault with that.

AP: Your answer lets me limit my next questions to two other essential points. First of all, what is your opinion of yourself, considering the intransigence that you've always brought to the defense of Surrealism?

AB: To . . . the defense of Surrealism? You see how we come back to Surrealism in spite of ourselves. Oh, I'm well aware that intransigence is no longer in style! Our vocabulary has been so

undermined and sabotaged in the last few years that you say "intransigence," and people think of absolutism and dictatorship. What does that mean: the intransigence I've brought to the defense of Surrealism? I went with what I believed was right, what I believed was liable to make the human condition less unacceptable. To the extent that others—a fair number of others, as we know—had expressed the same concerns, I believed that in the case of a breach of contract on their part, even an implicit one, they should be called to account for their change of heart. As you can imagine, I'm rather pleased to have maintained Surrealism's initial postulates, against all odds!

It's not hard for several people to fundamentally agree on a given body of ideas in their youth, but we mustn't ignore the fact that life is quite adept at breaking up forces that were once united. You see what happened to Saint-Simonism, for example. And besides, material demands become more pressing as time goes on. And then there are women . . . In short, everything happens as it does in Victor Hugo's lovely poem, "La Chanson des aventuriers de la mer." If fate wishes one to take the helm after, as he said,

> *In Malta, Olfani became a monk*
> *And Gobbo a harlequin . . .*

it's clear that one must guide this helm with a firm hand.

AP: Of course. But what is your feeling about yourself, considering the battle you've waged, the long series of hardships and rifts—and sacrifices, too?

AB: Well, I feel that I've lived up to my youthful aspirations, and to my mind that's already quite a lot. My life has been devoted to what I thought was beautiful and right. All things considered, I've so far lived as I had dreamed of living. In the battle I've waged, I've never lacked for companions just as determined as I; thanks to them, I've never been deprived of human warmth. It's true that I

had to part from some individuals who were dear to me, and that others have left me. There are those whose memory long haunted me, whose memory still assails me at certain times of the day, and I won't deny that it's like a wound being reopened every time. But I believe this was necessary in order to preserve the initial stakes, and that this was the price if anything was to be won. And to a large extent, the battle has indeed been won. I don't wish to sound conceited, but it's fairly commonly admitted today that Surrealism contributed much toward shaping our modern sensibility. Furthermore, it managed, if not entirely to impose its scale of values, at least to make these values be taken very seriously. If we refer back to the title of a magazine like *La Révolution Surréaliste*, which at the time seemed hyperbolic, it's no exaggeration to say that such a revolution did take place in men's minds. Just think, for example, of all the figures from the past that Surrealism brought out from the shadows, and who today are recognized as *lantern bearers*; and of all the false lantern bearers that it pushed back into the shadows. On this score, we couldn't have hoped for anything more.

It was in another domain that enormous obstacles blocked our path. Which domain? The one in which we felt bound to participate actively, yes, to contribute, from our specific position and with our specific resources, to the social transformation of the world. History will tell if those who've claimed a monopoly on that transformation are really working toward man's liberation, or whether they're condemning him to an even worse form of slavery. The fact remains that Surrealism, as a defined and organized movement, in trying to respond to the greatest possible will toward emancipation, could find no point of entry into their system. Even if this must be counted as an indisputable failure and in some ways represents a lot of lost time, perhaps it wasn't pointless. First of all, it was important that we attempt the experiment, and report our findings as they happened, from 1925 to 1950. And besides . . . Surrealism, that little particle of free thought, when compared to many forms of subjugated thought (and without prejudice to the outcome of the struggle), is rather like David and Goliath, you know . . .

AP: We can obviously trust in the judgment of history, but do you believe that Surrealism's current audience reflects its true importance?

AB: I have no complaints on that score. Eminent men have died, having every reason to believe that obscurity would forever be their fate; for others it took eighty years of posthumous neglect before the ears able to hear them even existed. Without putting myself on their level, I believe I can consider myself more favored than they: perhaps I had a luckier star, who knows! But twenty years ago, I was already asking how certain people could believe they were participating in the Surrealist spirit while still being concerned about their status in the world. Surrealism's current status? I don't know if it's been given its due, but I have no objections; and if its status were less prominent, I still wouldn't mind. In the word "status," there's always an aspect of official consecration that bothers me. I've already had occasion to say that, by temperament as much as or more than by reasoning, I fell in with the *opposition*; I was ready, come what may, to join an indefinitely renewable *minority* (so long as it aimed toward greater liberation, of course). This is scarcely compatible with the imperialistic designs that apply to the many academic theses I've forbidden. For my taste, it's already too much that they've begun teaching Surrealism in schools—no doubt in order to diminish it. When I was young, what helped me understand Baudelaire or Rimbaud as they *should* be understood was the fact that they weren't on the syllabus . . .

AP: Allow me a gratuitous question: if Surrealism had been discovered in 1951, would you have thrown yourself into the fray with the same enthusiasm?

AB: There's always something pointless about that kind of speculation. To answer with some measure of pertinence, I'd have to take into account both the changes that some thirty years have produced in myself, and the changes in the world during the same time. On top of which, it's clear that my own changes depended

on the changes in the world, and on a certain number of other factors. At twenty or twenty-five, one's will to struggle is inspired by the most offensive and intolerable things one sees around oneself. In this regard, the sickness that the world exhibits today differs from the one it exhibited in the 1920s.

In France, for example, the mind was threatened back then with coagulation, whereas today it's threatened with dissolution. All kinds of major fissures, which affect the structure of the globe as well as human consciousness, had not yet appeared (I'm thinking of the implacable antagonism between the two "blocs," of totalitarian methods, of the atomic bomb). It's perfectly obvious that such a situation calls for different reactions from today's youth than the ones provoked in us, in our youth, by *another* situation. At the same time, I believe that this in no way invalidates Surrealism's principle theses on poetry, freedom, or love. What has to be rethought on the basis of new data is the social problem. In this regard, and if only to indicate what I considered right, I'd like to stress that I didn't hesitate to look behind Marx, and, in my *Ode to Charles Fourier*, to call for a reevaluation of those parts of his work that are still valid. Moreover, I was one of the first to join the "Citizens of the World" movement, whose goals seem to me the only ones with sufficient breadth to meet the circumstances. Whatever difficulties such an action inevitably encounters, I still have complete faith in Robert Sarrazac and those around him, who inspired and organized it.

AP: But how do you feel about your former comrades-in-arms, some of whom abandoned you—even betrayed you?

AB: I've already gained enough distance to be able to make this judgment as dispassionately as possible. I was deeply impressed by the opinion that my friend Ferdinand Alquié expressed on this subject in his study on "Surrealist and Existentialist humanism." Pondering the division that has occurred in Surrealism, as earlier it occurred in Romanticism, between those who have opted for "social action without dreams" and those who prefer "an attitude that least repudiates their initial ideals, but also implies

the least commitment," he believes he can state that both sides were equally sincere and faithful, and that, in short, it's neither side's fault if "the moral dimension and the historical dimension" cannot be reconciled. Insofar as I've always been an active participant in this debate, it would obviously be too much to ask me to subscribe to this opinion; but objectively, it seems very wise. I admit that Surrealism's inclination was twofold, that there were and—as recent splits have shown once again—that there still are reasons for tearing away from it. Above and beyond anything that might have separated us, and the passions that got in the way (some of which have never died down), my desire would be to attain that point of serenity from which one contemplates the jointly followed path without remorse; from which one gives unreserved thanks to what fervently united a certain number of individuals around the same cause, even if the individuals themselves changed from time to time . . .

AP: I don't believe any Surrealist inquiry ever took happiness as its subject. Could you tell us what role it has played in your life?

AB: We'd first have to be clear on what we mean by "happiness." A certain degree of satisfaction, stemming from various ideas and the reactions these ideas might have elicited, cannot be equated with lasting well-being. But I believe that some people, myself among them, aspire more than anything to that kind of satisfaction, even if the cost is high. I've already said that the worst drawback of an activity such as the one I've engaged in resides in the fact that the emotional ties it creates between those involved can't withstand significant ideological divergences. So this happiness is of the most checkered sort. But I think there's something truly happy in being able to say that the landscape of one's youth has not silted up in middle age, that the same inalienable expanses are still uncovered every time the wind brings the accents of poets and a few others, who were once the great sources of exaltation.
   Speaking of happiness, I can still hear Gide reading us a text he'd written—I was with Aragon and Soupault—which began with the words: "All of nature surely teaches that man was made

for happiness . . ." That's rather debatable, I said to myself. It isn't happiness I sought in love, either: it was love.

AP: Even though you might refuse to answer this question, I'd like you to clarify what promise Surrealism holds today for various techniques: film, radio, etc.

AB: As early as the first *Manifesto*, I purposely stated that future Surrealist *techniques* didn't interest me. This is all the more the case, it goes without saying, for applications of Surrealism to a given technical means of expression. And moreover, in what category would you put certain of Duchamp's works? Do some canvases by Max Ernst, Magritte, or Brauner concern poetry any less than they do painting? Can cinematographic criteria exhaust the content of a film such as *L'Age d'or*? This kind of discrimination would be petty. No more petty than to wonder, about those of our friends who developed a taste for solo navigation, such as Miró or Prévert, to what extent they are or aren't Surrealists. We need only transpose the problem to Romanticism, or even to Impressionism or Symbolism, to see how inane it is . . .

AP: This series of interviews, which has highlighted your activity and that of the Surrealist movement for more than thirty years, naturally leads us to ask toward what horizons you're now steering your spirit and your action?

AB: If it's true, as I've admitted, that Surrealism, which for so long was a tumultuous river rushing under an open sky, has more recently followed a rather prolonged underground channel, I repeat that this is an entirely external impression, which is due only to the present lack of a group periodical. With all due respect to those who, as you know, have dug Surrealism's grave two or three times yearly for the past quarter century, I maintain that the principle of its energy remains intact. I can think of no better proof than this recent declaration from May 1951, which is all the more precious to me in that I owe it to seven of my youngest friends: "Up to now, only Surrealism seems to have defied the

processes of petrification that spare neither systems nor men. To tirelessly alert that which has not yet been struck by aphasia, to constantly demolish the economic and moral dogmas that mire men in secular oppression . . . , and to seek the untried remedies required by the extent and virulence of the disease: these are the imperatives that ensue from the principles that have always been Surrealism's own. . . . You have constantly defined the trajectory between the conscious and unconscious aspects of mental life, between revolutionary action and the exaltation of desire, between materialism and idealism. Starting at the point at which you have intersected it, we can only travel this trajectory, which is the very trajectory of Surrealism, from the outset, and make it ours in its totality." One can imagine that for me, at the end of an account encompassing the—already exceptionally long—existence of a movement with which no one can deny that my life has formed one body, nothing can equal such a testimony.

AP: If you wouldn't mind, let's end our conversation with this question: what sustains your faith in the remarkable human adventure on which you've embarked?

AB: Speaking in America in 1942 to the students of Yale University, I underscored the fact that "Surrealism was born of a limitless affirmation of faith in the *genius* of youth." For my part, I have never renounced this faith for an instant. Chateaubriand says superbly: "As a son of Brittany, I like the moors. Their flower of indigence is the only one that has not wilted on my lapel." I, too, come from those moors; they have often torn me apart, but I love that light of will-o'-the-wisp that they keep burning in my heart. To the extent that this light has reached me, I've done everything in my power to pass it on: all my pride comes from the fact that it hasn't yet gone out. At stake, as I saw it, were my chances of not failing the human adventure.

II

Answers to Other Questions

(1941–1952)

INTERVIEW WITH CHARLES HENRI FORD (*VIEW*, NEW YORK, AUGUST 1941)

C. H. FORD: Have you ever dreamed of Hitler?

ANDRÉ BRETON: That would make a good survey topic. If the question were put to enough people, I believe it would help elucidate the most troubling psychological aspects of this war. Even before it began, it was with some trepidation that I saw certain individuals removing Hitler from the sphere of reality and ascribing his successes to superhuman powers. This was the case with poet Pierre-Jean Jouve, who didn't hesitate to equate him with the Antichrist; and from the outset popular opinion—in France, for example—has demonstrated a suspect interest in the most outlandish things said about him: that he only drank water, was chaste, made no decisions without consulting his astrologers, was never so happy as when he was alone with several virgins, chosen from among the most beautiful in Germany. Obviously, this portrait was sketched for the needs of far-ranging propaganda, which we can only hope will not reach America. In France, this was all it took to accredit the widespread idea during the war that girls and women from all over fed the enemy information, simply out of love for Hitler (this was the period when Stuttgart radio broadcasts featured the daily menu of the Polish commander in chief, who had set up headquarters in Angers). This is no doubt the origin of the collective psychosis that resulted, in the months preceding the

armistice, in practically everyone owning a copy of the *Centuries* of Nostradamus. At least in the rather large area that I saw at the time, that extremely hermetic opus enjoyed an unprecedented vogue in the army's ranks, and gave rise to laughable interpretations. Imagine that they also passed around a prophecy of unknown origin, which was tailor-made for demoralizing the soldiers because it predicted that the war would last for seven years. This prophecy is based on simple addition, whose exactitude can be verified using the duration of France's two previous wars against Germany. You simply write the date of the declaration of war, then put the following year below it, and add the two numbers:

$$1870 \quad 1914$$
$$\underline{1871} \quad \underline{1915}$$
$$3741 \quad 3829$$

The difference between the sum of the first two and last two digits of the second line gives the *number* of years the war will last; the sum of the first two digits of the total gives the *day* hostilities will end; and the sum of the last two digits of the total gives the *month*. It turns out that the Franco-Prussian War of 1870, which lasted one year, ends on May 10, 1871; and that World War I, which lasted four years, ends on November 11, 1918. Applied to the current war, the same calculation:

$$1939$$
$$\underline{1940}$$
$$3879$$

gives us a duration of (6 + 1) years: for if the difference between the sum of the first two and last two digits of the second line is in fact 6, we have to carry over 1 because we need to subtract 12 from the total number of months (16). The current war, then, should last until April 11, 1946. You see to what extent the irrational had

overshadowed the rational. Instead of fighting him, there were plenty of people who dreamed of Hitler, and the war, with their eyes open. As for myself, I don't remember ever having dreamed of Hitler: I don't believe he's a part of my mythology. If by chance I had dreamed of him, it's clear that his appearance in the dream's manifest content would not in itself allow us to gauge my degree of interest in him, any more than the appearance of any other element. Only analytic interpretation could draw some conclusions in that regard.*

CHF: Instead of talking about New York itself, I believe you'd rather tell us about the countryside around New York . . .

AB: I was very impressed by what I've seen of the area along the Hudson and its green islets—the Floating Island—which retain something secret and menacing, no doubt from the books I read as a child. I was extremely pleased to recognize for the first time the uniquely *spectral* light that hits the grass at five in the afternoon, and that bathes, to the exclusion of all others, certain of Poe's poems, such as "Ulalume." At André Masson's house in Connecticut, in the heart of a small wood, I was enchanted to discover the little "Indian pipe," so fearful and ambiguous, that more than any other plant is part of that light. It was also with Masson that, freely inflecting every shade of leaf, I was able to admire the "scarlet tanager." For me, Surrealist flora strictly speaking have been enriched by a new species: the staghorn fern suspended from ceilings in its superb tortoise shell. But above all, I've begun my initiation into the mystery of American butterflies. How splendid and enigmatic the lunar moth is! Don't you find it intolerable that man cares so little about butterflies? Should the description of a plant be

---

* At this point, the original publication contains an additional sentence, which was cut from the French book version. This is how it reads in *View*: "In an ambitious way, not usual with me, I dreamed while in the throes of a great exaltation at Ciudad Trujillo that I was Zapata, making ready with my army to receive Toussaint L'Ouverture the following day and to render him the honors to which he was entitled."

allowed to ignore that of the caterpillar,* or of the larva that lives on it more or less by choice? Isn't the affinity it shows with such an animal organism just as significant as its type of flowering, for example? But the mania for classification tends to win out over every true means of knowledge. I fear that the philosophy of Nature hasn't taken a single step forward since Hegel . . .

CHF: Given current events, do you think that anything can be changed in art?

AB: A new spirit will emerge from this war. We mustn't forget that the tree of 1870 bore *The Hunting of the Snark*, *Maldoror*, *A Season in Hell*, and *Ecce Homo*. The tree of 1914 brought the works of De Chirico, Picasso, Duchamp, Apollinaire, and Raymond Roussel to their culminating points, as it did with Freud, whose influence would be felt worldwide by the entire modernist movement. No doubt it's still too early to judge what is alive and laden with promise on the tree of 1940, or what has died in its shadow. It's already clear that whatever is flourishing in the present circumstances, as if nothing had happened, has condemned itself to extinction. I'm particularly wary of things that deck themselves more and more heavily with jewels: I'm afraid they're only standing upright artificially, and that the fascination they exert is that of embalmed corpses. The time has come for a general survey on the widest possible scale: I believe that in art this survey should not saddle itself with any systematic viewpoint *a priori*, with any technical prejudice. All that matters are the "new intellectual thrills." As always in such moments, when human life becomes almost worthless on the social level, I believe that we must be able to read and look through the eyes of Eros—Eros who will be called upon, in the days to come, to restore the balance that has tipped in death's favor. Nothing seems better suited to meet the challenge than two paintings, chosen from extremely different sources, both of them outside of Surrealism: Edward Hopper's *New York Movie* and Morris Hirshfield's *Nude (at the Window)*. The

---

* The magnificent caterpillar called *samia cecropia*, which I discovered here, seems to be one of the sources of that blueish opaline light to which I referred above. This light is entirely unknown in Europe. [*Breton's note*]

very beautiful young woman lost in her daydream, standing apart from what the others find so absorbing; the heavy mythical column; the three lamps of *New York Movie* seem laden with a symbolic meaning that seeks an exit through the curtained stairway. Interestingly, it is also between curtains—one raised, the other drawn aside—that Hirshfield's nude offers herself, in the single spotlight of the magician's show that the artist has captured. He is the first truly mediumistic painter. The space between the curtains, where the figure is placed, even describes an admirable Greek vase, of a "paranoiac" value much more troubling than what the present vogue has borrowed from children's puzzles: find the hunter (or Voltaire).* I'm realizing that a half-drawn curtain also played a major part in my long-standing attraction toward De Chirico's *most 1914* painting: *The Child's Brain*. (When I glimpsed it in a window on Rue La Boétie, an irresistible force pushed me to get off the bus and run back to ponder it.) It seems to me that in times of serious external crisis, this curtain, which expresses the need to pass from one era to the next, must somehow make its presence felt, visibly or not, in any work able to confront the viewpoint of tomorrow.

CHF: Have you read the recent article by Aragon in the Hollywood magazine *The Clipper*?

AB: Yes, and I regret still having eyes to see such recantations. "It is peace that the people desire": and yet he did his best to call them to war, before and after Munich! And the rest: "When we met in the shop in Brest, I was buying some ribbon for the *croix de guerre* of my first citation. I have received a second (with palm) and I was awarded the *médaille militaire*. I look very respectable indeed with all my decorations and my hair whitened by age." "Respectable" is really a find (especially if one recalls that the author of these lines is the same one who wrote the last page of *Treatise on*

---

* As many readers at the time would have recognized, this is a jab at Dali's 1940 *Slave Market with Invisible Bust of Voltaire*. Dali had been officially excluded from Surrealism in 1939 (see Breton's remarks to Parinaud, above).

Style)!* But no sense getting worked up over it. I've sometimes wondered if certain intellectuals aren't like certain women, whose "youthful bloom," so-called, is only a function of age, and leaves behind no trace. But this viewpoint turns out to be far too limited when applied to the most striking cases of individual failure: Barrès, Valéry, Derain, De Chirico—didn't it also threaten Apollinaire?—Aragon, Desnos—and, I'm afraid, Eluard, etc. (you'll notice that I've refrained from mentioning "Avida Dollars"). We won't get anywhere until we've made a clinical study of this specifically modern illness (no relation to the silence of Rimbaud), which leads these intellectuals to radically change their opinions and renounce their own testimony, masochistically and exhibitionistically; to champion causes diametrically opposed to the ones they had earlier served with such brilliance. This illness should be described like any other mental disorder, with its etiology, symptomatology, etc. Perhaps I'll try it myself, once I'm convinced that the public life of the men in question *authorizes*— and that the risk their deceptions cause others *justifies*—certain intrusions into their private lives, without which nothing decisive or conclusive could be achieved.

CHF: What is Surrealism's present orientation?

AB: That's the same as asking to what extent events in Europe are liable to influence my and my friends' activities. Once again, these events carry such emotional weight, and are bound to have such decisive consequences on so many levels, that no intellectual process will emerge unchanged—whether contradicted, weakened, verified, or reinforced. Surrealism, as you know, has always tried to respond to two kinds of concerns: the first kind has to do with the *eternal* (the mind grappling with the human condition), the other with the *current* (the mind as witness to its own evolution: for this evolution to be valid, we maintain that, *in reality just*

---

* Aragon's *Treatise on Style* closes on this antimilitaristic note: ". . . it is my pleasure, here, in this book, on this page, to say very deliberately that I shit on the French army in its entirety."

as much as in dreams, the mind must reach beyond the "manifest content" of events and rise to an awareness of their "latent content"). These tendencies naturally lead me, as I believe anyone who has a predetermined attitude must be led, to clarify what is ending, what is continuing, and what is just beginning in Surrealism, in view of the general crisis we're living through.

WHAT IS ENDING: the illusion of art's independence, even transcendence. Despite precautions taken by Surrealism at the outset, and repeated warnings since, this deviation has not been totally avoided. It shows itself in *egocentrism* (the poet or artist comes to overestimate his own gifts, disdaining Lautréamont's dictum, "Poetry should be made by all, not by one," which remains one of Surrealism's fundamental watchwords); leads to *indifference* (he puts himself "above the fray," believes he is entitled to an Olympian attitude); and is generally ratified by *stagnation* (he quickly depletes his individual resources, and is finally able to produce only sapless variations on a dried-out theme).*

WHAT IS CONTINUING: Surrealist activity along the three paths on which it was most deeply engaged before the war, and which the critical efforts of my friends Nicolas Calas in New York and Georges Henein in Cairo have recently situated with utmost clarity: *disorientation of sensation*, in accordance with Rimbaud's precept that one becomes a "seer" by a careful derangement of all the senses; in-depth exploration of *objective chance*, the place where natural necessity and human necessity are reconciled, the peak of revelation, the pivot of freedom; and the prospecting of *black humor*, the ultimate means for the "ego" to surmount the traumas of the external world, and above all to show that the remedies to the "ego's" great ills, in the Freudian sense, can only come from the "id." My personal contribution to the Surrealist canon thus

---

* In *View*, this paragraph ends with another deleted passage: "We see today where this has led Eluard: collaboration in *La Nouvelle Revue Française* of Paris (a new series sponsored by the Germans) with a poem that is very careful to appeal to all tastes, little else than a vain language of fruits and flowers which would not be out of place in an old number of *Keepsake*; and Avida Dollars, in New York, hunting sensational publicity to illustrate the pitiful rapport of a badly made woman's foot and a worn-out shoe, the beginning of his 'classical period.' It is clear that neither the one nor the other, even though they persist in advertising it, has anything more in common with Surrealism."

defined will consist in the forthcoming publication of an "anthology of black humor," from Swift to the present day, which was prohibited in France by the censorship board. I also intend to publish a poem called *Fata Morgana*, which I wrote last winter in Marseille and which the censors also rejected. This poem states my resistance, which is more intransigent than ever, to the masochistic enterprises in France that tended to restrict poetic freedom or to immolate it on the same altar as other freedoms. A typical example of such enterprises, in fact, is a recent manifesto by Aragon on the supposed need for a return to poetry with fixed forms and "rich" (!) rhymes. What is continuing, what must be maintained in living poetry, is the great modern tradition inherited from Baudelaire:

> . . . we can plunge
> to Hell or Heaven—any abyss will do—
> deep in the Unknown to find the *new*!*

WHAT IS BEGINNING: in Surrealism, anything that can realize the ambition of applying bold solutions to the problems posed by current events. These events and the commentaries to which they give rise, as well as the notorious poverty of perspectives that one gets from them, prescribe the overthrow of ways of thinking that

---

* This quotation is followed in *View* by the passage: "In the French language this conception is upheld and illustrated by Benjamin Péret, Pierre Mabille, Nicolas Calas, Julien Gracq, E. L. T. Mesens, René Char, Alice Paalen, Valentine Penrose, Aimé Césaire, René Ménil, Jacques B. Brunius, Maurice Blanchard. It is this conception in painting which, in the latest period, renders more and more necessary, and dazzling with truth and life, the productions of Max Ernst, André Masson, Yves Tanguy, René Magritte, Wolfgang Paalen, Kurt Seligmann, Victor Brauner, Leonora Carrington, Kay Sage, S. W. Hayter; which leads us to expect the best from the researches of Oscar Dominguez, Wilfredo Lam, Matta Echaurren, Gordon Onslow-Ford, Esteban Frances, Joseph Cornell, David Hare. Collective activity, such as has always been practiced in Surrealism, will appear again soon in a *card game* for which a model was devised in Marseilles at the beginning of 1941, with another in preparation in New York. This game, of which the significations and figures were debated among us at some length, interests me not only because, in such a troubled time, it proposes to throw an ideological bridge between two worlds but also because, aside from the very different contingencies that witnessed its elaboration, it shows plainly the *unity* of aspiration that exists between Surrealism here and over there."

have been honored for centuries. I say that not one of these ways of thinking can satisfactorily explain what's happening in the world today. Generally, people expect the outcome to be decided by a pure and simple superiority of arms: of course this is out of the question, since it's unforseeable—as if communications between the outer and inner worlds were cut. When I leaf through works here in America that claim to draw lessons from France's defeat, I'm struck by the lack of breadth, not to say sterility, of the views expressed. Both victors and vanquished, moreover, seem to me to be running toward the same abyss if they don't put the forces that set them against each other on trial while there's still time. And in fact, in the course of such a trial, the exhaustion of the conflict's economic causes would underscore the common misery of our contemporaries—which in the final analysis is surely ideological. The world is dying from rationalism, *closed rationalism*: physical violence is unconsciously accepted, justified as the outcome of mental passivity. The least permeable philosophies—Cartesianism, for example—will no doubt be the first to crumble. This is so true, the withdrawal is so widespread, the despair so great, that some people are wondering—I've been told that a strong current of this exists in America—whether man's salvation doesn't demand his "de-intellectualization," in favor of a revaluation of his deepest instincts. It is certain that in matters of faith, ideals, and honor, from every corner we can observe *the survival of the sign over the thing signified*. Faith, ideals, and honor must be reestablished on new bases: meanwhile, all those rags that don't even cling to the body anymore are to be shaken off. In this regard, Surrealism will never find a period more favorable to its intent, which is to restore to man the concrete empire of his faculties: the descent in the diving bell of automatism, the conquest of the irrational, the patient comings and goings in the labyrinth of probability calculations have hardly been brought to term. The present circumstances have stripped them of their utopian aspects and uncovered a *vital* interest in them, on a par with laboratory research. These activities are in no way restrictive: on the contrary, Surrealism's practical goal is to multiply them. Today I see two existing fields, which Surrealism

cannot avoid without compromising its own procedures: it seems to me extremely urgent to compare our results, on the one hand with those of *Gestalt* theory, which in particular states that any distinction between sensory and intellectual faculties must be rejected; and on the other hand with those of Camille Revel's "theory of chance," which states that anything conceivable is possible and everything possible tends to be manifested (all possibilities tend to repeat themselves an equal number of times), so that anything representable tends to be manifested. I've become convinced that such a comparison would allow for many new discoveries and certainties.*

* The original publication ends with the following exchange: "CHF: Do you think that a 'Third Manifesto of Surrealism' is in order? AB: Absolutely."

INTERVIEW WITH RENÉ BÉLANCE (*HAITI-JOURNAL*, HAITI, DECEMBER 12–13, 1945)

RENE BELANCE: In your view, what is the future of poetry after the terrible war that has just swept the earth?

ANDRE BRETON: Poetry would betray its immemorial mission if historical events, even the most painful ones, pulled it away from its *royal road*, and made it turn around in circles at a crucial point in this road. Its role is to move ever forward, to explore the field of possibility in all directions, and to emerge—come what may—as a force of *emancipation and divination*. To do so it has to keep in touch, above and beyond the convulsions that shake regimes and societies, with the primitive heart of humanity—anguish, hope, creative energy—which has proven to be the only inexhaustible reservoir of resources.

RB: Given the political necessities in this period of confusion, when the most divergent interests are already facing off, can Surrealism maintain the freedom that you have always demanded for the artist?

AB: Whether or not Surrealism can continue to demand complete freedom for artistic research is a life-or-death issue. In this regard, I'll confine myself to the terms of the manifesto called "For an Independent Revolutionary Art," published in 1938 and signed by Diego Rivera and myself. This declaration already

made generous allowances for the political necessities you mention. It nonetheless affirmed the urgent necessity of reconciling the *transformation* of the world, which is bound by certain disciplines, with the *interpretation* of the world, which must remain fully the master of its own means.

RB: Do you believe, then, that Surrealism will be able to sustain itself and flourish, even given the current vogue of occasional poetry and realistic painting?

AB: Occasional poetry written in wartime is an eruptive phenomenon with no future. I admit that it conveyed utterly praiseworthy sentiments, at a time when they were not allowed to take any other form of expression. Its contribution to the struggle at hand might be its justification. We lack the necessary distance to say for sure whether, out of all that ephemera, they've managed to make something eternal spring forth. What is certain is that, today, occasional poetry has lost all right to live on, at least as a dominant genre. Let's wait and see, not without some trepidation, how those who have devoted themselves to it make out—those who owe it their more or less dizzying success (which has nothing to do with true poetic merit).

The return to "realistic" painting, as seems to be the case in France (but not in England or the United States), marks a pure and simple *reaction*, resulting from the unchecked and blind speculation that affects paintings as it does everything else. This kind of painting has absolutely *no future* because it runs counter to the historic determinations of painting itself—which moreover are inseparable from those of poetry, philosophy, or the sciences—because it prides itself, brazenly or naively, on blocking the march of time.

RB: You surely know better than anyone the criticisms that have always been leveled against Surrealism; its obscurity, for example, which according to the movement's detractors keeps the mainstream public from appreciating its beauties . . .

AB: The charge of obscurity comes from an overestimation of *one* of language's virtues: its power of immediate exchange. Paul Valéry has already observed that the poet aims at "simultaneously manipulating sound, sense, thought, rhythm, and images," which gives rise to "many causes for obscuration." But Surrealism, by offering texts "captured under the dictation" of the inner voice, declines all responsibility for the unclarity of its texts. The manifest content of dreams is not clear, and even the analysis of these dreams at best clarifies their broad lines.

RB: I know that one of Surrealism's primary aims is the abolition of "differences that exist between men." Do you think the methods you promote have the potential to bring this about? What advantage can people of color, the eternal target of imperialism, gain from embracing Surrealism's way of thinking, feeling, and living?

AB: Yes: keeping in mind class and other barriers that we must first overcome by other means, I believe that Surrealism aims, *and is the only one to aim systematically*, at abolishing these differences. You know that with Surrealism the accent was moved off the *ego*, which is always somewhat despotic, and onto the *id* common to all men. But this would lead me to retrace the entire development of Surrealism over the past twenty years.

Surrealism is allied with people of color, on the one hand because it has always been on their side against every form of white imperialism and banditry, as demonstrated by the manifestoes published in Paris against the Moroccan War, the Colonial Exhibit, etc.; on the other hand, because there are very deep affinities between so-called "primitive" thought and Surrealist thought: both want to overthrow the hegemony of consciousness and daily life, in order to conquer the realm of *revelatory emotion*. These affinities were highlighted by a Martiniquan writer, Jules Monnerot, in a recently published work: *La Poésie moderne et le sacré*. I believe that reading Monnerot's book would prove this point.

RB: You have stated—I believe in your *Second Manifesto*—that Surrealism is the application of dialectical materialism to the realm of art. How do you reconcile this philosophical attitude with, first, your "search for a myth," which to me seems a rather characteristic procedure of this school; and second, with the interest you show in hypnotism?

AB: Among Surrealism's other tasks, I proposed *an intervention in mythic life* "which first of all, on the widest possible scale, takes the form of a clean-up operation." You see that I stressed the negative side of the undertaking . . . Nonetheless, I didn't fail to reserve possible rights for the *sacred*, freed from the degenerate ritualism that conceals it and restored to whatever might have given it its hold over the first human communities.

I believe that this sociological way of envisioning the question is not at all incompatible with *true* dialectical materialism. The Surrealist experiments with "induced slumber" demonstrated, on my part, no intention other than to overcome the resistances that consciousness sets against mental automatism, even when this consciousness is deliberately put into *abeyance*. I've always taken great care to point out that I considered the hypothesis of "spirits" ridiculous, and, in general, that I dissociated myself *a priori* from any spiritualistic interpretation of hypnotic phenomena. But I still believe that these phenomena require observation and study, the same as any other phenomena, and that only obscurantism benefits from the neglect into which they've fallen.

RB: Could you clarify the relations between automatic writing and Freudianism? Are there profound differences between the objective notation of dream imagery and the Freudian interpretation of dreams?

AB: I'm not sure I understand the question. Freud and his disciples had used automatic writing with their patients, in order to obtain a relatively uncontrolled mental production (or at least, less "censored" than a dream narrative, for example, whose fidelity is compromised by memory gaps). In the eyes of psycho-

analysts, automatic writing was useful only as a *means* of exploring the unconscious. For them, there was no question of studying the automatic product in and of itself, of subjecting it to the same criteria that apply to the different categories of consciously *elaborated* texts. "Thanks to automatic writing," Maurice Blanchot recently said, referring to its use in Surrealism, "language has enjoyed the highest promotion. It is now merged with human 'thought'; linked to the only true spontaneity, it is human freedom acting and showing itself." The interpretation of dreams, of course, can find only a point of departure or *basis* in the objective notation of dream imagery. But something else benefits from it: human *freedom*, which is revived in the perfect identification of man with his language. Until Surrealism, we had lost the secret of this identification.

INTERVIEW WITH JEAN DUCHÉ (*LE LITTÉRAIRE,* OCTOBER 5, 1946)

JEAN DUCHE: The bombing of Hiroshima affected everyone. Do you think it can help man to leave behind his "desperate condition in the middle of the twentieth century"? Or rather, will it give unexpected meaning to the famous statement, "Here begins the era of the *finite* world"? What do you anticipate from this death blow—our extermination or our salvation?

ANDRE BRETON: Yes, the shock was a rude one: the citizens of Hiroshima were not the only ones to suffer from it. Were it not for the human mind's inexhaustible and unfailing resources of insouciance—note that I consider this insouciance consonant with life, that I'm grateful for it as I am for the *wild grasses* that so quickly take over the ruins, getting a jump on any war reparations that might be undertaken—I don't know how we could recover; how any of us could still believe, without immediately feeling ridiculous, that we were freely able to commit to anything.

When I left New York four months ago, agitation with respect to this subject had reached a fever pitch: it brooks no comparison with the much more passive emotion I've seen here. Over there, atomic disintegration was widely held to be the most important discovery since fire; no one hesitated to make predictions about it, however romantic (ultrapessimistic or ultraoptimistic, depending on one's nature). But what struck the keenest minds, what for them constituted the great new fact was that man, realizing for the

first time that not only was his own life endangered, but that of his entire species as well, suddenly lost the perspectives (whether selfless or cynical) that until then had conditioned his own think-ing, and, in the best case, had justified his actions. Despite every-thing, the individual framework of birth and death had remained open until that point. Suddenly, however, a radical and well-founded doubt was introduced into the world's future, closing the old framework shut. Everything we'd entrusted to a distant to-morrow, for want of seeing it happen in our own lifetimes—but which implicated us nonetheless—now became futile: the great blue thread snapped in the eyes of our children. As for art and literature (I'm still speaking of America), professional psycholo-gists said that a profusion of works "made from pure despair and pure insanity" was unavoidable and just around the corner.

The intellectual situation created by the explosion in Hiroshima remains critical, and the reflections this event has inspired are still taking a dizzying turn. It goes without saying that we should do everything in our power, for as long as we can, to keep might on the side of life, to ward off and overcome this major scourge. In this regard, Denis de Rougemont's *Lettres sur la bombe atomique* [Letters About the Atom Bomb], written in such a lucid tone that it deliberately eschews any ringing of alarms, constitutes a healthy and exemplary act. The concrete suggestions it contains deserve to be debated and to bear fruit. This, of course, must in no way make us lose sight of certain facts, and in particu-lar does not absolve us from knowing *whose* hand governs the use of atomic energy in the United States (there are many details on the subject in the September issue of *La Revue Internationale*, from which the appropriate social conclusions can be drawn).

We are forced to concede that our role here is only to *propose*, while others *dispose*; be that as it may, it is the strict duty of intellectuals to denounce the progress of a murderous folly that no longer knows any limits. Small as it may seem, every time the irresponsible powers get their comeuppance, and every time se-duction and hope raise their heads, something is won. The use of atomic energy, as the irrevocable conquest of man, plants him dumbstruck at the intersection of two roads: one road leads to

collective suicide, the other to a greater good of the most unexpected kind. For man to choose the latter will require all his capacity for refusal, all the audacity and genius he can muster. He'll have to shake his habitual laziness, shatter the old frameworks, and then proceed to an overall recasting of ideas that have now become clichés, not one of which can be counted on.

Given the urgency of this choice, such an undertaking might seem fanciful. Nevertheless, a fundamental dissatisfaction is smouldering beneath the most varied and incompatible forms of conformity, not to mention a growing discontent, which might soon bear fruit.

JD: In 1942, you told students at Yale University that you were anticipating a spectacular discovery that would help reestablish "the most general contact, with no prejudice, between human beings" . . .

AB: As in other desperate moments throughout History, we can expect the world to make a jump that will restore its vital balance. It's not only social structures and mores that need to be modified from top to bottom: my personal belief is that nothing viable is possible if we don't quickly do away with outmoded aspects of universal assent. It was with this in mind that I recommended, in *Arcane 17*, an experimental and systematic effort to give *free rein* to *absolute* criticism and to the most *daring* plans of action. I have no doubt that such an activity would soon yield the expression of profound desire in our time, which everything is trying to simplify vulgarly, to obscure, or to shunt to one side. It seems to me that only this form of implacable elucidation—encyclopedic in nature—can reestablish human contacts, whose slackening is at the root of our anxiety, and can spawn a movement large enough to build a *new human era*.

JD: Our ways of thinking and seeing are more impregnated with Surrealism than the average man realizes: posters, shop windows, some poetry of the younger generation, certain paintings . . . Isn't this a veritable inflation?

AB: Those are external observations that perhaps apply more to New York than they do to Paris. As you can imagine, Surrealism's "applications" in advertising or fashion are of only minor interest to me. In the 1924 *Manifesto of Surrealism*, I said that I didn't expect the establishment of a conventional *Surrealist pattern* any time in the near future. Indeed, it took some twenty years for it to happen.

In the "Prolegomena to a Third Surrealist Manifesto or Not," published in New York in 1942, I was again forced to take a public stand against every kind of conformism, to "attack a Surrealist conformism that is all too obvious. Too many paintings, in particular, come upon the scene today all decked out in what cost the innumerable followers of De Chirico, of Picasso, of Ernst, of Masson, of Miró, of Tanguy, etc., absolutely nothing, people who are ignorant of the fact that there is no great expedition in art that is not undertaken *at the risk of one's life*, that the road to take is obviously not the one with guard rails along its edge, and that each artist must take up the search for the *Golden Fleece* all by himself." The moment I returned to Paris, I became convinced that this observation could be applied to the vast majority of poems written today. Nothing outstrips them for monotony, and the supposedly Surrealist leanings discerned in them are of a purely formal nature. It's high time to remind ourselves that Apollinaire—in his last essay, "The New Spirit and the Poets"—called surprise "our greatest new resource," and that Surrealism has not only abided by this opinion, but has made it one of its unimpeachable tenets.

I hadn't waited for the inflation you mention in order to contrast, in *Minotaure* shortly before the war, the work of art as a *happening* with the work of art as a *ribbon*, at so much per inexhaustible foot (thinking of "those art merry-go-rounds which revolve remorselessly around the same objects, the same effects, and of those poetry windmills which grind away, year after year, exporting sacks of the same flour to ever more distant countries"). To counter the deadly boredom that many so-called poetic publications distill today, the accent must be placed on the ability to go beyond, which is a function of *movement* and *freedom*. In this

respect, Reverdy, Picabia, Péret, Artaud, Arp, Henri Michaux, Prévert, Char, and Aimé Césaire remain so many *inimitable models*. The most sensationally new poetic text I've read in quite some time is Jean Ferry's "Le Tigre mondain," published in the fifth issue of *Les Quatre Vents*.

JD: Don't you find that painting, whether Surrealist or not, is losing steam? And in your eyes, who are the Surrealist painters of today?

AB: During the war and up until now, painting in France has followed a clearly regressive course, which we had already seen between 1918 and 1923. It has returned to a more or less whimsical form of imitation (which doesn't exclude distortion) of *physical appearance*, an imitation that Surrealism persists in considering historically outmoded. Here, I have to make a glowing exception for Brauner and Hérold, and another (despite certain concessions of his to a realistic vision) for Dominguez. Keep in mind that I haven't had time to visit every gallery and artist's studio (what are Picabia or Balthus up to, for instance?). During my recent explorations, I enthusiastically verified that in sculpture Giacometti had managed to reach a synthesis of his earlier preoccupations, on which the creation of a *style* for our times has always seemed to depend. Judging by the several gouaches that have arrived from New York, no Surrealist artist has shown greater capacity for renewal, nor moved further forward in the confirmation of his mastery, than Miró, who unfortunately is still held in Spain. But, just as during the preceding war, it's on the American continent that painting seems belatedly to have given off its finest shower of light: Ernst, Tanguy, Matta, Donati, and Gorki in New York; Lam in Cuba; E. F. Granell in the Dominican Republic; Esteban Frances, Leonora Carrington, and Remedios Varo in Mexico; Braulio Arenas and Jorge Caceres in Chile. We must bring together and confront these works in 1946, in Paris. I hope to organize this in the context of an upcoming international exhibit of Surrealism, with the help of Marcel Duchamp in New York,

who is the great hidden inspirer of the artistic movement—as much in the 1940s as in the years 1918 to 1923.

JD: It seems you had a hand in the Haitian revolution. Could you comment on exactly what happened?

AB: Let's not exaggerate. At the end of 1945, the poverty, and consequently the patience, of the Haitian people had reached a breaking point. You have to realize that, on the huge Ile de la Gonave off the Haitian coast, men earned less than one American cent for an entire day's labor, and that, according to the most conservative newspapers, children in the suburbs of Port-au-Prince lived on tadpoles fished out of the sewers. This situation was made all the more poignant by the fact that the Haitian spirit, more than any other, miraculously continues to draw its vigor from the French Revolution; that the striking outline of Haitian history shows us man's most moving efforts to break away from slavery and into freedom.

In a first lecture on "Surrealism and Haiti," I tried, both for the sake of clarity and out of deference to the underlying spirit of this history, to align Surrealism's aims with the age-old goals of the Haitian peasantry. In conclusion, I felt driven to condemn "the imperialisms that the war's end has in no way averted and the cruelly maintained game of cat and mouse between stated ideals and eternal selfishness," as well as to reaffirm my allegiance to the motto on the Haitian flag: "Union makes strength." The newspaper La Ruche, the voice of the younger generation, which devoted the next day's issue to me, said that my words were electrifying and decided to take an insurrectional tone. Its confiscation and suspension immediately led to a student strike, followed within forty-eight hours by a general strike. Several days later, the government was held hostage. Unions were being started everywhere and free elections were promised. Even without yet knowing the final results—since the nature of the Haitian revolution has been hotly debated—I'd predict that it should be truly beneficial, especially since one of the most intellectually and

morally respected men, the learned ethnologist Dr. Price-Mars, has been elected to a key government post.

JD: What benefit do you derive from all these masks, emblems, and strange objects I see around you? And where did you find those extraordinary dolls?

AB: Those are Eskimo and Indian masks, and some from the South Seas. I brought the dolls back from my visit to the Hopi Indians of Arizona. Look how these objects justify the Surrealist vision, and even give it a new impetus. This Eskimo mask represents the swan that in the spring leads the white whale toward the hunter (the swan, here reduced to its head and neck, emerges from the whale's mouth). And this Hopi doll evokes the goddess of corn: in the crenellated frame of her head you can see clouds over the mountain; in this little checkerboard in the center of her forehead, the corncob; around her mouth, the rainbow; in the vertical stripes of her dress, rain falling on the valley. Yes or no, isn't that poetry as we continue to understand it?

The European artist in the twentieth century can counter the desiccation of his wellsprings of inspiration, which rationalism and utilitarianism have brought about, only by reviving the so-called primitive vision, a synthesis of sensorial perception and mental representation. African sculpture has already made a dazzling contribution in this regard. Today, it's above all the visual art of the red man that lets us accede to a new system of knowledge and relations. Monnerot, in *La Poésie moderne et la sacré*, has moreover highlighted the affinities between Surrealist and Indian ways of thinking; I've been able to verify that the latter remains as vibrant and creative as ever.

JD: You once wrote: "Today, authentic art is linked to the activity of social revolution; like the latter, it aims toward the confusion and destruction of capitalist society." Is this still your position?

AB: I see you're not sparing me my most sensitive point. My conviction hasn't changed: even the singular aggravation of the

misunderstanding between artists and nonartists, in the revolutionary sphere, can't do anything about that. I think that on this subject the main points have been covered by Monnerot, in the book I just mentioned, and by Blanchot in "Quelques réflexions sur le surréalisme." For me to add anything insightful to their comments would force me to overstep the limits of this interview.

JD: The least one can say is that the motion recently passed by the Writers' Union in Leningrad gives you a resounding refutation . . .*

AB: The motion you're referring to didn't surprise or upset me overmuch. It's perfectly in keeping with a system of thought that I've never entirely managed to adopt for my own, despite numerous attempts. Imperious as it might be, this motion mainly expresses the USSR's need to counter what it currently sees as a growing threat, which it would be pointless to deny. But it's also impossible not to recognize that *art* has now been slapped with a prohibition (who could honestly think of finding an escape route for it through all those barriers?). It goes without saying, moreover, that the limits imposed on free speech by the Leningrad resolution are no less extreme for writers and artists subject to communist discipline outside the USSR than they are for those within its boundaries. Although the former necessarily enjoy far greater tolerance, I'm curious to see how they'll resolve this *matter of conscience*.

JD: Given these conditions, how will true art, today, play its role in the social revolution?

AB: It's part of human nature for some people to believe that they have to *devote themselves*—at least partially—to art and the *cause* of

---

* In reference to the resolution of August 14, 1946, decreeing that literature should have no connection with "the bourgeois culture of the West," and that its only function was to "illustrate the directives of the Politburo."

free expression (which after all are just as seriously threatened): it would be unfair to hold them responsible for a rift that has purely and simply been inflicted on them, without prejudice to other sanctions. For myself, I would not change a word of one of my statements from Mexico in 1938: "To those who urge us to consent that art should submit to a discipline which we hold to be radically incompatible with its nature, we give a flat refusal. . . . We recognize, of course, that the revolutionary state has the right to defend itself against the counterattack of the bourgeoisie, even when this drapes itself in the flag of science or art. But there is an abyss between those enforced and temporary measures of revolutionary self-defense and the pretension to lay commands on intellectual creation."

JD: Artistic freedom isn't the only thing at stake. Arthur Koestler's *Darkness at Noon* posited the problem of freedom in a state that has staged a social revolution. Do you defend freedom above all and *at any price*? Or are you prepared to give it up in order to bring about certain ideas?

AB: The trials that the concept of freedom has undergone since the eighteenth century are a constant source of surprise and excitement. Whereas, following the theological debates that systematically obscured it, this concept emerged in all its clarity in Helvétius (you'll find it beautifully explained in his work *De l'Esprit*); whereas for Marat and Saint-Just the idea of freedom proved so *compelling* as to forego any definition; you'll see that throughout the nineteenth and early twentieth centuries it suffered an acute crisis, and since then has had trouble regaining its courage. It's striking to note that the great social reformers were the first to restrict it: Saint-Simon, by assigning as the social state's goal not freedom, but the improvement of the worker's lot; Fourier, by considering freedom the simple result of the conquest of the seven primordial natural rights; Marx and Engels, by equating it with the knowledge of necessity; Lenin, by fitting it into the actual domination of every practical determinism.

   Darkness at Noon reveals the confusing prospects that result

when this latter viewpoint is taken to extremes. Even though it's been said that Koestler's book earned the Communist party an appreciable number of new memberships, it seems hard to deny that these memberships are of a rather *disturbing* nature. I believe many pairs of lungs will have trouble adapting to the rarefied air that blows through this book, and that brings it to its final explosion: "It was a mistake in the system; perhaps it lay in the precept . . . that *the end justifies the means.*"

Camus and I immediately agreed in New York that the remaining free intellectuals must combat this particular precept as categorically and as actively as possible. I believe that the only truly effective affirmation of freedom today resides in such an unbridled rejection. An energetic campaign, which I'm sure would attract many persuasive resources, must be launched immediately and *at all costs* to settle accounts with that old Jesuit precept, whose least evil is that it's extremely antidialectical—a precept to which even Trotsky himself subscribed, to our amazement, in *Their Morals and Ours*. Only by working to abolish this precept, which has gained monstrous vigor at the entrance to the inquisitorial den, can we claim to serve the cause of freedom—and *not* by vainly trying to reduce freedom to the arbitrary faculty of doing as we please. But for starters—to get some air back into our lungs and to avoid losing our taste for, even the sense of, freedom—once again I suggest reading Helvétius.

JD: Surrealism's original pessimism has been replaced by the pessimism of the absurd, the "myth of Sisyphus." Camus triumphs over it with the pride of despair, but doesn't entirely manage to do away with it. Do you think that one day we can emerge into the sunlight and remain there? And if so, how?

AB: I have express reservations about Surrealism's so-called "pessimism." This pessimism, as regards the illness of our time and the majority of remedies communally envisioned, at least has this in particular, that it goes hand in hand with a largely anticipatory optimism.

The Rock of Sisyphus? The Surrealists differ from Camus in

that they believe that one day or another it's going to crumble, abolishing as if by magic both mountain and torture: they tend to think that there might be a propitious way of rolling it . . . Tell me, is that optimistic enough! They don't consider the "fracture" observed by Camus between the world and the human mind to be irrevocable. They in no way accept that nature is hostile to man, but suppose that man, who originally possessed certain keys that kept him in strict communion with nature, has lost these keys, and that since then he persists more and more feverishly in trying out others *that don't fit*.

Scientific knowledge of nature can be worthwhile only on condition that *contact* with nature via poetic and, dare I say, mythic routes be reestablished. It remains understood that any scientific progress achieved within a defective social structure only works against man, and further worsens his condition. That was already Fontenelle's opinion . . .

JD: You've spoken of an all-powerful desire, capable of transforming the world. Is it on desire that you base your action?

AB: *Desire*, yes, *always*. We can rely only on this great key bearer. Just as freedom can't be equated with the impulse to do anything one wants, it goes without saying that I set this desire apart from certain forms of unrestrained bestial appetite, such as have recently been displayed. Even under the frantic guise it wears in Sade, we recognize desire, and duly honor it, as utterly *dignified*.

JD: Can you base a morality on that?

AB: Yes, or at least we could in another society founded on the certainty that all passions are good (this brings us back to Helvétius: "On the Superiority of Passionate Men over Sensible Men"); or more precisely, that it is not within man's power to change the nature or goal of these passions, but rather to modify their development to suit universal harmony. These passions, by their very diversity and their unexplored capacity for playfulness, are the potential guarantors of this harmony. I'm limiting myself

here to mentioning one of Fourier's seminal ideas, in which I see the cornerstone of any morality liable to gain our support. Naturally, such a morality could only be built on experience. For the moment, it can at most be conjectured in its broad outlines.

JD: I've heard that you're about to publish a poem in honor of Fourier. What concordance of ideas have you found with him?

AB: Fourier is immense, and my greatest ambition is to stem the tide of oblivion that has engulfed him—which already says something about the *loss of knowledge* in our time. The fact that his name was scandalously misused by a few Vichy hacks won't keep me from celebrating the man who, as Engels said, "handled dialectics with as much power as his contemporary Hegel," and who "is at his greatest in his conception of the history of society." Coming from Engels, that's no small praise.

But what captivates me most of all in Fourier, in connection with his discovery of *passional attraction* (whose invaluable benefit has yet to be realized) and his attitude of *absolute doubt* toward traditional modes of knowledge and action, is his attempt to furnish a hieroglyphic interpretation of the world, founded on the analogy between human passions and the products of the three natural realms. Here, Fourier is making a cardinal juncture between the concerns that have animated poetry and art since the beginning of the nineteenth century, and plans for social reorganization that run a strong risk of remaining embryonic if they refuse to take these concerns into account.

JD: This brings us back to the question I asked at the start of these interviews: how can man reach unity? How can we reestablish contact between human beings?

AB: I cannot stress too heavily that Fourier must be one of our primary guides, not to say a major contributor, to the potential establishment of a new *myth* on which we could base a durable cohesion (I'm thinking of his marvelous *ongoing* cosmogony, of his

concept of the "aromal shell," home of the "transmundanes," etc.).

Bataille, in an excellent essay on "the moral meaning of sociology" for the first issue of *Critique*, is right to say that I'm completely in favor of seeing such a myth constituted, whose scattered elements exist and are only waiting to be brought together. In everything that has to do with the development of this myth, I think that Bataille, as much for the breadth of his knowledge and views as for the remarkably untamed nature of his aspirations, is qualified to play a vital role. I don't believe that the passage from myth to activity—if this activity resolutely takes such a passage as its goal, and if it manages from the start to keep idle and merely curious souls at bay—will encounter serious obstacles.

INTERVIEW WITH DOMINIQUE ARBAN (*COMBAT*, MAY 31, 1947)

DOMINIQUE ARBAN: Whatever the value of automatic writing might be in the final analysis and after twenty years' experience, one cannot deny its influence on so-called "non-Surrealist" poetry, nor that this influence has been considerable. Despite this fact—or because of it—would Surrealism grant automatism the same credit today?

ANDRE BRETON: Verbal automatism, as a generating principle of Surrealism, seems amply to have proven itself: 1) Though its outflow has been "torrential" only at certain times, at least it acted by continual infiltration, and one can say, after these twenty-odd years, that it "mined" the field of expression from end to end. 2) It has been contagious enough to impose itself rather quickly as a "common" need in every part of the world, or at least where totalitarian regimes have not blocked its spread: by not basing itself strictly on the determinations specific to modern French poetry, it has proven to be of universal value. 3) Reaction against it hasn't "paid off"; we've seen proof enough of this in the pathetic drivel, spouted with full political fanfare, that has been heaped on us by some former Surrealists whose penchant for overstatement can only find an outlet in repudiation. Once we're rid of the monopolizing and terrorizing techniques they've used so often (which even now are losing steam), I have no doubt that their efforts will widely be deemed reactionary, and their pitiful

achievements treated as they deserve to be. Surrealism, moreover, has little cause to complain: every day these renegade dupes are repelling young minds more and more effectively, even within the party that they call their own. I can assure you that psychic automatism and the larger cause it entails are hardly at the mercy of these clowns who, at the end of every winter, take their idle curiosity in hand and start up once again.

This said—and to move on to more important matters—the crisis of automatism is hardly new: scarcely had it appeared than some individuals boasted of "domesticating" it (they were domesticated long before it was). Others who, out of common spite, strove to immolate it on the altar of "reason" managed only to singe their own wings on the flames of the phoenix. Still others imitate it, and these are not the least dangerous. The most serious thing is that, along the way, the hostile surroundings in which we operated often caused us to legitimize automatism via rational arguments, which more or less belied its nature. Which only goes to show that, at least in current society, disputes between "passionate men" and "sensible men" seem vain: the former are led to "rationalize" their passion once they try to impart it, the latter to inflame their rational stance in the most irrational way. Primacy, on one side or the other, is the only thing that can be considered decisive in this domain, even if by a rather cruel irony one spends one's life fighting with the enemy's weapons.

DA: Does automatism, which originally seemed essential, remain absolutely linked to Surrealism's fate?

AB: The primacy of passion has turned out to be the great constant of the Surrealist movement, and we must never separate automatism from it, or sacrifice automatism to it. Automatism has always guaranteed and amplified passion. On this score, we know the old refrain only too well: there's also no shortage of disciples ready to preach psychoanalysis so long as one masks certain pansexual views that govern it; or Marxism, so long as one agrees to leave out class struggle! I suppose it's fair enough to lay blame on the constituent parts, rather than on the inessentials. But such

attacks are spiteful, and old hat besides. Even if automatism, sure of its abilities, no longer needs to stand in the foreground, it goes without saying that in Surrealism it is under no threat of disfavor. More than that, I believe it is destined to spread much more widely, once we've found the (mechanical) means of sheltering it more securely from self-criticism, which is an open invitation to its negation.

DA: It seems that, in principle, Surrealism has counted heavily on the liberating aspect of Surrealist poetry. On the other hand, whatever its achievements, its audience seems definitively limited, and so it has failed. Do you consider this failure essential, or accidental and temporary?

AB: We've never aspired to the role of "public writers," which presupposes a taste—unlike ours—for cultivating clichés. Against those who would impudently reduce things to their lowest common denominator, against demagogical hacks, we continue to affirm a stance of free research and exploration of the unknown. As soon as one embarks on this path, one is forced to renounce all claim to a mass audience, which is too uneducated to hear anything new. On top of which, this renunciation of a large following is hardly final: look at Stendhal, or Baudelaire. How can we properly speak of a Surrealist "failure" in such conditions? Before us, they talked about the failures of Rimbaud, Mallarmé, Cézanne, and Van Gogh . . . At least such "failures" were subsequently compensated. Fortunately, certain successes were compensated, too. In the meantime, Surrealist liberation, which we've often said will not become fully effective until social exploitation is suppressed, has hardly remained utopian. The objective proof is that young people are being attracted to and tempted by Surrealism in greater numbers than ever before.

DA: Does the liberation that Existentialism is trying to bring about have any connection with Surrealist liberation?

AB: No doubt. I've already stressed the possibility of linking

Surrealism with Heidegger's thinking on myth. Such a link exists: the work of Hölderlin, which Heidegger has superbly analyzed. For my part, I'm also very taken by Jaspers's efforts to "ground" responsibility anew, which these days rests only on a cloud. Closer to us, I hold Sartre in great intellectual esteem, despite his *Baudelaire*, which, as you can imagine, hardly reflects my own viewpoint, and despite our very different intellectual backgrounds.

Note in passing that when someone tries to set one modern movement against another, even when these movements operate on very different planes, it's almost always for suspect reasons. To disappoint such persons once and for all, I'll add that, free from any competitive afterthoughts, I take only the most favorable interest in Isidore Isou's book *Pour une nouvelle poésie* [For a New Poetry], and that I in no way consider Lettrism an enemy.

DA: Do you see Surrealism as a system of morals?

AB: Initially, Surrealism was conceived as "dictated by thought, etc., exempt from any aesthetic or moral concern." This formula, today, applies only to automatism. In other respects, moral imperatives have emerged, at least as far as the behavior of individuals is concerned. This said, I won't be intimidated by those who claim that I'm bowing to Christian morality: it's true that Hegelianism and Marxism have toppled traditional morality, and that many have taken advantage of this to grant themselves full license—to lie, defile, or kill, for example. But a post-Christian morality (just as there were "pre-Christian" ones) judges such individuals without even being formulated. We were talking before about repudiation: isn't it precisely Jaspers who calls it "equivalent to a veritable spiritual suicide"? Don't you think that even in an age as troubled as ours, no matter what, it's still fairly easy to recognize an honest man?

INTERVIEW WITH AIMÉ PATRI (*PARU*, MARCH 1948)

AIME PATRI: Since your return from the United States, a number of people have been claiming that Surrealism is dead, or that it is nothing more, in this second postwar era, than a vestige of the past. I suppose these are the same people who believe that one should write only for one's time and that, when all is said and done, only fashion counts. Without entering into these issues, I'd like you to tell me what you yourself consider dead and what you consider living in the spirit of Surrealism from 1924. I mention 1924 specifically, since it was the date of the first *Manifesto*.

ANDRE BRETON: Dead or living? You'll forgive me, but I find the question rather nearsighted, narrowly keyed to utility and efficiency. It's precisely a steady diet of such questions that will be the death of us. If I recall correctly, that vogue was started by Benedetto Croce: *What Is Living and What Is Dead of the Philosophy of Hegel*. It will soon be forty years since then, and you know how much dirty, reddened water has passed under that bridge. Certainly, in 1948, it would be useful and expedient to be able to say what is dead and what is living in Hegel, among others, but I fear the scales we're judging by are illusory. And what would you say of the question: what is dead and what is living of Marxism? As it stands, we humans are a wretched lot, led by a passion over which routine has managed to gain the upper hand. To choose, to discriminate *a posteriori* would be the ideal. But you know very well

213

that even posterity doesn't choose, or does so very sparingly. As far as Surrealism is concerned, I'm particularly ill placed. I'm not joking when I say that I don't have enough distance from it. It's obviously not what some of my former friends have *become* since leaving Surrealism that could set me off in turn down the path of compromise. A group of ideas capable of being sorted into the living and the dead? No. I prefer to stick with the old dilemma: to be or not to be.

AP: How do you currently situate the technique of automatic writing? Do you believe that a work deserves the name "Surrealist" only if it has been obtained by this method? Looking at the *Ode to Charles Fourier*, whose technique is reminiscent of Mallarmé's *Un Coup de dés* and whose inspiration is obviously premeditated, it seems to me that you yourself don't make exclusive use of it these days.

AB: You cannot know how automatic writing, and everything it carries in its orbit, remains dear to me. And yet, I don't believe that anything was ever less understood. Its time will come . . . Meanwhile, to my knowledge, no one has ever noticed that when we spontaneously express ourselves point-blank, we use only one verbal *structure*, to the categorical exclusion of any other structure that apparently conveys the same meaning. For example, you might say, "You can't mean that," when theoretically you could just as well have said, "That's impossible" (or vice versa). Too bad if rationalism sees this necessity as being of scant importance! Personally, I consider it the sole guarantee of affective authenticity in language, and (beyond language, of course) in human behavior. Besides, no matter how you care to envision the automatic state, not just anyone can attain it, nor, still less, remain in it for a set amount of time.

AP: In short, if I've understood you correctly, you believe that there's something irreparable and definitive about the spontaneous juncture of thought and word, which the detours of premeditated thought will never recapture. Is that it?

AB: Yes, but it's very difficult. One has to have *cut one's ties* from so many things. In this regard, I don't hesitate to use the word "asceticism." This asceticism plunges old *littérateurs* like Roger Caillois into despair only because it is beyond them. Of course, historical and other circumstances have had their way with us, displacing the stress that we'd originally put on the automatic message; but nothing can keep this stress from having been the voice of *desire* captured at the source, closely related to the desire of primitive peoples who *assigned names* to things, and of revolutionaries who believed—or will believe—in *restoring* man to a world he no longer finds alien. As I see it, certain "nonautomatic" works are Surrealist, so long as they situate themselves to some benefit, and with some stringency, along that curve that life has imposed on us; whereas far too many works today, whose automatism remains external, not to say merely simulated, are not Surrealist. In automatism's favor, as I originally conceived it, I'd stress once again that as a universally accessible form of expression, harboring no secrets, it remains the best thing yet invented for countering literary and artistic vanities, which take a more revolting turn with each passing day. You'll agree with me that these vanities are merely the outbursts of ridiculous little "egos," from the "greatest philosopher of modern times" to the poet-messiah who believes that those who can understand him have not yet been born. This illness of our age seems to me, on the whole, one of the most miserable. Far from sharing in this infatuation, I can assure you, the *Ode to Charles Fourier* stands on that curve I spoke of. It takes automatism as its point of departure, but doesn't absolve me from dealing with certain obligations that might arise along the way. In this case, the link with automatism is the personality of Charles Fourier himself, and the greatest constructive work ever to have been based on unconstrained desire. It's true that I feigned here to bow to occasional poetry, but rest assured that it was merely in order to kill it.

AP: After Dada in 1919 and Surrealism in 1924, it seems to me that, if we follow a well-known dialectical rhythm, we should arrive at a third term. I'd like you to explain what poetic and

historical function you currently grant to notions such as myth and utopia, which don't appear in Surrealism's theoretical writings from after the First World War. Also, what role do you ascribe to the initiatory tradition? On this subject, even some of your intimates have reproached you for abandoning the old Surrealist revolutionary spirit, in order to espouse another which would entail an escape toward the past or outside of time . . .

AB: That's a seemingly harsh question, so I'll be all the more careful not to sidestep it. Are you quite sure that the dialectical compound isn't itself inherited from initiatory tradition? No matter. Among the many abuses to which the word "myth" gives rise, I currently know of none more misleading. Here I see a Sallust who says: "The universe itself is a myth" (between you and me, he might be right); there I hear a Georges Bataille confide to me (one couldn't be more nostalgic) that the absence of myth is perhaps today's true myth. Personally, I've long held that, when it comes to the relative degree of importance granted *manifest* content and *latent* content, it is the same thing for waking life—even when taken very objectively—as it is for dreams. The first is a subject for historians and politicians, and they're welcome to it. The second interests sociologists, but also, exceedingly, poets and artists. It is in fact this latent content, and it alone, that constitutes the raw material of poetry and art.

Myth is what this content becomes through the efforts of the latter. In periods of great division and abdication such as this one, myth follows a somewhat underground channel, all the while remaining the fundamental concern of a few individuals. I've become convinced in my travels that the fate of human communities can be evaluated by the power that the myths conditioning them still hold. To a large extent, that is how they resist both secular oppression (in the case of the Hopi Indians) and extreme economic poverty (in the case of the Haitian blacks). At least they're preserved from the threat of massive collapse, such as we saw hanging over France—a country whose officials had pushed it so far down the road of skepticism and indifference—in 1939 and

1940. And has anything happened since then that has failed to refute the most widely held beliefs of the time? Perhaps some people use the word *utopia*, accompanied by a shrug of the shoulders, as the most poisonous weapon of all. Like it or not, we've had to admit that this word required more careful use. Provided we not insist on utopias in the strict sense—dreams that to all appearances are impracticable—I believe that many predictions hastily branded with the same discredit should be reexamined closely for anything viable they might contain. This is particularly the case with the so-called social "utopias" (which moreover have led to very appreciable partial realizations). Let's not forget that Trotsky, at the end of the darkest dilemma he ever pondered, shortly before his assassination, was forced to conclude that Marxism itself might be a utopia.* Even so, it's not my aim to dismiss Marxism as a museum curiosity, or to forget the precious tools of orientation that it has given mankind. Poets and artists in particular would be inexcusable if they tried to guard against "utopias," when the very nature of their creation leads them to draw, at least initially, from the vague realm where utopia reigns. In some instances, this utopia might prove fruitful in reality, thereby revealing itself as having been not such a utopia after all.

What role do I ascribe to the initiatory tradition? With all due respect to those faithful followers who hypocritically worry about me, an increasingly important one. Observe, my dear Aimé Patri, that the best things said in France since the Liberation (a latent Liberation if ever there was one) aim at the long-overdue elucidation of the bonds that make the modern conceptions of poetry, revolution, and love part of the occult process. In this respect, I believe that we're progressing, at least in terms of deeper ideas. Think of the beginning of the twentieth century, when utter

---

* Here is the particularly important reflection of Trotsky's alluded to above: "If, writes Trotsky, the war provokes 'not revolution but a decline of the proletariat' and if, consequently, Marxists must recognize that Bureaucratic Collectivism, not Socialism, is the historical successor to Capitalism, then: 'nothing else would remain except openly to recognize that the socialist program, based on the internal contradictions of capitalist society, ended as a Utopia.' " (Dwight Macdonald in "The Root Is Man"; *Politics*, April and July 1946.) [*Breton's note*]

cretins such as Edmond Rostand or Pierre Loti could become famous: how far we've come since then! What a *restitution* of thought since that time, and particularly since the last war. And what vindication for occultism, which bore almost the entire brunt of it. Remember, it's not really a matter of knowing whether a strict oral or written tradition has managed to stretch secretly from Antiquity to the present day (even though this is the vulgate's persistent objection), but rather of finding out whether the works that continue to influence us maintain appreciable—even if impure—ties with this tradition. I consider the matter beyond dispute when it comes to Hugo, Nerval, Baudelaire, Rimbaud, Lautréamont, and Jarry (and I believe it's only a matter of time for Fourier, for example, or Mallarmé). Between you and me, this is rather serious. I'm saying that the thinking of these authors only reflects (albeit remarkably well) esoteric thought as it was available at the time, often in bits and pieces. I'll simply refer you to Georges Viatte's *Victor Hugo et les Illuminés de son temps* [Victor Hugo and the Illuminati of His Day]; G. Le Breton's *Nerval, poète alchimique* [Nerval, Alchemistic Poet] and Jean Richer's *Gérard de Nerval et les doctrines ésotériques* [Gérard de Nerval and the Esoteric Doctrines]; George Blin's *Le Sadisme chez Baudelaire* [Sadism in Baudelaire]; Jacques Gengoux's *Lâ Symbolique de Rimbaud* [The Symbolics of Rimbaud]; *Maldoror* by Marcel Jean and Arpad Mezei; Maurice Saillet's postscript to *L'Autre Alceste*; etc.—not to mention everything that might support my thesis in a masterwork such as Raymond Abellio's *Heureux les pacifiques* [Happy Are the Peace-Loving] or in the journal *Cahiers d'Hermès*, edited by Rolland de Renéville. In the last issue of this journal, in fact, a study by Michel Carrouges on "Surrealism and occultism" refutes the accusations you've cited against me. This study shows that I've remained not only true to my lifelong convictions, but also fully consistent with the *afterthoughts* that form part of every veritable, autonomous thought—afterthoughts that were perhaps awaiting maturity to start coming forward. Be that as it may, for the past twenty-five years this way of seeing has always been implicit in Surrealism. Those who claim the contrary are lying, and shout themselves hoarse trying to maintain an untenable position.

AP: I remember that one issue of *La Révolution Surréaliste*, which I believe came out in 1925, announced on the cover the end of Christian civilization; and the latest Surrealist writings show that you've remained faithful to that notion of historical perspective. But how do you see it?

AB: Nothing will reconcile me with Christian civilization. In Christianity, I reject the entire masochistic dogma based on the insane concept of "original sin," no less than the idea of salvation in an "other world," with the sordid scheming it entails in this one. As you might imagine, this doesn't prevent me from taking some interest in Christian mythology and the speculations it has inspired, just as I'm interested in Egyptian, Greek, Aztec, and other mythologies. Since this interest brings some highly emotional forces into play, I'll add that, as far as Christianity is concerned, my preference goes straight to the heretics. These are the inclinations I set once and for all against attempts at alteration and confiscation, to which—after Baudelaire, Rimbaud, and more recently even Sade—Surrealist thought has become subject in turn.* As for Christian *civilization*, is there any need to add that the *mortal* grievances we hold against it go far beyond a fundamental disagreement over its constituent principles? We condemn it for its increasing infidelity to its own premises. Old relic, absurd by-product that Christianity is, for more than two centuries— let's say since the death of Pascal—we've supported that witch, whose sole remaining power is a little spite. The only way we'll finally be rid of her is by again codifying a corpus of ethical precepts, some of which go much further back than Christianity, and some of which were developed outside of it or in reaction against it. Whether we like it or not, the ethical level here remains dependent on the mythic level, because of the *eternal vigor of*

---

* At this point, the interview as published in *Paru* contains the following sentence: "That today someone can announce a book whose title features my name preceded by the word 'saint' constitutes so flagrant a provocation that it would be unforgivable of me to reply." Breton is referring to a proposed volume by Catholic writer and critic Claude Mauriac, which was finally published the following year under the less controversial title *André Breton*.

symbols, which imposes on human behavior a constant harmonic reference to certain irrational, fabulous facts about origins and endings. For this new order to come about, all that's needed is for sociology (an active, not a passive, sociology) and poetry (finished with its mumbling and restored to its highest prerogatives), at the point they've reached, to mysteriously come together and engender it.

INTERVIEW WITH CLAUDINE CHONEZ (*GAZETTE DES LETTRES*, JULY 31, 1948)

CLAUDINE CHONEZ: You've been accused of having lowered your guard against the bourgeois world—of letting yourself be adopted by *Le Figaro*, for example . . .

ANDRE BRETON: The bourgeois world is so undermined from within that the very idea of maintaining one's guard, as you say, strikes me as being obsolete. Can you really believe that this world has any chance of recovering from what the last war did to it? Those whom you call my detractors are like people who, with great fanfare, would amass battering rams against the House of Usher. This wouldn't matter if I loved their law, but I've already seen too many applications of it that have wrung my heart. In my concept of a necessary well-being in times to come, no one lies, no one cheats, no one seeks to accredit the most desperate false witness at death's door, no one destroys the mind with a pickax.

Have I been "adopted" by *Le Figaro*? Today the conditions of struggle are such that one can't choose one's forum; and the fact is, the most I did was to grant an interview to *Le Littéraire*, as I'm granting you this one. The important thing is to continue to speak freely. Who is really going to believe that I've adopted the political line of whatever newspaper carries my statements?

CC: What is the current relation between Christianity and Surrealism? Isn't it true that you'd like to replace Christian morality

with a "morality of passion," whose instigators were Sade, Freud, and Fourier?

AB: In a new collective Surrealist text, which will be published under the title *A la niche*, Surrealism's attitude will be defined both with respect to the exorbitant idea of the "death of God," which in our eyes is absolute nonsense (you'll agree that for someone to die, he first has to exist), and to the "Luciferianism" with which we intend to confound it.

I grant you that the morality Surrealism aims at promoting is still in its intuitive phase. It's quite certain that for the famous "Each man according to his abilities," "his works," or "his needs" (materially speaking), not only Surrealism but all poetry worthy of the name has substituted an "Each man according to his desires." Is that so much more ambitious, when you think about it? Who says that a good overall management wouldn't be enough to bring desire into order? In return for abolishing the "verboten" in every tongue, I have no doubt that the most extreme, and even most antisocial, points of desire would soon be absorbed. Keep in mind that we're speaking about desire and not *license*. License is what is at fault. Because it hides, because it schemes (but let's not forget that it's the product of constraint). Sade, Freud, Fourier: you've named the three great emancipators of desire.

CC: Fourier in particular?

AB: Fourier, yes, especially so. He's the one who took the bull by the horns—the unpleasant bull of human bad conscience. There is no way for me to briefly characterize a contribution at once as rich and as original as his. It absolutely defies "digests." Today's intellectual slovenliness will have to rouse itself and refer directly back to his works.

CC: Nonetheless, hasn't your morality evolved since the time when you said that the simplest Surrealist act would consist of firing blindly into the crowd? Isn't Roger Vailland, who harshly attacks you in *Le Surréalisme contre la Révolution*, right when he says

that in 1925 you would have welcomed the age of the atomic bomb?

AB: Few people pass up the chance to remind me of the phrase you've just quoted, but I'm not overly concerned about it! I won't deny passing through periods of giddiness in the course of my life ("Giddiness" [Vertige], moreover, is also a *culpable* poem of Rimbaud's). Too bad for the paroxystic forms their expression might have taken. The important thing in my eyes—and perhaps in others'—is that I've always tried to be heard even in darkness, and to render a faithful and lasting account of my few variations. In *La Lampe dans l'horloge* [The Lamp in the Clock], which is about to come off press, you'll see that I have no trouble explaining this crucial variation: the lyrical aspiration toward the end of the world and its subsequent retraction, owing to new facts. Those who claim that I would have welcomed the atomic bomb in 1925 are too pigheaded to grasp the importance of these facts, or more likely are scoundrels.

CC: Forgive me for pursuing my questions on such an accusatory tone; this is simply my way of trying to reach your thoughts more directly . . . Many consider you to be a "rebel" and not a "revolutionary," standing "to one side of social conflicts." Sartre, in the same way, underscored your "ineffective clerkship" . . .

AB: In the pamphlet *Inaugural Break*, my friends and I refuse to let ourselves be ensnared in the false dilemma of *ineffectiveness* or *compromise*. More than ever I believe in the need to transform the world in the direction of the rational (or more exactly, the surrational) and the just. Just because a certain political party claims a monopoly on the process of that transformation, doesn't mean I'm ready to join its disintegrating ideological ranks and employ its means, which I find repugnant. I prefer to continue seeing man's future clearly, and not in the gigantic shadow thrown over it by that prison cap. I regret the fact that this has momentarily barred me from political action, but at the same time I'm resigned to it,

not being someone whose vision is strictly limited to current affairs.

CC: But how would you answer Sartre when he accuses you of being only "destruction"? Do you continue to take a mocking view of the *human condition*—whereas, for the Communists, only *living conditions* are pitiful?

AB: Don't you think that that's playing on the word "condition"? Indisputably we have to change current living conditions, which by definition are remediable (although at the same time we need to have confidence in the means adopted, to be assured that they don't carry the seeds of other unacceptable living conditions). Furthermore, it's puerile to believe that a rectification of living conditions, even a radical one, would put an end to conflict: conflict would resurface in other spheres, because of the power of man's desire and its fundamental dissatisfaction.

CC: So you believe in the metaphysical impact of evil?

AB: Why not? Good and evil are condemned to engender each other indefinitely. The "pitiful aspect of the human condition" is of an "existential" order; it results from the flagrant disproportion between the breadth of man's aspirations and his individual limitations. Here again, his greatness and his poverty are one.

CC: But what about the golden age you seem to be promising in the *Ode to Charles Fourier*?

AB: According to Fourier himself, a rising curve must be followed by a descending curve. It's possible that all of humanity evolves like a single living organism. Meanwhile, the most urgent thing is to combat every manifest proliferation of evil, such as we see today on the social level. And still, in doing so, we would have to take care not to desperately aggravate moral evil by stripping man of the idea of freedom and by compromising the notion of justice.

CC: But is the "pitiful aspect" of the human condition, if I may say so, intact for Surrealism today? Haven't you come to believe more and more that there is a magic or poetic "key" to the world? That love is not only a human invention, but the law of the universe?

AB: It's true that Surrealism, which began mainly as a protest, has found itself, in moments of rage, occasionally butting against doors that caved in, discovering access to what might well be "real life." Love was one such access. I'd like to know if this, too, is "destruction." In love, human misery finds its purest revenge, even approaches its own negation. Today, Malcolm de Chazal sees sensuality as the line of interference between birth and death, the ideal point from which these two merging phenomena might be apprehended. He could be right.

As to the idea of a "hieroglyphic" key to the world, it more or less consciously existed before all high poetry, which can only be moved by the principle of analogies and correspondences. Poets such as Hugo, Nerval, Baudelaire, and Rimbaud, or thinkers such as Fourier, share this idea with the occultists, and likely also with the majority of scientific inventors.

CC: At what point does that involve you in a restoration of the "sacred"? You have become increasingly interested in studying magic and the occult, in Indian thought, which is essentially religious. And you have written that it was necessary to "reinvest the artist with his religious functions" . . . I have to admit that this is the most disturbing of Vailland's charges against you.

AB: Should I be registered in the "American party" because I admire the surviving art and philosophy of the American Indians, an oppressed people if ever there was one (and by whom, more-over)? With all due respect to certain bureaucrats, man's mythical thought, which is in constant development, always walks alongside rational thought. To deny it any outlet is to let it become harmful and lead it to erupt into the rational, which it then deteriorates (raving worship of leaders, two-bit messianism,

etc.). Did I say "that it was necessary to reinvest the artist with his religious functions"? When and where did I say that? That's a lie and a forgery. It's really something to read this—presented as if it were my statement—in a pamphlet whose quotations are "certified absolutely faithful to the source." Is that a product of judgment or contempt?

But I'll go straight to the author's name: simply refer to the meeting minutes that open the special issue of *Variétés* called "Surrealism in 1929." These minutes mention the exclusion of a single individual, out of the entire group that the Surrealists formed at the time with the editors of the magazines *Clarté* and *Le Grand Jeu*. A journalist for *Paris-Midi*, this individual pushed his conformist zeal to the point of becoming the sycophant of Chiappe, the fascist police commissioner. Listen to this article. It begins: "Mr. Chiappe is a little like a grandfather who smothers his grandchildren with gifts . . . " and ends: "Let's hope that Parisians will be just as delighted to hear in their public squares the hymn called 'Chiappe-Martia,' to the glory of the purifier of our capital." Well, the skilled mercenary of twenty years ago and the forger of today are one and the same. It's especially laughable to see him try to "act Marxist" by digging into Jean Prouvost, the ex-publisher of *Paris-Midi*—whose favor, it would seem, he was instead trying to curry at the time. What could I possibly add to that? That he is hardly out of place among the repentant Maurrasians and Hervéistic neopatriots who constitute the principle ornaments of the "French" Stalinist party . . . Please, let's deny these obsequious servants-for-hire the right to speak of liberating thought.

CC: What do you hope, or what do you fear, for the future of the world?

AB: I believe in the forthcoming constitution of a United States of the world.

INTERVIEW WITH FRANCIS DUMONT (*COMBAT*, MAY 16, 1950)

FRANCIS DUMONT: What exactly were you hoping for from communism in 1925, when you drew closer to it over the Moroccan War?

ANDRÉ BRETON: I was hoping that it would radically put an end to a social situation whose arbitrary, inequitous, thoroughly revolting character was becoming more evident with each passing day. Only communism struck me as having the requisite *framework* to put an end to conflicts such as the ones between exploiters and exploited, idle rich and impoverished workers, nations of prey and brutally "colonized" peoples, which to my mind foster an open wound within the spirit.

When we first turned to communism, there were still not too many dark spots in the picture: a few stains all the same, like the repression of the Kronstadt sailors, or the pocketing of Lenin's will. And also a few worries of a more fundamental nature: the German revolution had failed; in flagrant contradiction with the doctrine, the dogma of "Socialism in a single country" was taking the lead; from certain signs given by the opposition, we also feared that democracy did not reign within the Party. Nonetheless, our great hopes subsisted: we wanted to believe that nothing essential had been compromised.

FD: What do you expect from communism today?

AB: Given its current identification with Stalinism, I can expect only atrocities.

We have seen one man order the assassination of his best comrades-in-arms; we have seen procedures, borrowed from the Inquisition and refined, that were used to degrade these comrades-in-arms before taking their lives; we have seen concentration camps that in scope and horror are every bit the equals of Hitler's; we have seen the abrogation of every freedom worthy of the name; we have seen the systematic use of lies, slander, forgery, and blackmail as tools of propaganda. Instead of an effort toward "more awareness," which I persist in considering socialism's utmost objective, they've substituted the watchword of fanaticizing the masses. The divinization of the leader ("the man we love best"), who these days even has to be smothered with presents, crowns this edifice, the impudent negation of what it claims to represent.

To speak of "communism" in this context is obviously insane. Beyond the deadly malaise that such an imposture entails, we would have to go back to the time when the worm first crawled into the fruit, the better to rot it. Whatever it might cost many of us, we'll have to subject certain aspects of Lenin's, and even Marx's, thinking to intense criticism, insofar as they stem from what is most debatable in Hegel—the *Philosophy of Right*, for example.

FD: What did you hope for from esotericism?

AB: On several occasions, I've stressed the interest that poets have constantly shown in esoteric thought, from the beginning of the nineteenth century to the present day (once again, I need only mention Hugo, Nerval, Aloysius Bertrand, Baudelaire, Lautréamont, Rimbaud, Mallarmé, Jarry, and up to Roussel and Kafka). To the extent that Surrealism follows the historical determinations that pass through these poets, it could not avoid rubbing shoulders with esotericism. But only of its own accord—that is, borne by motives that to me seemed strictly poetic—was it led to "intersect" with certain fundamental esoteric theses.

FD: So this is the case with the oft-quoted sentence from your *Second Manifesto*: "Everything tends to make us believe that there exists a certain point of the mind . . . the hope of finding and fixing this point"?

AB: For example. Keep in mind that poetry, ever since Rimbaud assigned it the task of "changing life"—entrusted it with a "Promethean" mission, as they say—has been following the path of that "internal revolution" whose perfect accomplishment could well merge with that of the Great Work, as alchemists understand it. Nonetheless, twenty years ago I had only a premonition of this.

FD: And today, what do you hope for from esotericism?

AB: More and more I believe that "History," as it is written, is a web of dangerous nonsense, which makes us take a merely external, fallacious projection of events for reality. Its brilliant coloring comes only from the hemoglobin of battles. But trying to destroy anything of such History is basically as vain as claiming to interpret dreams solely on the basis of their manifest content.

Beneath these various facts, which are of greater or lesser import, runs a thread that we very much need to unravel. It's there that myths have been entangled since the beginning of the world and—whether rigid Marxists like it or not—that they find a way of coming to terms with the "economy" (which in a certain modern acceptance of the term is perhaps just another myth). Considering the scope that esotericism lends our need for investigation, we have to admit that it makes historical materialism, as a system of knowledge, seem laughable. As soon as we stand before the enigma of these myths, we are forced to realize that esotericism teaches us most about them. No need to tell you that to my mind, "fideism" is to be avoided here just as much as anywhere else. In particular, we must be wary not only of ratifying the many suspect works that have tried to pass themselves off in this light, but also of the idea that a secret "tradition" has been handed down to us more or less intact.

FD: As far as you are concerned, what respective positions do these two methods of human liberation occupy?

AB: The two necessities that I once dreamed of making one and the same—Marx's "transform the world" and Rimbaud's "change life"—have, in the course of these past fifteen years, become more and more separate and opposed. But I haven't lost hope that one day they'll find each other again.

Currently, the great obstacle barring their meeting is Stalinism. By distorting all revolutionary values, Stalinism has *burnt the bridge* that, since the time of Saint-Simon, Fourier, Abbé Constant, Enfantin, and Flora Tristan, has allowed those who strove toward the liberation of men and women, those who aimed at spiritual emancipation, to communicate freely; the bridge that made them indistinguishable from each other. At that time, it was possible to work on both levels without being accused of Illuminism. Today the yoke is the same as before, except that it can be exchanged for another, still heavier one. And yet, the solution is not to take refuge in abstract concerns, but rather to maintain the integrity of human aspirations, the only source from which we can draw the strength to cast off these yokes one by one.

INTERVIEW WITH J.-L. BÉDOUIN AND P. DEMARNE (FOR THE RADIO PROGRAM *WHERE DO WE COME FROM? WHERE ARE WE? WHERE ARE WE GOING?* JULY 1950)

J.-L. BEDOUIN AND P. DEMARNE: We wonder if you would kindly tell us about the situation of Surrealism in 1950, with respect to the problems facing the human condition, and with respect to everything that tries to bar people from seeking true solutions to these problems.

ANDRE BRETON: What if I spoke instead about the question that provides the excuse for this series of broadcasts? My sense is that it wouldn't be quite so evasive.

Where Do We Come From? Where Are We? Where Are We Going? It's a shame there are no television cameras here, so that we could discuss it in front of Gauguin's famous painting, a corner of which bears these words on a golden background! In that triple question resides the one true enigma, next to which the one that legend places in the Sphinx's mouth is a pathetic cliché. I've always been astonished by the platitude of that interrogation, which caused Oedipus to assume such grand airs . . . But with it, we're in the heart of Greek myth, and specifically facing one of the first plots aimed at persuading man that he is master of his circumstances, that nothing that surpasses his understanding can block his way; aimed at *infatuating* him, in short, by making him value his powers of elucidation, even if it meant taking away the sense of his own mystery. Gauguin was very clear on that point. You'll recall that

he said, "Always keep the Persian, the *Cambodian*, and a little of the Egyptian in mind. The great error is the Greek, no matter how beautiful it is."

JLB AND PD: The error was to progressively reduce the life of the mind to a simple manipulation of ideas, by systematically stifling all its irrational manifestations. We could say that this error has reached its peak today. As for the tradition that spawned it, hasn't it been petrified for quite some time?

AB: Greco-Latin culture is in its final throes. Not long ago I read a magazine article on the subject that was one long cry of alarm—at once very revealing and entirely futile. "Until recent times," its author observed, "literary or artistic revolutions were made in a climate of respect for the old values. Culture was a continuity; one did not repudiate one's origins. Today we are seeing a widespread attempt at subversion, which aims at fundamentally altering our scale of values." And he laments that these days, Laclos has been eclipsed by Sade, La Rochefoucault by Vauvenargues, the "major" Romantics by the "minor" Romantics (major or minor according to the outmoded viewpoint of study guides). The same author also worried about the invasive space taken up in young minds by the works of Lautréamont, Rimbaud, Jarry, Roussel, and others, which tend increasingly to limit one's interest in the literature that is still on the curriculum. But *that's how it is*, and there's no use regretting it. For better or worse, I think that we have to come to terms with it and try to grasp the phenomenon in its entirety.

JLB AND PD: For us, the essential thing is to remove the mind from the destruction of established systems that threaten to drag it down into their ruins . . .

AB: The question was beautifully examined by René Huyghe, in his introduction to the catalogue of last year's Gauguin exhibit at the Orangerie. It's all the more noteworthy in that this exhibit allowed us to rediscover the great painting from 1897 called *Where*

Do We Come From? Where Are We? Where Are We Going? which hadn't been shown in France for some twenty years. It's precisely on that painting that René Huyghe based his study. The remarkable thing is that this painting led him to rigorously determine the boundary that separates the old world from the modern. After noting that the prevailing concept in the West emphasizes the preponderant influence of Aristotle over Plato, he endeavors to show how this concept, to which we owe our certainties and successes, is also the one that has increasingly brought home our failings and limitations—failings and limitations that, he says, "so many primitive and Eastern societies" do not know.

JLB AND PD: This is why the products or remains of these civilizations still matter to us, even as "European" civilization has expanded its material influence.

AB: The regular—and indisputable—progress of technology from Greek Antiquity to the present has been accompanied by a no less perceptible, regular regression on other levels. Mr. Huyghe marks its stages: the Roman Empire, the rise of the bourgeoisie in the eighteenth century, and the affirmation of bourgeois positivism from the fifteenth to the nineteenth centuries. We have to admit that at the point we've reached, rational certainties seem outmoded. The accumulation of technological successes has taken a threatening, catastrophic turn. Man finds himself before a veritable "call to order"; everything tells him that he's made a wrong turn, everything cries out in warning . . .

JLB AND PD: Don't you think we can find a remedy to the danger you've just spoken of—which must certainly be at the root of the current, widespread disarray—in the work of certain poets and artists (especially the ones you mentioned earlier) who act as beacons for our time?

AB: The same author underscores the fact—an antidote, whether he likes it or not—that "since the beginning of the nineteenth century, many minds have been troubled by the desic-

cation and stifling that they see all around them. Horrified," he says, "they have seen . . . the sources of internal life, and of its renewal, run dry; they've been appalled by the sterilization in which the Greco-Roman tradition deteriorated, in which it became increasingly cramped and limited with each passing day, particularly under the influence of bourgeois rules. . . . A huge effort was made to get back in touch with the soul." He shows how this line begins with Novalis and Nerval (naturally we could take it much further back), then passes through Gauguin and Rimbaud. It's clear that it ends with Surrealism. That's why, rather than appearing to "blow my own horn," I've preferred to yield the floor to an art historian, an impartial witness of life and intellect, someone whom no one can reasonably accuse of acting as judge in his own case. Let me simply point out that what Mr. Huyghe states is precisely what Surrealism has always proclaimed and violently felt.

To come back to Gauguin's painting, and to the questions that it asks us more and more urgently: "Where Do We Come From? Where Are We? Where Are We Going?" you of course haven't forgotten that they date back to the time when he'd decided to kill himself. "So," he said, "before dying I wanted to paint a large canvas I had in mind, and for an entire month I worked day and night in a state of incredible fever." That fever, within several tenths of a degree, might not fundamentally differ from the one gripping us today, except that it's not an individual who has chosen to disappear, but the entire human race. And each man, on the few yards of canvas left, will try to paint for himself, to the best of his abilities and better than the others, the strange human adventure of this century—caught between the tumble of his birth, quasi-clandestine but individual as always, and the tumble of his death, spectacular and widespread . . .

JLB AND PD: "Paint for himself" . . . Do you mean man's chances of giving the strange adventure into which he's been thrown willy-nilly an overall interpretation—an interpretation that humanity is surely lacking at present, and whose foundations Surrealism is trying to rediscover? Don't Gauguin's high spiritual

expectations, particularly in this painting, prefigure the ones that must now motivate any artist worthy of the name?

AB: Without claiming to explain it, of course, I'm struck by how valid the *fabric* of Gauguin's painting still is today, perhaps because of the universality of the questions it raises. It's a kind of emotional "pattern" from which the interplay of human anxiety and insane tranquility cuts its lights and shadows, which are constantly interfering with each other. Man is at the center, preoccupied with gathering fruit, which is life. Behind him a squatting figure, seen from behind—or as Gauguin said in a letter to Monfried, "an intentionally enormous figure, despite the perspective"—watches amazed as two other figures pass, dressed in purple and "daring to ponder their fate." That's more or less the state we're in. The course of human existence unwinds on the painting from right to left, with its childishness, its grace, and the splendors that can make you forget everything—for starters, its way one should live. As the same Gauguin said, "Everything takes place by a stream in the woods." Only carnal beauty and desire manage to blossom in that muted light, which brings us the sleeping child in the right-hand corner, and chases the old woman toward the left—the same woman (along with others) whom Gauguin elsewhere gives the treacherous advice: "Be in love, and you will be happy." As if it were the result of a spiritual desertion, of the mind's fundamental inability to meet the specific tasks facing it, love itself—to which everything here draws us, as a last resort—takes on a venomous character.

JLB AND PD: Among other clues in Gauguin's work, there's the title of one painting: *The Spirit of the Dead Watches*. As we know from Gauguin himself, this "spirit" comes from the mythological tradition of the Marquesas Islands. Shouldn't one look toward this for signs of a strength that until now seems to have been missing from the picture?

AB: Standing over the scene is an "idol" that Gauguin introduces into the landscape, which he himself tells us is related in his dream

"to all of nature, reigning in *our primitive soul*." A young woman appears to be listening to this idol in the foreground, squatting, or so it seems, near a person who will soon die. I said: so it seems, for it's understood that every figure in the painting occupies a separate space, a kind of "time-space" blended together in an arabesque. Without there being any question of trying to exhaust the painting's symbolic—or prophetic—intentions (without Gauguin's own confidences, we'd never know that the strange white bird to the left, which resembles a puffin, represents "the uselessness of vain words"), you'll note that magic—for that's what it's about—here asserts its supreme potency, that it stands as the great overseer: the "idol" is beautiful, all strength is luminously absorbed into it.

What does this have to do with the problems currently facing us—the Korean situation, for example? Well, I persist in believing that it has *everything* to do with it. This is the point man has reached: he's gambling with his fate (and even—what more could you ask?—the fate of his race). He's gambling without knowing it—that much goes without saying—and without even caring any more about grasping the situation in any way, which is very serious. And worse still, the deck with which he's playing has been stacked (he's beginning to think it might have been stacked).

There are a lot of digressions in all this. You'll say that I've dwelt inexcusably long on the description of Gauguin's painting. But what do you want, it's the only positive statement we have on the question . . .

JLB AND PD: There are many who prefer in this domain not to go beyond the doctrines of "professional" philosophers. In this regard, what do you think of the opposition between so-called "materialist" and "idealist" tendencies—an opposition that the proponents of each side claim is irreconcilable? For you, doesn't this opposition have mainly an historical importance?

AB: The quarrels between materialism and what is set against it, as well as what it sets itself against, are absolutely vain when faced with the unity of the human condition and the precariousness of

this condition, which is at its height. A day will come, tearing itself out of the ledger that for the first time keeps silent about the future, when man will emerge from the labyrinth, having felt his way in the dark back to the lost thread. This thread is that of poetry, as still only a few of us can hear it; the kind of poetry that, following Lautréamont and Rimbaud, we hoped would change life itself. This thread is one with the thread that winds endlessly on the spool of the occult tradition, to the rhythm of the myths that pass and remain. The mistake is to think that this tradition could be handed down intact, transmitted with greater or fewer hazards. Against all odds, it seems to me to vouchsafe the continuity of human life, in the sense that it can be conceived indefinitely only as both generated and generative.

JLB AND PD: For now, we can only hope that life will again plunge into those deep waters, far from the increasingly vain turbulation on the surface.

AB: Buried or not, the talisman remains. It's unthinkable that we won't find it again sooner or later, among the layers of the heart, by endeavoring to restore man's *primordial* feeling about himself. Positivist rationalism has corrupted this feeling, led man to the paroxysm of his misery after having stripped him even of the sense of his greatness—even though the two were inseparable for so long.

INTERVIEW WITH JOSÉ M. VALVERDE (*CORREO LITERARIO*, MADRID, SEPTEMBER 1950)

JOSE M. VALVERDE: How do you feel about *neo-Surrealism?*

ANDRE BRETON: There is no such thing as "neo-Surrealism." Anything that presents itself as such or, these days, sports the label "revolutionary Surrealism" is a counterfeit enterprise and must be denounced as an imposture. And for a good reason: from the sole fact that Surrealism, at the outset, claimed to be the codification of a state of mind that has manifested itself sporadically in every age and in every country, one cannot ascribe an end to it any more than one can pinpoint its beginning. Goya was *already* a Surrealist, as was Dante, or Uccello, or Lautréamont, or Gaudì. Centuries from now, any art that takes new paths toward a greater emancipation of the mind will be Surrealist. The events of the past thirty years have not fundamentally modified the premises that gave birth to Surrealism as an *organized movement*. If, despite everything, there are noticeable differences between the Surrealist attitudes of the 1920s and the 1950s, it's because our field of investigation has considerably widened: though more or less limited to the poetic domain at first, it has now extended way beyond that.

JMV: What do you think of the recent proliferation of Surrealist schools? How should we interpret the branches that have grown out of it?

AB: Let's not speak about Surrealist "schools." The notion of a Surrealist "school," or even "group," is absurd; it was treacherously introduced into public opinion by Surrealism's adversaries, avowed or not. Surrealism has never been anything other than a free, spontaneous association of men who all sought to pursue the activity that they considered most closely related to their shared ways of thinking and feeling. From the start, a kind of charter was established among them, broadly defining a poetic, social, and philosophical attitude that could not be transgressed without entailing a break with the spirit (and community) of Surrealism. It is possible not to be a Surrealist, or to be one, or to have stopped being one. People like Aragon in 1930, or Dali in around 1935, or Eluard in 1938, stopped being Surrealists. What I mean is that, by acting in a way that ran counter to the Surrealist viewpoint that they themselves had shared up until the dates in question, they excluded *themselves* from Surrealism. The notification we gave them of this exclusion was no more than the consecration of an established fact. It's a total error in judgment to try to see their subsequent activity as "dissident Surrealism." It's pure mental laziness to believe that they still have anything to do with what motivated them in their youth. So there can be no question of "branches" or "proliferation," but rather of deviations and repudiations, pure and simple.

JMV: What was the primary factor in Surrealism's evolution? Did the results obtained meet your expectations?

AB: In the course of its history, Surrealism has confronted most of the philosophical movements that have shown some vigor in our time; it has grown by defining its position with respect to them. Its influence is still spreading, and no one can now deny that it has been one of the constituent forces of the specific mentality of our age. The Surrealist concepts of love and freedom, and of a certain extrareligious "sacredness," have moved and in large part shaped today's sensibilities.

JMV: Have Surrealism's ideals and ways of seeing been

profoundly modified over the years? What is the current position of Surrealism with respect to politics and religion?

AB: These ideals and ways of seeing do not fundamentally differ from their earliest expression. It always comes back to the need, the hope of "changing life." More than ever, the life that has been imposed on us has proven unacceptable; it's been ten or twelve years since anyone has even tried to defend it. An operation of great breadth is indispensable and urgent: the main thing is to know what the action should be exerted on. To that question, Surrealism has always answered that it must act simultaneously on the external world (its economic and social structure) and the internal world (human understanding). Moreover, this was as much the view of a reformatory genius such as Fourier, as it was of a poetic genius such as Rimbaud. Today it's well known that Surrealism wants nothing so much as to make the mind cross over the barrier set against it by antinomies such as action and dream, reason and madness, sensation and representation, etc., which constitute the main obstacle of Western thought. In its continual effort in this direction, it has never stopped evaluating the footholds it found in the dialectics of Heraclitus and Hegel (given recent rectifications stemming from the work of Stéphane Lupasco); in the "yin-yang" relation of Chinese thought and its culmination in "Zen" philosophy; or again in so-called "traditional" thought, as it is authoritatively expressed in a work such as René Guénon's *The Great Triad*. But the Surrealist procedure only found reassurance in these supports. It never sacrificed its independence to them.

On the political level, the conditions offered humanity today (the fraudulent bankruptcy of the words "peace," "freedom," "democracy," etc.; the reign of the police; the threat of a new world war, and of atomic or some other form of destruction) seem to call for the formation of new frameworks. It's in this spirit that I support "banning" all currently existing parties. But nothing will happen so long as public opinion, largely fanaticized, has not taken itself in hand. For that to happen, it needs new goals, which transcend the former ones and yet are within everyone's reach. We

have one such goal in the action of the "Citizens of the World," who have already attracted hundreds of thousands of members in every country and can boast concrete results: the "globalization" of ten French *départements*, and of several cities in Germany and India; the opening of a "global highway" that has every hope of stretching all the way around the world, like a cordon sanitaire.

As for religion, the Surrealist position remains as intransigent as ever. There is an irreconcilable tension between, on the one hand, the Surrealist will to penetrate the meaning of ancient myths and to recapture the secret of their gestation; and on the other, the channeling by certain religious dogmas of our need for marvels, to the benefit of a church discredited in principle and forevermore disgraced by its actions.

JMV: What direction are your personal efforts currently taking? What are your most immediate projects?

AB: What tempts me most at present is to return to the problem of dreams, on which John W. Dunne's book *An Experiment with Time* seems to have shed new light. By so doing, I hope to free myself from some remorse left by one of my books, *The Communicating Vessels*, in which I sacrificed too much to the "materialism" of the day. I haven't given up the idea of further exploring the question of whether Surrealism truly meets up with "traditional" thought—let's say, that of Swedenborg, or Fabre d'Olivet—to the point of eventually merging with it; or if it only intersects it at various points. As for entertainment (for you have to think of that, too), my friend Benjamin Péret and I would like to prepare the ground for a "universal history," the need for which is becoming increasingly pressing as a counter to national histories (histories of Spain, France, etc.). Notably we'd like to publish a history—of France, let's say—that would try to disentangle actual events from the myth that takes over and distorts them; and, correlatively, to establish the definitive portrait of a "great" man (Charles the Fifth, for example, or Napoleon), conceived as the result of what has been said about him from his own day down to the present, and from the site of his exploits to the places farthest from it.

JMV: How interesting do you find recent contributions in the Spanish language to intellectual life? Can a work such as Neruda's *Residence on Earth* properly be considered Surrealist?

AB: Unfortunately, I'm largely forced to decline giving an opinion. Years have passed since anyone here has been able to keep abreast of intellectual activity in Spain, which has not gone entirely without giving rise to a certain sense of mutilation. Communication was nonetheless maintained through painting and, first and foremost, through the painting of Joan Miró, which so many times has delighted us; it is to Miró's art that Surrealism owes the most beautiful feather in its cap. Given the current state of my information, I'd add that the Spanish-language poet who most touches me is Octavio Paz, a Mexican, and that for me the most ductile philosophy in Spanish comes from Antonio Porchia, an Argentine whom Roger Caillois introduced to France by translating a volume of his *Voces*. This without prejudice, once again, to what has been written in Spain itself over nearly the past fifteen years. I do not know Pablo Neruda's *Residence on Earth*, but in any case I could judge its potential affinities with Surrealism only retrospectively: the noise that its author recently caused by gathering professional howlers in a pack around persecutions against him, disproportionately inflated for propaganda, is enough to disqualify him totally from the Surrealist point of view.

JMV: It's being said that Surrealist activity is running up against obstacles . . .

AB: There is a beautiful painting by Picasso from 1913 (during the early days of aviation), whose title is one of the "slogans" of the period: "Our future is in the air." Certain ideas are "in the air," and from the moment that they've found a way of *being configured*, no one can prevent them from becoming a reality.

TWO INTERVIEWS WITH ANDRÉ PARINAUD

1.

(*OPÉRA*, OCTOBER 24, 1951)

ANDRE PARINAUD: There hasn't been a Surrealist periodical since the publication of *VVV* in America during the war. What are the reasons for this silence?

ANDRE BRETON: We're no longer living in an age when the costs of starting a magazine can be borne by its contributors, each one donating what he can. This was the case for *La Révolution Surréaliste* and *Le Surréalisme A.S.D.L.R.* At least this way, we guaranteed our total independence. Today, we're forced to work with a publisher, or take on a silent partner. Nothing has yet been decided, but the several overtures made to us have left us hesitant, because they aimed at creating an "art" periodical, whereas Surrealism, now just as much as before, can only fully make do with a combat magazine.

The affirmation of Surrealism as an ongoing movement has a conspiracy of powerful, organized forces against it. The tactic used by these adversaries consists of trying to limit Surrealism to the period between the two wars, and of burying the revelation of what it *is* under incessant reminders of what it *once was*. This method aims at masking or reducing the meaning of certain dissidences. No one wants a *new* Surrealist magazine, something living, whereas we had to decline an offer to republish all twelve issues of *La Révolution Surréaliste*, which died more than twenty years ago.*

* This republication was finally realized by Editions Jean-Michel Place in 1975.

243

AP: Do you think that the forms of expression currently made available to poets, writers, and painters by the press, publishers, and visual art media demonstrate ecclecticism and sufficient guarantees?

AB: I don't think so, at least as far as the possibility of showing works liable to constitute *tomorrow's* values is concerned. The places in which they seek each other out and manage to come into contact are increasingly rare. The disappearance of a good number of young periodicals (such as *Confluences*, *Fontaine*, and *Les Quatre Vents*) and the putting to sleep of several publishing houses turned toward the avant-garde have greatly dimmed the prospects in this regard. Here as elsewhere, financial interests have won a sure victory, with everything this entails: the level of workmanship is lowered by mass production. A work's chances of "selling" are about to win out definitively over its intrinsic qualities: whence, notably, the degrading rush toward literary prizes. In such conditions, it's doubtful that works corresponding to what, in their time, were the first books by Pétrus Borel or Jarry, will ever see the light of day.

It is no more certain, because of the conditions imposed on art today, that the equal of a Daumier or a Gauguin will be able to "penetrate." The network of "art galleries" that arose with the twentieth century, and the commercial speculations that regulate them ever more stringently, are apt to falsify relations between artists and art lovers. Because of this, certain works, such as those of Matisse, Rouault, Utrillo, or Picasso, enjoy—and suffer from—an outrageous promotional inflation, which it is unforgivable of these artists to permit. The true innovator today, barred by dealers and critics—for reasons of fashion—from taking any route other than the "nonfigurative," has little chance of being noticed.

AP: Has freedom of artistic expression evolved in France since the Liberation? Is it greater than during the years 1922 to 1944?

AB: No doubt. In recent years a certain number of "taboos" have

been lifted. In particular, we've seen the publication above board of books that before were sold only "under the counter." But as you know, repression continues; and if it is not even more active in this domain, it's only because it would have too much to handle. In fact, freedom of expression is more limited than before, and by much more astute means, which do not depend on the powers that be. This limitation above all follows the international climate. The constitution of two warring blocs who dream only of, and prepare only for, the other's annihilation and the subjection of whatever remains, leaves little room for free expression in the sense that we still understand it. If you prefer, what it limits today is not so much freedom of expression as space for free expression, which comes down to the same thing.

AP: What are the conditions you'd like to see adopted by the press, publishers, and visual art media for free expression to become a "reality"?

AB: You ask too much of me! The Stalinists have a host of publications at their disposal. With the intellectuals that serve them, they're able to gain a huge audience. A sort of oath binds these men, which allows them to spread the same untruths in unison, as well as to coat the most inimical actions with soothing words. The Americans, who are inundating this part of Europe with their "digests," are in no position to provide the appropriate ideological rebuttal. The fact nonetheless remains that these gentlemen are ripping the printing paper out of each other's hands. At the very least, I believe that every publishing house, art gallery, and periodical that cares about its independence should stay resolutely closed to these warring factions, and make absolutely no exceptions for either side. This is no doubt a utopian wish, and yet freedom of expression cannot be reconquered so long as contact is maintained with those who have disposed of it.

AP: Could you name the poets, painters, and works that to your knowledge have not been published or exhibited in at least five years, owing to some form of censorship?

AB: This censorship is exerted much more subtly. It doesn't entirely bar the writer from publishing, or the artist from exhibiting, but—when it can't do any better—it blunts the work's statement by organizing a campaign of silence around it, or by burying it under *tangential* comments. This way, one avoids the threat of similar statements in the foreseeable future. The Stalinists, who have long been posted up and down that road, were the first to lead us to this dust heap. They've systematically depressed the emotive terrain, and the latter has begun to crumble from one end to the other. Today's youth is feeling this very keenly. The letters I receive from unknown young people, most of them isolated, express a more or less radical doubt about the possibilities of real—by which I mean consequential—intervention by means of poetry and art. This worry also translates, for certain writers in love with great adventure, into too much impatience, feverish agitation. There's a crisis of resonance even more than there is a lack of instruments.

AP: Do you think the audience for poetry and painting is as large as it was before the First World War?

AB: Did you say, "before the First World War"? With that caveat, yes, it's undeniable. Back then, the largest audience was reserved for poetasters such as Rostand or Anna de Noailles, and for a few Salon hacks. The taste for works of quality did not extend beyond the limits of a small number of "cliques": Rimbaud and Mallarmé, even Baudelaire and Nerval, were kept at a distance by the public; gibes at Seurat, scornful laughter at Douanier Rousseau. Fortunately, that's no longer the situation. This said, I believe that the "Resistance" period, which swelled poetry's audience considerably, hardly achieved the famous Hegelian "passage" from "quantity to quality." A veritable poetic inflation resulted from it, as well as an attempt to reinstate the worst kind of "occasional verse." I know that Goethe said, at the end of his life, that all his poems were "occasional verse." But as Roger Ayrault recently stressed in his introduction to Goethe's poems, this can only be understood with respect to his belief that the work of art

must be "true" and not "real," which is the diametrical opposite of "socialist realism."

AP: What new prospects are offered by poetry and painting?

AB: The prospects do not change fundamentally from decade to decade. A greater emancipation of mind, and not a greater formal perfection, must remain the principal objective; this greater emancipation can be expected only from constantly renewed means and expanded freedoms. It's not easy to pinpoint the common denominator between a certain number of seemingly divergent processes, which to my mind stand out today by their power to alert. I'll simply mention a few: the works of Raymond Abellio and Malcolm de Chazal, for their penetration of the world by the occult path; for their detection of new kind of fantastic, *Le Visage de feu* [Face of Fire] by Jean-Louis Bouquet and *Soleil des loups* [The Sun of Wolves] by André Pieyre de Mandiargues; for their lyrical cryptaesthesia of the lower depths, the novels of Maurice Raphaël; and for its apprehension about the future, J.-M. A. Paroutaud's *La Ville incertaine* [The Uncertain City]. In the same period, theatrical poetry has produced two masterpieces: Julien Gracq's *Le Roi pêcheur* and *Monsieur Bob'le* by Georges Schehadé. In the category of publicly "recited" poetry, a genre normally prey to the worst superficiality, I place at its true height Jean Tardieu's astounding *Monsieur Monsieur*, which, in its own original way, equals the marvels of Charles Cros.

AP: Can a movement such as Surrealism be limited to poetic or pictorial forms? If you had the choice, in which domains would you find it useful to express Surrealism's positions?

AB: It hardly matters. The main thing is for Surrealism to express itself regularly, and globally. Its incursions in different domains would thus be much more perceptible. We are arbitrarily reduced to fragmenting our viewpoint, to parceling it out piece by piece, as the opportunities arise. At best—but this is too seldom—a special issue of a magazine gives us the chance to take

stock. This week, for example, a Surrealist double issue of *L'Age du Cinéma* is coming out: we could state our position without any restraint, but it goes without saying that we were basically forced to stick to the topic of film. Still, it seems to me that such an issue allows one to take Surrealism's current pulse, and I have every faith in it. Likewise, should we get the chance, we have all the talents required to prepare a Surrealist publication on architecture, for example; but this would make sense only if placed in a wider context, in other words on condition of finding the more general outlets that are currently lacking. Only then can the various Surrealist initiatives be given free rein, and especially be coordinated and combined. As it is, these initiatives remain far too indecisive, even though they are constantly being reenergized by the current of life itself.

2.

(*ARTS*, MARCH 7, 1952)

ANDRE PARINAUD: In their disciplines and aspirations, art and science have been separated for centuries, after having been identified with each other for so long. Nevertheless, don't you think that in the middle of the twentieth century, art and science have moved closer together in a certain number of ways (two examples: the revelations of psychoanalysis as used by poets; primitive artworks as studied by psychologists and sociologists)? Do these connections strike you as coincidental, or do you believe that historical evolution naturally leads scientists and artists to find common ground?

ANDRE BRETON: *I don't see why* science and art should so soon stop looking askance at each other. The way civilization has been going, in a direction that along with Rousseau and Fourier I consider unnecessary and even totally absurd, *I don't see how* the two labyrinthine roads of science and art could converge. That occasionally a man following the path of art might—I won't even say meet, but, through openings in the wall, catch sight of a man following the path of science (the reverse is much more doubtful), cannot lead us to think that they will walk together toward mutual knowledge. This would be comforting, of course, but it's hardly likely. When I say "science," it's understood that I mean the hard sciences, and that my judgment loses its rigor as it slides toward the speculative sciences: doctors, for example, often prove to be enlightened art lovers . . .

AP: And yet, you can't deny that certain relations have been established!

AB: Yes, it's indisputable that the revelations of psychoanalysis have greatly influenced the poetry and art of our time. Surrealism in particular used them as a springboard. But let's not forget that with psychoanalysis, we were dealing with an emerging and very particular science—in this case an extremely lively offshoot, stemming from a root that had been the teachings at the Salpêtrière hospital. Mistaken as it might have been from many viewpoints, this teaching, by favoring certain explorations of the human soul, inevitably ended up revealing the underground layer into which art, too, thrusts its roots. If we recall that by 1881 Scherner had discovered the symbolism of dreams, it becomes clear that Freud, with all the genius that I've always accorded him, was tilling soil that had already been optimally cultivated so as to let him be heard by both artists and analysts. Between art and science as he understood it, it looked like a veritable honeymoon. But you know that it was nothing of the kind, and Freud was the first to abandon the dialogue. Here's what he wrote me twenty years ago:
". . . a confession, which you will have to accept with tolerance! Although I have received many testimonies of the interest that you and your friends show for my research, I am not able to clarify for myself what Surrealism is and what it wants. Perhaps I am not destined to understand it, I who am so distant from art."

AP: Some answer indeed!

AB: You see . . . But you were speaking about the interest that sociologists and psychologists are beginning to have in primitive art? You're not suggesting that this creates appreciable bonds between them and the artists who are their contemporaries! No: with very few exceptions, those you mention are slaves to a belief in *progress* (technological or otherwise) that, up to a certain point, is perhaps justified in science, but that in art does not hold up for an instant. Between the artist who *feels* the primitive artwork and

the man who lectures on it (almost always with the underlying conviction that a child could do better), there is no hope of a common language.

AP: In your view, what sciences have concretely influenced painters and poets? Without judging the bonds that might have formed between scientists and artists, I'd like you to explain whether a particular state of mind doesn't modify their relations.

AB: I fear this won't be pleasant for scientific minds, but, to the extent that they cared about the science of their era, the poets and artists I've known seem to have adopted a dissident attitude toward it and have deliberately chosen the path of regression. To mention only the painters ("realists" obviously left aside), I'll briefly try to specify their main temptations:
De Chirico is touched only by enigmas. He aims to reinstate the divinatory arts of Antiquity.
Kandinsky, as his book *Concerning the Spiritual in Art* makes clear, has from the start been inspired solely by metaphysics.
By nature, Duchamp chooses to speculate on chance, in a way that is totally independent of scientific theories on the subject . . .

AP: And Picabia?

AB: Picabia! His "mechanical period" should leave no illusions. His taste for machines hardly excludes an impulse toward sabotage. In the same way, Max Ernst, although very up on scientific evolution, draws his inspiration from timeless fantasy and myth. Arp refers, but altogether poetically, to embryogenesis. Tanguy has always struck me as examining the "Mother realm," in the Faustian sense. Magritte has thrown doubt on traditional optics, by premeditating all its modes of telescoping. And I could go on . . . Brauner, who long devoted himself to studying hypnotic phenomena, has since begun concentrating on the symbolic. Toyen has created for herself, completely on the side, a cynegetics of apparitions. Lam has drawn his greatest dynamism from Voodoo. Seligmann, influenced by heraldry, later demonstrated a

preference for alchemy. Leonora Carrington, in life as in art, has never tried to see any way but through magic. Hérold only turned to mineralogy in order to master its sparks. Dorothea Tanning has put all her frenzy into depicting marvels that fortunately have nothing in common with the kind found in science fairs . . .

AP: This enumeration is obviously peremptory. What conclusion do you draw from it?

AB: First of all, that scientific theories have hardly had an all-consuming influence on painting, especially Surrealist painting . . .

AP: But what about Dali?

AB: Yes, it's true that Dali formulated—for his own use above all—the so-called "paranoia-critical" method, which presupposes a keen awareness of psychiatric views, the better to overcome them. It's also true that with Matta it was once a question (with more bravado than substance) of "psychological morphology." But of all my friends—present or past, no matter—only Paalen has kept his eye on scientific curiosity and, in particular, tried to put stock in the new physics of Louis de Broglie. And even he is not immune to what might lead an artist to go backward: in his case, Indian totemism. In an article called "Le Grand malentendu (art et science)"[The Great Misunderstanding], published during the war in the Mexican magazine *Dyn*, he very rightly pointed out that science and art seem condemned to live in discord, given the fact that they respectively answer a temptation to interpret reality, one *quantitatively*, the other *qualitatively*.

AP: So you don't think that the physical sciences, which have been modifying the structure of our concept of the world for the last fifty years, have influenced the work of artists?

AB: I say that artists have unanimously, or nearly unanimously, been uninterested in quantum mechanics and Heisenbergian

physics. I'm not claiming that it's better this way, but what can you do, that's how it is. Naturally, there are plenty of artists who also endeavor to change the current concept of the world, but it's by totally different means. Science's most recent applications, which have hung an unprecedented threat over men's heads, are hardly liable to strengthen the bonds. The artist, like the man in the street, more than ever has the right to glower at the scientist. Physics professor though he might have been, Lichtenberg once said: "Mathematics is a very fine science, but mathematicians often aren't worth a damn. It's almost the same for mathematics as it is for theology . . . The so-called mathematicians often demand to be taken for deep thinkers, even though their heads are most often filled with junk." What more could we say about *atomic scientists*?

AP: That there are others—I really believe this—to whom artists owe quite a lot . . .

AB: Certainly. I grant you that the bridges are not entirely burnt, owing to a few thinkers such as Gaston Bachelard, thanks to whom Surrealism has notably seen itself reflected in a "surrationalism"; and Stéphane Lupasco, who not only has put affectivity back in favor in philosophy, but also, at the end of his *Essai d'une nouvelle théorie de la connaissance* [Essay on a New Theory of Knowledge], particularly answering the wish of poets, has replaced the principle of noncontradiction with the principle of "contradictory complementarity."

AP: On another level, it seems that scientific technology today allows artists to gain knowledge of the aesthetic contributions of peoples from all over the world, and from every period. To what extent can this phenomenon influence the artist's aesthetic?

AB: I wish I could share your optimism, but I don't see how. The scientific technology you're speaking of—the kind that governs film and radio, am I right?—does not seem to me, at least not so far, to be a source of artistic enrichment: quite the opposite.

Nothing in it can rival a visit to the Egyptian wing of the Louvre, or to the Jeu de Paume, or to the Musée de l'Homme, or to the exhibits of Popular Arts and Traditions; or even more so, deep contact with nature, followed by a withdrawal into oneself for as long as is needed. The artist didn't need these techniques of mainstream popularization in order to learn everything that has happened in space and time. To my mind, he won't benefit from this technology in any way, shape, or form.

AP: But do you believe that beauty, in the sense that modern artists are seeking it in every form, can be enhanced by the future revelations of science?

AB: Artists are not necessarily seeking beauty, any more than modern poets are. What the Surrealists in particular wanted was much less to create beauty than to express themselves freely, which meant expressing their inner *selves*. As such, taken together, they could not help expressing their times as well. In this sense, we can say that for the Surrealists the need to know and make known has always predominated over the need to please and be admired. Moreover they thought, and still think, that this is their only chance of encountering a truly *living* form of beauty, as opposed to a dead one.

AP: What final frontiers would you like science to explore?

AB: The only sciences whose revelations could be of value to artists are the psychological sciences. Once more, psychoanalysis had no secrets for the Surrealist painters and poets from the start, such that on many occasions they have *consciously played* on the sexual symbolism attached to it. This alone should heap scorn on the attempts of that psychiatrist who recently, in public lectures at the Sorbonne, claimed to subject the canvases of Max Ernst, Dali, and Brauner to the same investigations, and to reach the same conclusions about their authors, as if they'd never heard of Freud before painting them.

The "theory of form" (*Gestalt* theory) is of no less importance to

art than it is to psychoanalysis, and if their common outcome in Rorschach's "psychodiagnostics" were better known, no doubt it would put an end to the exorbitant pretentions of so-called "abstract" painting. Moreover, I consider all these "projective techniques" obtained by means of "tests" captivating for an artist. Psychiatry, when applied to concrete cases—I mean when its statements are supported by drawn or written documents—can also be of great value. A very fine example was recently furnished by the publication of two books by M.-A. Sechahaye: *Journal d'un schizophrène* [Diary of a Schizophrenic] and *La Réalisation symbolique* [Symbolic Achievement]. This tour of the interest that poets and artists might have in the psychological sciences seems to me to come full circle on that which, in metapsychics, particularly concerns cryptaesthesia and mediumistic activity. It's only in these various directions that art can expect new revelations from science, ones liable to influence it in the future.

Acknowledgments

9 Stanza from "Anne" translated by David Paul, in Paul Valéry, *Poems*, trans. David Paul, *The Collected Works of Paul Valéry*, vol. 1, Bollingen Series 45 (Princeton: Princeton University Press, 1971), p. 51.

36 Excerpts from *The Magnetic Fields* translated by David Gascoyne, in André Breton and Philippe Soupault, *The Magnetic Fields*, trans. and intro. David Gascoyne (London: Atlas Press, 1985), pp. 72–5 [translation slightly revised].

58 Excerpt from "Introduction to the Discourse on the Paucity of Reality" translated by Bravig Imbs, in André Breton, *What Is Surrealism? Selected Writings*, ed. Franklin Rosemont (New York: Monad Press, 1978), part 2, p. 18.

68 Excerpt from *A Corpse* translated by Richard Howard, in Maurice Nadeau, *The History of Surrealism*, trans. Richard Howard (New York: Macmillan, 1965), p. 235.

90 Excerpt from *Legitimate Defense* translated by Richard Howard, in Nadeau, *The History of Surrealism*, p. 248.

101 Excerpt from *Nadja* translated by Richard Howard, in André Breton, *Nadja*, trans. Richard Howard (New York: Grove Press, 1960), pp. 108, 111.

113 Excerpt from *The Communicating Vessels* translated by Mary Ann Caws and Geoffrey T. Harris, in André Breton, *The Communicating Vessels*, trans. Mary Ann Caws and Geoffrey T. Harris (Lincoln: University of Nebraska Press, 1990), pp. 146–47.

123 Excerpt from *The Immaculate Conception* translated by Samuel Beckett, in Breton, *What Is Surrealism?*, part 2, p. 53.

135 Excerpt from *Mad Love* translated by Maria Jolas, in Breton, *What Is Surrealism?*, part 2, p. 166.

146 Excerpt from *Fata Morgana* translated by Jean-Pierre Cauvin and Mary Ann Caws, in *Poems of André Breton*, trans. and ed. Jean-Pierre Cauvin and Mary Ann Caws (Austin: University of Texas Press, 1982), p. 142.

168 Excerpt from "On the Road to San Romano" translated by Charles Simic and Michael Benedikt, in Paul Auster, ed., *The Random House*

Book of Twentieth-Century French Poetry (New York: Random House, 1982), pp. 195, 197.

183 Restored passages from "Interview with André Breton" from *View*, vol. 1, no. 7–8 (Oct.–Nov. 1941), pp. 1–2.

188 Lines from "Travelers" by Charles Baudelaire translated by Richard Howard, in Charles Baudelaire, *Les Fleurs du Mal*, trans. Richard Howard (Boston: David R. Godine, 1982), p. 157.

The translator also wishes to acknowledge existing translations of works cited more briefly, and particularly the following translators: Roger Shattuck (Apollinaire), Helen Weaver (Artaud), Samuel Putnam (Ehrenburg), Alexis Lykiard (Lautréamont), Wallace Fowlie (Rimbaud), Barbara Wright (Tzara), Martin Sorrell (Vaché), Richard Seaver and Helen R. Lane (*Manifestoes of Surrealism*), Simon Watson Taylor (*Surrealism and Painting*), Stephen Schwartz ("Leon Trotsky's 'Lenin' "), Robert Greer Cohn ("The Situation of Surrealism Between the Two Wars"), and Dwight Macdonald ("For an Independent Revolutionary Art").

Index